1993

W9-DAQ-125

A NIGHT IN TUNISIA

Imaginings of Africa in Jazz

by
NORMAN C. WEINSTEIN

The Scarecrow Press, Inc.
Metuchen, N.J., & London
1992

Four chapters and a poem appeared in different form in various publications. Grateful acknowledgment is offered for permission to reprint the following:

"The Creation of Time": copyright 1988 by *The Village Voice*. Reprinted by permission of *The Village Voice*.

"Louis Armstrong's Second Happiest Moment": copyright 1989 by *The Village Voice*. Reprinted by permission of *The Village Voice*.

"Traveling Through the Jungle With Pierre Dørge": copyright 1988 by *The Absolute Sound*. Reprinted by permission of *The Absolute Sound*.

"John Carter": copyright 1988 by *Jazziz*. Reprinted by permission of *Jazziz*.

"A Spiritual Exercise: An Interview With Ronald Shannon Jackson": copyright 1989 by *Rhythm*/Music Maker Publications Inc. Reprinted by permission of *Rhythm*/Music Maker Publications Inc.

Appreciative acknowledgment is offered to the following publishers for permission to reprint previously published materials:

MCA Music Publishing, a division of MCA Inc., New York, NY 10019, for "A Night in Tunisia" by John "Dizzy" Gillespie and Frank Paparelli, © copyright 1944, 1947, 1949, 1976 by MCA Music Publishing. Used by permission. All Rights Reserved.

New Directions Publishing Corporation for *Alphabetical Africa* by Walter Abish, © copyright 1974 by Walter Abish. Reprinted by permission of New Directions Publishing Corporation.

"ABC's (2)" by Charles Olson, © copyright 1987 by the University of Connecticut Library. Reprinted by permission of the University of Connecticut Library.

The author will donate 10 percent of royalties from sales of this book to The Africa Fund to further health, educational, and agricultural programs for Africans.

British Library Cataloguing-in-Publication data available

Library of Congress Cataloging-in-Publication Data

Weinstein, Norman C., 1948–
    A night in Tunisia : imaginings of Africa in jazz / by
Norman C. Weinstein.
        p.   cm.
    Discographies: p.
    Includes index.
    ISBN 0-8108-2525-2 (acid-free paper)
    1. Jazz—History and criticism.   2. Music—Africa—History and
criticism.   3. Afro-Americans—Music—History and criticism.   I. Title.
ML3506.W44   1992
781.65'156—dc20
                                                            92-3476

Contents

146, 452

List of Tables

Preface

Once considered beneath the dignity of scholars, jazz has spawned a vast literature as this century draws to a close. Books abound in most categories: technical analysis, histories, biographies, both those bordering on hagiography as well as character assassination, discographies, even the occasional tome linking jazz to other art forms.

What appeared missing, in my perception, was an attempt to chronicle the development of a key motif that some jazz has explored. Even a cursory perusal of jazz records in a library or store reveals certain topics and images fascinating to jazz musicians which they have tried to capture musically. I began exploring the image of "Africa," remembering my initiation into loving jazz, a quarter century ago, with repeated listenings to "A Night in Tunisia."

This project began reluctantly. The initial burst of research left me wondering just how significant this theme would be. Added to my doubt was the fact that I had read numerous distinguished jazz critics who debunked the idea of a motif analysis of "program music," considering any jazz which attempted to suggest extramusical images and ideas a throwback to the worst excesses of nineteenth-century romantic classical music.

As this book unfolded, and as hundreds of recordings linking jazz and Africa came into my hands, I began to perceive the complexity and depth of the motif. And grew astonished that the theme had never been systematically analyzed in print. Interviews with musicians and discussions with critics and record company producers brought it into clearer light.

The vastness of the topic was difficult to contain. I decided to concentrate on jazz recordings exclusively, however fascinating jazz tours across Africa, or migrations of musicians between the continents, or political ramifications of the topic might have been. The accessibility of recordings made this the approach of choice, as did the fact that readers could use the discographies to further explore the motif on their own, or find clarification for ideas not immediately comprehensible in the book.

Images and ideas about Africa explored musically are not static; like jazz and Africa, they are constantly in flux. Therefore, I have avoided the notion that there is any one "correct" interpretation of jazz related to Africa. My role has been that of a chronicler detailing the way jazz composers creatively have struggled over time with the African theme. Those who expect a doctrinaire reduction of the "meaning" of jazz in some Parnassian final judgement had best read this book with caution, if at all. The goal of *A Night in Tunisia* is to raise questions about the relationship of Africa to jazz— not to contain the music in its multifariousness only in an African-shaped mold.

The word "imaginings" is offered in the title not to suggest that Africa is a flimsy fantasy for jazz composers. *Imagining* here implies an energetic force which constellates, in ever new and changeable configurations, ideas and images surrounding notions of Africa. Imagination comes to mind when one reads how Sidney Bechet moved to France in order to become closer to Africa. Not just literal miles illuminated his description. In Guy Davenport's telling phrase, Bechet was describing "the geography of the imagination," where Africa reigned in the center of his musical consciousness. It was this capacity of jazz musicians to put Africa in the forefront of awareness when playing that was repeatedly moving.

So many topics jazz has been "about": African-American urban life, religion, politics and folkways, left-wing bohemianism, sexual freedom, modernism. Let this book add the theme of "Africa" to this catalog. More than just another topic, it has represented a major perspective crafted by jazz practitioners (mostly African-American, but also, significantly, from other peoples). This perspective is explained in the opening chapter as "Afrocentric." The ideal reader of *A Night in Tunisia* would be one who attempts to enter this perspective—attempting as much as possible to see the world through African eyes. The rewards for seeking this perspective surely transcend this book's subject.

This book was written by an enthusiastic booster of many jazz styles. I have tried to be a passionate explicator of the works of thirteen key figures—but hope that my passion has not lessened my critical acumen. This analysis is accessible to non-musicians, eschewing intensive technical analysis of the music in favor of evoking something of the "feel" of the jazz. I hope technically minded academics will forgive my sins of omission, as African ancestors will forgive my writing about musical evocations of a continent I have never experienced except through recorded jazz and imagination.

If this book inspires jazz lovers to listen anew to any of the recordings celebrated here, I will feel, whatever academics and ancestors might think, that my purpose has been realized.

Norman Weinstein
Boise, Idaho

Acknowledgments

"Igi Kan Ki S'igbo" is a Nigerian proverb which Yusef Lateef has translated as "One tree cannot make a forest." Many hands helped in the making of *A Night in Tunisia*. Special thanks must be given to two outstanding musicologists who have been faithful correspondents over the years, Doug Seroff and Ken Bilby. Another correspondent whose ideas strongly influenced these pages was Professor John Szwed, Department of Anthropology, Yale University. Of authors whose books were particularly central to my writing, two of Szwed's Yale colleagues need mention: Professors Robert Ferris Thompson and Christopher L. Miller. Others whose books were seminal included Henry Louis Gates, Jr., Houston A. Baker, Jr., Paul Oliver, Samuel Charters, and John Storm Roberts. The psychological perspective on imagination shaping this study owes much to the writings of Carl Jung, James Hillman, and Gaston Bachelard.

The grail hunt of obtaining the necessary records needed to complete this study was simplified through albums supplied by the following companies: New Music Distribution Service, Worlds Records, Original Music, Rykodisc, Gramavision, Fantasy Records, Caravan of Dreams Records, MCA Records, P & O Compact Discs, Polygram Special Imports. Special thanks also to The Record Exchange in Boise, Idaho.

Securing esoteric texts was facilitated by the patient and resourceful reference staff of the Boise Public Library, Grove Koger and Lisa McMillin-Dennis. Also helpful were Janet Stanley, Chief Librarian of the African Art Museum Library of the Smithsonian Institution; Beverly A. Gray, Head of the African Section of the Library of Congress; and Betty Odabashian of the Schomburg Center for the Study of Black

Culture. Data even these individuals could not unearth were supplied by Professor Michael Coolen, Department of Music, Oregon State University; Professor James Robertson, Department of French, Boise State University; plus Roger Steffens, Harvey Brown, Monique Goldstein, Orrin Keepnews, Gary Giddins, and Don Schlitten. Thanks also to Janice Carruthers for her typing of the manuscript.

Four chapters were previously published in abbreviated form in various publications. My appreciation to *The Village Voice, Jazziz, The Absolute Sound,* and *Rhythm* for permission to reprint my features on Sunny Murray, John Carter, Pierre Dørge, and Ronald Shannon Jackson. Special thanks to artist Betye Saar for the right to reproduce a photograph of her assemblage, "Africa." Permission to quote from "ABC's (2)" by Charles Olson was generously given by Richard H. Schimmelpfeng, Head of Special Collections at the University of Connecticut Library. Appreciation also goes to New Directions Publishing Corporation for permission to quote from *Alphabetical Africa* by Walter Abish; to *The Village Voice* for permission to reprint my poem, "Louis Armstrong's Second Happiest Moment"; and to MCA Music Publishing for permission to quote the lyrics to "A Night in Tunisia."

Finally, my appreciation is offered to my family and friends for their various demonstrations of sensitivity and support.

This book's dedication is dual. It is dedicated to the musicians celebrated in its pages as well as to my wife, Julie. Without the musicians, the music, and my wife, this life would be infinitely less worthy of celebration.

Remembering the Nigerian proverb, it is hoped that all parts of this "forest" forgive any shortcomings on the part of this "tree." They are not responsible for blemishes in the undergrowth, and deserve credit for any green splendor these pages might hold.

CHAPTER ONE

Opening Night in Tunisia: An Introduction

> He realizes the essential Pan-Africanism is
> artists relating across continents their craft,
> drumbeats from the aeons, sounds that are still
> with us. —*Ishmael Reed*[1]

There is a guiding image in my mind as I open this book: a teenager is sitting in his bedroom in the early 1960's listening to a recording by Art Blakey and the Jazz Messengers. The album's graphics, a Middle Eastern cityscape, mosques outlined against a star-lit landscape, create the apotheosis of exotic romance. The title cut is evocative of a place far removed from the boy's Philadelphia home. The music's rhythms suggest "Africa," a place he hasn't one salient bit of information about. Some schools in the early sixties deemed African history worthy of three paragraphs in a world history textbook. But the music begins an enchantment, a spell encompassing both jazz and Africa.

Nearly three decades have passed since I heard that recording, the first remembered instance of hearing jazz as an artistic force with a beauty and energy which would transform my understanding of myself and the world. That moment of enchantment has blossomed into this book.

Over a period of years I have realized that a very significant group of non-African jazz musicians has developed an Afrocentric tradition evoking Africa in their music, cultivating a musically grounded channel for Pan-African imagination. Rather than evading or trivializing the key influence of Africa in the development of jazz, these musicians have

1

emphasized African sources inspiring jazz. The recorded compositions of thirteen jazz composers are profiled here, and hundreds of others are mentioned.

The purpose of this investigation is not simply to reduce the essence of jazz to some common African denominator, as Rudi Blesh vulgarly does in *Shining Trumpets* (Da Capo, 1975) by implying that the only supposedly "pure" jazz most obviously showcases its African musical roots. Nor would I imply that only hard-core spokespersons for various forms of black nationalism have the hidden keys to the kingdom of comprehending, once and for all, the chief meaning of jazz. The purpose is to map the importance of the African theme as one among several in jazz history, and to suggest that an understanding of the African theme not only can heighten one's comprehension and appreciation of a significant body of the music, but can also reveal a Pan-African consciousness permeating various strata of African-American culture and daily life.

Although this is the first book-length treatment of the relation of recorded jazz to Africa, attention to the issue is nearly as old as jazz itself. Witness this headline from the September 19, 1926, *New York Times:*

AMERICAN JAZZ IS NOT AFRICAN

Derived From It and Rhythm Is Similar, But Ours Is Much Simpler, Says Well-Versed Authority of Negro Music[2]

Sunday *Times* readers could therein discover the "scientific" discoveries of Nicholas George Julius Ballanta of Sierra Leone, who directed readers to listen to "coon songs" and spirituals rather than jazz for evidences of melodies heard in African jungles. A half century later the distinguished musicologist Paul Oliver would follow Ballanta's suggestion in his *Songsters and Saints* and *Savannah Syncopators*. But perhaps jazz researchers, with a handful of distinguished exceptions like Marshall Stearns, Richard Waterman, Gunther Schuller, and Amiri

Baraka, have been as certain as Ballanta that all jazz had in common with African music was rhythm.

Attempts to "prove" Africanisms retained in jazz have been the subject of scholarly debate for so many decades that one can empathize with musicologist Richard Waterman when he entitles an article: "On Flogging a Dead Horse: Lessons Learned From the Africanisms Controversy."[3] While I am clearly on the side of those musicians and scholars who share the conviction that jazz is heavily indebted to African music, *I am more involved with the issue of how jazz musicians who recognize their African connection create music to acknowledge their profound artistic debt to Africa, how they celebrate one of their chief wellsprings of musical inspiration.* Whether a certain quantity of the melodic, harmonic, and rhythmic vocabulary of jazz is ever finally proven in scholarly discourse to be of African origin is of less consequence to me than what a jazz musician does who assumes the authenticity of his or her African connection. What occurs when musicians wish to create a new music out of that imaginative focus?

How these jazz artists perceive and celebrate an African connection is an issue that must be examined in the broader historical context of African-American history, a history marked by various swings in attitude toward Africa manifested in an encyclopedic range of images. African-American folklore tackles the African connection with characteristic wit:

"Tell me, Lord, how come I'm so black?"

"You're black so that you could withstand the hot rays of the sun in Africa."

"Tell me, Lord, how come my hair is so nappy?"

"Your hair is nappy so that you would not sweat under the hot sun in Africa."

"Tell me, Lord, how come my legs are so long?"

"Your legs are long so that you could escape from the wild animals in Africa."

"Tell me, Lord, what the hell am I doing in Chicago?"[4]

In a more serious vein, historian Harold R. Isaacs writes:

> Down through the generations Africa has persisted as a
> hazy presence in the universe of Negro Americans, an
> image now receding, now advancing, taking on different
> shapes, occupying different places in Negro mental
> landscapes. Now it is an ancestral land, dimly known,
> forgotten, denied, or thrust away both as a place and as
> a memory, dark, torrid, dangerous, a deeply unwanted
> piece of oneself. Or now it is, as the white man has said
> and his Providence has ordained, a savage, heathen land
> awaiting a tardy redemption on which even Negro
> slavery in America could be seen as a deposit. Or again,
> it is the shadowy wisp of a far past, nostalgically or
> romantically remembered, or woven unrecognized into
> bits and corners of a great folklore. Or a promised
> land . . . .[5]

The dynamically ever-changing image of Africa in the
"mental landscapes" of African Americans in general, jazz
musicians in particular, comprises much of this book. These
varieties of African images held in the imaginations of African
Americans will be examined in light of various historical
developments among African Americans: slavery days, the
migrations to metropolitan areas in the northern U.S., the rise
of Garveyism and various forms of Pan-African political
expression, the Harlem Renaissance. Contrapuntally, references will also be made to how Africa has been stereotyped
and flattened into a one-dimensional image by colonizers, by
white travellers, and by artists with a colonial consciousness
("It's quite a small place—our Africa, I mean. You could
squeeze the whole of it into the Place de al Concorde . . . "
says a character in novelist Norman Douglas' *Fountains in the
Sand*). The development of jazz compositions which keep
images of Africa in strong focus will be examined through
these various perspectives.

This discussion linking jazz to African imagery raises the
question: How does jazz evoke Africa? The simplest sign of a
connection, the title of a musical composition which mentions

Africa, can be deceptive. Eubie Blake relates a tale about the
origin of his most famous piano rag, "Charleston Rag." His
fellow composer and erstwhile manager, Will Marion Cook,
received Blake's newest rag with enthusiasm, promptly titling
it "Sounds of Africa." Blake was led in hand by Cook to
Schirmer, the largest New York music publisher at the time.
Blake performed "Sounds of Africa" on piano for Curt
Schinder, Schirmer's manager. The manager immediately
signalled his approval and wrote a one hundred dollar check
for advance royalties. Here the tale took a surprising turn:

> Then Schinder says to me, very friendly—he bought the
> number already, remember. He says, "I see you go from
> a G flat to E flat without any preparation or modula-
> tion." Now he don't mean nothin' at all. He *bought* the
> tune. He's just curious. Then suddenly Cook gets very
> indignant. He says, "How dare you criticize Mr. Blake?
> What do *you* know about genuine African music. That's
> *genuine* African music."—he's lyin' now. "I insist you
> apologize to him."[6]

No apology was tendered; the sale was lost. Cook's folly
only restored to Blake the composer's prerogative of titling
his composition in a manner suggesting a landscape closer to
home.

But as musical titles are sometimes an inaccurate indicator
of what music connects to Africa, critic and composer
Gunther Schuller even takes the position that most jazz titles
are irrelevant to musical content. Then what does surely
signal jazz related to Africa?

In spite of the various academic controversies surrounding
the African origins of jazz, there are six general characteristics
of most African music which should be considered when
exploring this connection. Although generalizations about so
massive a musical continent should be made with trepidation,
these insights are general enough to apply broadly, though
not exclusively, to African music:

1. *Multileveled rhythmic activity forms the core of many musical events.* Polyrhythms arranged in interlocking arrangements are a commonly found organizing device, particularly in West African traditional music. Batteries of percussion instruments establish a central musical focus with other instruments in contrast interacting through a dynamic dialogue. Rhythmic development seems more primary than melodic and harmonic development, particularly to non-African listeners.

2. *Improvisation is a key performance value.* Parts of performances, or entire performances, might be created on a moment-by-moment basis, without strict reliance upon a rigid and all-encompassing *a priori* form (transmitted orally or through printed score) to guide and finally determine performance outcome.

3. *Musical events invite collective participation.* Attempts are made to reduce formal physical and psychological barriers separating musical performers from audience. This often means performers empowering audiences to enter call-and-response modes, bringing vocalisms, body percussion, and dancing into the event. Music making is a vocal and instrumental event with dancing integral to the proceedings.

4. *Vocalization styles, realized both through human voices and instruments, emphasize the rhythms and colors of passionate speech.* Microtonal contour shifts are present, as are broad changes in vocal tone accomplished through shouts, grunts, moans, wails, bends, and glides.

5. *Musical events have a moral, political, and spiritual function coterminous with their entertainment function.* These events contribute to the daily social construction of African reality in a manner necessary as well as

appealing to the senses, hearts, minds, and souls of community members.

6. *Music can be directed to generations of deceased ancestors as well as the living and yet-to-be-born.*

While these six characteristics are found in non-African musical traditions, they are particularly and peculiarly emphasized in African music. They provide an infrastructure for much of jazz, to a greater or lesser degree. Jazz strongly partaking of these characteristics can be labeled "Afrocentric." This is music integrally tied to a vigorously developed image of Africa in the mind of its creator. Such labelling does not imply any discounting of the musical and cultural value of jazz beyond this classification. The goal here is to illuminate one facet of a multifaceted art form and to consider the musical and extra-musical consequences of working with the African theme.

Apart from participation in these six qualities largely found in African music, what other characteristics demarcate jazz tied to Africa? Consider the following:

1. Traditional African melodies and harmonies are partially or totally utilized by jazz composers in formal compositions and improvisations.

2. Traditional African instruments (mbira, kora, drums, various hand-held percussion instruments) are used as they would be played in African contexts. Or they are modified in design (mechanically or electronically) to meet the needs of Western jazz artists.

3. African musicians are invited to play with Western jazz artists in informal jam sessions, rehearsals, concerts and recording sessions both within and outside of Africa's borders.

4. Jazz composers provide extra-musical texts (album liner notes, which may include clarifications of musical titles evoking Africa, concert notes, published interviews) explicating the African content of their jazz.

5. Non-African jazz musicians may choose to visit, work, study, teach, and record in Africa.

While this catalog of African qualities in jazz suggests the ingredients found in the jazz showcased in this book, it doesn't answer the question of why this music deserves such extensive attention. What does it matter that there is a strain of jazz saturated with African characteristics and images?

Not only does the study of this line of jazz illuminate jazz history and enhance musical appreciation, it also furthers understanding of an Afrocentric tradition imagining Africa through artistic creativity. Out of that vast spectrum of images of Africa held by African Americans which historian Harold R. Isaacs has cataloged, there is a particular spectrum held by African-American artists in general, and jazz musicians in particular. An exploration of the musical imaginations of these jazz artists promises to reveal much about African-American life and its ties to Pan-African thought. Hearing this tradition of jazz through this matrix, through this interpretative lens, brings the study of the African diaspora into a new perspective. What anthropologist Clifford Geertz writes about his analysis of a Balinese cockfight is relevant here:

> What it does is what, for other people with other temperaments and other conventions, *Lear* and *Crime and Punishment* do; it catches up these themes—death, masculinity, rage, pride, loss, beneficence, change—and ordering them into an encompassing structure, presents them in such a way as to throw into relief a particular view of their essential nature.[7]

In other words, the study of Afrocentric jazz catches up these themes—the relation of African Americans to Africa, pride,

rage, power, loss, masculinity and femininity, and liberation—and orders them into a structure wherein the nature of
one's affinity to Africa is a central concern.

How do musicians with musical imaginations centered
upon Africa bring images of Africa into their art? Pianist
Randy Weston and hornman Yusef Lateef have chosen to
spend years living and studying music in Africa. Drummers
Art Blakey, Max Roach, and Ronald Shannon Jackson have
developed jazz based upon visits to Africa. Some musicians
(John Coltrane comes to mind in this instance) never had
actual contact with Africa but developed their art based upon
literature, African music recordings, street lore, family
stories, classroom encounters, religious experiences in and
out of church, and mass media presentations. Whatever the
source of African inspiration, musicians involved with Africa
have had to develop imaginative visions of Africa in contradis-
tinction to the African visions sustained by colonizers,
businessmen, evangelicals, and others who brought to their
actual or imagined African encounters various racist stereotypes. It is hard to believe that twenty-five centuries of human
"progress" have passed since the Greek sailor Hanno offered
his glimpse of Africans as they came gradually into focus
along the shoreline while his crew sat in a craft offshore,
terrified of landing, seeing

> . . . a wild tribe who inhabited a mountainous area
> swarming with wild beasts; Troglodytes of strange
> appearance able to run faster than horses; . . . and
> another whose pipes, drums, and cymbals terrified the
> explorers.[8]

That enormous span of centuries compresses to a moment
when Mr. Ian Smith, former Prime Minister of Rhodesia
(now Zimbabwe), offers his 1987 historical revision of the
meaning of the transatlantic slave trade:

> The white Americans were really saving these poor
> people, and I don't miss an opportunity to tell Ameri-

cans when I'm over there how taken aback I am at this guilt complex of theirs, which is absolutely false and unnecessary.[9]

Twenty-five centuries have carried us from the vision of Africans as bizarre-looking cave dwellers to pitiable cases who needed slavemasters as social workers to raise their stations in life. Fortunately, centuries have lessened, to some degree, the impact of this racism. Africa is now almost entirely governed by its own peoples who hold proudly their place in a community inclusive of Africans and worldwide citizens of the African diaspora. This Pan-African awareness certainly did not exist in Hanno's age and was written off as an escapist and politically subversive idea during the colonial era in which Ian Smith participated.

A small but very significant advance in that area of African Studies concerned with colonial and post-colonial images of Africa in the minds of blacks and whites has occurred through the publication of Christopher L. Miller's *Blank Darkness,* Philip Curtin's *The Image of Africa,* William Cohen's *The French Encounter With Africa,* George Fredrickson's *The Black Image in the White Mind,* and Joseph Boskin's *Sambo.* Harold R. Isaacs' research, cited in *The New World of Negro Americans,* also had a major impact in calling attention to the proliferation of African images in ever-changing forms among African Americans. Particularly insightful are his accounts drawn from prominent African-American political leaders and artists about the traumatic nature of school textbook images of "savage Africans" upon their self-esteem and sense of connection to Africa. Hanno's wild African cave men and Ian Smith's poor human wrecks found life in the pages of countless school books, in Hollywood's Tarzan movies, in the logo of the smiling Negro servant or mammy on the cereal and pancake box, to cite but a few examples drawn from a vast image-repertoire held by racists committed to the notion that Africa was "a dark continent."

What I am identifying as "the Afrocentric imagination,"

manifest through jazz recordings celebrated in this book, is a counter-racist imagination: an imagination that has been informed by the writings and other activities of such seminal thinkers and artists as W.E.B. DuBois, Marcus Garvey, Langston Hughes, Zora Neale Hurston, Claude McKay, Sterling Brown, Amiri Baraka, and others. The term "Afrocentric" was coined by cultural analyst Molefi Kete Asante, who defines it in *The Afrocentric Idea:*

> . . . it suggests a turnabout, an alternative perspective on phenomena. It is about taking the globe and turning it over so that we see all the possibilities of a world where Africa, for example, is subject and not object . . . The crystallization of this critical perspective I have named *Afrocentricity,* which means, literally, placing African ideals at the center of any analysis that involves African culture and behavior.[10]

Asante's perspective is timely not only for African Studies in general, but also for study of the arts produced by citizens of the African diaspora. While not denying the American invention of jazz, it enables us to begin to hear and view jazz through an Afrocentric vantage point.

In amplifying Asante's ideas, I am linking the word "Afrocentric" with "imagination" in dealing with jazz. Any piece of music might inspire various imaginative images in listeners. But I am suggesting that African-American artists produce art in the context of combating centuries of racist-constructed imaginations of Africa. Faced with centuries of distorted visual and written accounts depicting Africans as uncivilized ape-men inhabiting a savagely dark continent, faced with the horrors of the slave trade and European colonialism and neo-colonialism, Africans and many African Americans have developed a counter-racist imagination of Africa. This unique form of imagination can best be understood by looking at the specialized definition of "imagination" offered by the philosopher and critic Gaston Bachelard. In contrast to the commonly used notion of imagination as representing a whimsical escape from reality, Bachelard's understanding of imagination highlights its engaging and constructive function:

> Imagination . . . is essentially a rejection of the tyranny of forms, primarily of forms given by reality but also of forms evoked by the imagination itself—of all these fixed images which offer themselves to imagination.[11]

Applying Bachelard's use of imagination to this study suggests that African-American artists in search of their African connection must initially deconstruct the fixed body of distorted African imagery that racists have historically disseminated in multitudinous forms. After these images are deconstructed, various elements can be recombined so that new perspectives can be gained, materialized through the energetic movements of artists under the spell of Afrocentric imagination. The chapter on Duke Ellington's music will offer insights into how one musician took the racist notion of Africa as a primitive jungle and deconstructed that stereotype through his music so that listeners could see a fresh Africa. A parallel to this alchemy of African imagery can be seen in the work of the contemporary African-American visual artist, Betye Saar.

In her *Africa* (see page 14), an assemblage within a small wooden box completed in 1968, she combines a seemingly mysterious set of objects: part of an animal vertebrate, a tin toy elephant split apart at the seam, a mink pelt, buttons, ribbons, a mirror, a picture of a "savage" of apparently African identity. Close examination, enhanced if the viewer puts his or her face eye-level with the box, reveals an astonishingly rich set of interrelated images evoking the artist's sense of Africa as the cradle and crucible for her art. The ribbons display traditional and religious color symbolism. The "savage" face stares with unitary gaze at the observer— but the observer's face is rendered in fragmentary fashion by the mirror in the box. The bones in the box are not only a grisly reminder of the mass murders various Europeans and white Americans perpetrated upon African humans and animals, they also hint at the presence of the Spirit world lurking around the African boneyards. Or they can cause one to reflect upon how African elephants lovingly sort through the bones of their departed ones, part of a mysterious ritual not yet comprehended by biologists.

Even the wooden box itself, lid open to observer, raises questions and concerns about Africa. Is the box a coffin for all things African? Is it a safe, a secret chamber, an alchemical alembic assuring the safety and purity of sacred African elements? Whatever else Saar's box is, it is clearly an art object providing a site for an interrelated set of images evocative of the Africanicity of African Americans. It is as artfully arranged as the shrine of sacred objects created by practitioners of the Afro-Cuban religion of Santeria, called "A House of Images." Saar's assemblage displays what Bachelard in his theory of imagination calls "a culture complex." Imaginary images are chosen and drawn together into a constellation, a pattern reflecting transmissions of the artist's culture. In Carl Jung's terminology, an artist's favored images constantly transformed in imagination reflect that artist's contacts with archetypes having life within "the collective unconscious." Archetypal energy is summoned by the animal bones in Saar's box, suggesting the easy intimacy between humans and animals in traditional Africa. These bones collide with the mass-produced tin toy elephant in the visual field, an object conjuring up the mass mechanization threatening the human spirit in the West. This multidimensional field of objects capable of being read, simultaneously, both in light of Africa and in light of the American experience for African Americans, can be interpreted metaphorically, applying the perspective Asante offers in examining various statements by leaders of the Back-to-Africa movement:

> Standing above the movement's rhetoric is the metaphysical Africa, encompassing and activating the quest

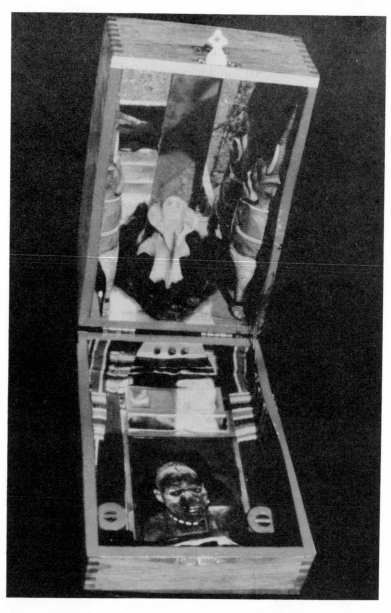

Africa—1969, Betye Saar. Mixed media assemblage 9½″ × 5¾″ × 11¾″. Reproduced by permission of the artist.

for unity, security, and liberty. "Africa" signifies an escape from racial discrimination and an epitomized pride in heritage. The metaphor becomes the message.[12]

Yet Saar's box cannot be easily read as simply signifying an unqualified hooray from one African American to the Motherland. It is far more complicated than that since the objects are arranged so that multiple interpretations of their meanings are constructed by the viewer. Different stories about a relationship to Africa can be conjured up, depending upon how the objects are connected together in viewer consciousness, a process parallel to what any reader of this book might do while listening to recordings of Afrocentric jazz. The rich play of meanings suggested by Saar's art underscores Bachelard's point that "Imagination creates images, but above all, it creates a world which opens anew with each image."[13]

Shifting from the visual arts to jazz, that same richness of associative imagery can be found in a number of the musical compositions considered in this book. Max Roach's *Freedom Now Suite* juxtaposes South African screams of protest against Apartheid with sounds drawn from the American civil rights struggle. Ellington even dares to incorporate flying saucers into his *A Drum Is A Woman,* mixing cosmic and occult imagery into a drama tracing the birth of jazz from Africa through the Caribbean to New Orleans. John Carter combines the storytelling of an elderly uncle about post-Civil War Southern life with sounds of modern Ghanaian drummers in his set of five suites, *Roots and Folklore.* None of these works are simply about Africa in any one-dimensional way. Like much of the recorded music honored in this book, these are works which engage the listener on several planes. And central to this engagement is an awareness of the key significance of Africa.

How do certain musical works suggest a sense of a certain place to listeners? Ponder the ways that various classical composers suggest specific locales. The image of a New England town center on the Fourth of July is called forth by mighty brass choirs battling for noisy supremacy, a rioting explosion of raggedy dissonance, in Charles Ives' Fourth Symphony. Closer to the spirit of the music examined herein, Louis Moreau Gottschalk suggested images associated with *A Night in the Tropics* through his buoyantly syncopated rhythms. The pastoral clime of Finland is musically known by millions who have never visited the place through *Finlandia,* by Sibelius. The music historian John Burke offers a unique examination of how various romantic English composers evoked their homeland in his *Musical Landscapes.*

As this book examines music by thirteen African-American jazz composers, it will go beyond previous studies of how musicians have evoked a sense of place. Not only have jazz musicians heralded Africa as a place, they have also evoked additional themes intrinsically tied to Africa. Here are the five themes that persistently came to mind as I studied Afrocentric jazz:

Place
Compositions reflect the composer's engagement with images of African rivers, deserts, mountains, and jungles. Occasionally, ancient or modern cities are evoked.

Portraits
Compositions include a range of ancient and contemporary leaders (ranging from Ethiopian emperors to contemporary prime ministers), artists, depictions of historically notable (often archetypally charged) figures like Cleopatra and Nefertiti, and youths.

Nature
Compositions include references to specific forms of animal life as well as general images of African flora and fauna.

History
Compositions include references to major historical events transmitted through mythopoetic storytelling or through conventional Western historical narration. Of particular importance are the struggles related to the transatlantic slave trade and the modern struggle for release from colonial rule.

Liberation
These compositions deal with one or more dimensions of Africans in search of political, economic, and spiritual release from chains of bondage so that people might attain greater fulfillment of their human potential within contexts of community.[14]

A listing of recorded examples of jazz embodying these aspects of the African theme will be found at the conclusion of each chapter, cataloging the contributions by each of the thirteen musicians at the cornerstone of this study. A discography listing recordings by musicians not in this core group concludes the book.

Putting the notion of an Afrocentric imagination at the heart of an analysis of a large body of jazz raises a thorny question: Can a white American really understand and meaningfully participate in such a form of musical imagination? My ancestors, for example, came from Eastern Europe, and probably never gave a thought to Africa. Is it appropriate for this white American to speak of the Afrocentric imagination?

One of the few literary studies dealing comprehensively with the nature of the Afrocentric imagination, Stephen Henderson's *Understanding the New Black Poetry*, hints that only black Americans can really have access to black imagination.[15] Henderson bases this on his belief that only those who have experiences living as a black in the U.S. can fully appreciate what meanings lurk beneath the images and sound textures of black poetry. Only lived experience as a black entitles one to unlock the mysteries hidden in black art.

While there is a commonsensical grain of truth in Henderson's stance, he neglects to take into account that some of the major themes articulated by black artists find striking parallels in the works of non-African based artists. This paradox was compellingly stated by musician and activist Paul Robeson who marvelled about his natural affinity for learning both the Russian language and Russian songs. What Robeson suggested might explain his seemingly intuitive grasp of the language and music was the fact that both African and Slavic peoples knew the meanings of slavery deep within their collective unconscious. The theme of liberation marks the music and poetry of both peoples.[16]

To make the connection as Robeson did is not to deny the uniqueness of the African heritage as made manifest by the artists of the African diaspora, or to bypass Henderson's point that there is no substitute for having lived black in order to comprehend some meanings in black art. But I am strongly affirming that art created by African Americans exercising their Afrocentric imaginations can be appreciated by and enriching for anyone. Almost everyone is capable of imagining a world where Africa assumes a center-stage position, as well as being capable of developing an image-repertoire reflecting a counter-racist perspective. That African Americans can bring an enormously richer body of life experiences to the cultivation of an Afrocentric imagination seems unquestionable. The subject matter here, jazz and Pan-Africanism, are largely creations of members of the African diaspora.

And these descendants of Africans also have a significant advantage over others in creating and appreciating Afrocentric art through their direct participation in a tradition extending from centuries old ancestors to those yet-to-be-born. A cynically minded white scholar of Pan-Africanism, Imanuel Geiss, can write that "one of the wittiest definitions of Pan-Africanism is that it is 'a delayed boomerang from the time of slavery' "[17] but those of African descent do not possess Geiss' sense of "delayed boomerang." As literary historian James Olney notes:

> The ancestors, though individually long dead, have not been shunted off to heaven or hell: they are right there in the soil, in the air, in the life of present descendants, no matter how many generations removed; and there, too, exist the children and grandchildren who have yet to achieve physical embodiment.[18]

Although I can never be a direct part of that sacred pact the dead African ancestors have made with generations of the African diaspora, I have tried to establish a place among the community gathered around the tribal musicians. Years spent listening to and thinking about the jazz of Duke Ellington, John Coltrane, and the others celebrated here have made them "ancestors" to me, if only artistically and spiritually. I hope their spirits will accept this book in the spirit of reverence with which it is offered.

Certain readers may accuse me of being "sentimental" or "romantic" about jazz and Africa. It is currently the fashion among some American journalists to manifest a cynically "realistic," debunking attitude about Africa and its global influence. The very real problems Africans face at the close of this century are suddenly being sensationalized in ways frighteningly redolent of the most hate-infested colonial literature of a century ago. In what ostensibly is a book review of a text by a fellow journalist involved with Africa, David Lamb writes:

> Africa's external debt stands at 135 billion. In some countries, upwards of 40 per cent of the leaders are infected with AIDS. The continent, which fed itself in 1960, now must import two fifths of its food. And as the food supply shrinks, Africa's population growth today— 3.2 per cent—is the "highest seen anywhere," anytime, throughout human history.[19]

So this litany of Africa's sins invites despair—or correction. One can look at African problems Afrocentrically, viewing

African lives as if through African ideals and values. A study of Afrocentric jazz can begin to offer that perspective. This vision is all the more vital as Africa's problems are tackled increasingly by armies of foreign visitors, armed with non-African varieties of capitalism, communism, religions of every stripe.

I would like to image one of these non-African "helpers" packing his or her suitcase for an African journey. Recalling the prankish teenage boy in love with Art Blakey's jazz, I would like secretly to plant an audio cassette of jazz in a suitcase. Let that tape contain, among its selections, a tune composed by Dizzy Gillespie.

Imagine that look of the visitor's face when that mysterious tape falls out of the suitcase upon arrival in Africa, is placed in a tape player, and the opening bars of "A Night in Tunisia" fill the African night air.

CHAPTER TWO

Earliest Intimations of a Return to the Motherland

> The high school fraternity dance of 1919 was planned to be an important affair. We had heard of a hot Negro band down in Louisville, and I signed them unseen and unheard . . . Louis Jordan's Band (This was not the Louis Jordan from Arkansas who had a popular band in the thirties) . . . Jordan's men broke into Russian Rag as a grand march. We did a wild shuffle of moaning pleasure. They changed the rhythm to a fast fox trot. The day of judgement was upon us. I shouted: "I'm a Congo medicine man!"—*Hoagy Carmichael*[1]

Who can trace the origin linking American musical ecstasy with African magic? One highly plausible source for the connection would be nineteenth century minstrelsy where the term "Ethiopian" was bandied about with regularity. (The term was generalized to mean any dark-skinned performer, natural or cosmetically masked.) *A Dictionary of American English* offers a citation from an 1855 *Putnam's Monthly* about how "Ethiopian Serenaders and Congo Minstrels will draw crowded houses at three dollars a seat."[2] Minstrelsy scholar Hans Nathan reports that short dramatic skits with singing and dancing were called "Ethiopian Operas." And on the cover page of the sheet music for Stephen Foster's "Old Folks at Home" appears the subtitle: "Ethiopian Melody."[3]

The history of the word "Ethiopia" provides a key to the significance of the American use of the term in minstrelsy.

The Greek word translates as "burnt face," and was used by the ancient Greeks to refer to those residents of Africa south of Egypt. Historical and literary citations in fourteenth-century England suggest "Ethiopian" was used to signify anyone of a swarthy complexion. From the Greco-Roman classical period to the Elizabethan, one could be assured that the popularly published descriptions of "Ethiopians" were surrealistically fantastic and often focused upon the qualities of black skin. In a controversial attempt to prove the absence of racism in ancient Greece, Frank M. Snowden offers ample proof to the contrary:

> There was a belief in certain circles that the color of the Ethiopian's skin was ominous, related no doubt to the association of the color black with death, the under-world, and evil. It was noted, for example, among omens presaging disaster that ill-starred persons were known to have seen an Ethiopian before their misfortune.[4]

Continuing the theme of connecting black skin with misfortune, Elizabethan England contemplated a remedy to right skin hue. Emblem books by the Italian illustrator Andrea Alciatra swept sixteenth-century England with an illustration of white men scrubbing a black man to rectify his color. The image is framed by:

> You wash an Ethiopian; why the vain labor? Desist. No one can lighten the darkness of black night.[5]

But the wish was there for "Ethiopians" to look like Europeans, a wish persisting into the New World. Leave it to Dr. Benjamin Rush, the father of American medicine, to contribute to a solution:

> Dr. Benjamin Rush gravely informed the members of the American Philosophical Society that the complexion of Africans was indicative that they were the victims of endemic leprosy. . . . Dr. Rush was carried away by his imagination. He claimed that the African's "naturally

white flesh" could easily be restored by bloodletting,
fear, forbearance from any indulgence of appetite,
hydrochloric acid and "the juice of ripe pears."[6]

While pears lacked the efficacy of a cure, one can be
reminded that as simple a nostrum as burnt cork long had the
power to cure a Caucasian of whiteness, a fact that Shakespeare's audiences appreciated when watching Othello, then
as, occasionally, now. And it was curious how black skin, so
identified with evil and tragedy could be acceptable, even
desirable on stage, paralleled by the no less curious fact of the
currently emergent acceptability of black actors in white face.
Such transformations of flesh were expected on the imaginative platform of the stage where shocking reversals of
everyday reality were relished by theater goers. One wonders
what sixteenth-century actors, steeped in the racist stereotypes of Africans as savages without conscience or active
intellect, thought when they donned black face? Did a
fleeting second of imagining the humanity of the Africans
they portrayed cross their minds?

That same question can be asked of performers in the
heyday of American minstrelsy when the actors again were
largely whites in black face. But unlike black-face characters
in the complex dramas of Ben Jonson and William Shakespeare, minstrels could indulge in acting out absurd character-
izations of blacks to the hilt. The form of minstrelsy itself
actively encouraged such indulgences, such frontal mockeries
of the intellect, posture, sound, and surface appearance of
blacks. And yet, even within a dramatic form that was a tissue
of cartoonish stereotypes, a moment of humanity would
surface, albeit subconsciously, accidentally. Central to minstrelsy, its most lasting legacy, was music. Through an
examination of its most famous song, later resurrected in jazz,
a glimpse through the racist trappings of minstrelsy can be
caught.

No composer of minstrel music was as popular as Stephen
Foster, whose songs take on the guise of "folk music" today,

standards, "the songs America loves best." And "Old Folks At Home" (also known as "Way Down Upon the Swanee River") is so identified with the heart of the American popular music legacy that John Tasker Howard, a Foster biographer, writes without any apparent irony that the song "disarms all who would criticize or analyze it."[7]

Forget the rustic dialect used, often dropped in modern versions. Forget also the banality of the melody. It was the image of the black slave longing for the warmth of the old plantation that rang true for music lovers in 1851 when the song was first published. For anyone with a non-racist orientation in this century, the only way to tolerate hearing the song is to contemplate the exact opposite of the song's message, to imagine a slave pining for an African home. Intriguingly enough, transposing from the South to Africa is easy due to the non-specificity of location in the lyrics. The plantation is only described as a "little farm" in the second stanza, and only "one little hut among de bushes" is offered in the rarely sung (on record) third stanza, an image that sounds to modern listeners as African as American.

But a modern listener to this chestnut might find most pleasure in Africanizing Foster to interpret "old folks" as African ancestors. An enormous part of the spiritual dislocation African slaves experienced on these shores had to do with removal from the distant burial sites of ancestors. There was a cause for spiritual longing that was mightily captured in African-American spirituals. However Foster's song is contemplated, there is a heartbreak in the pivotal word "home."

In one sense, this entire book tracing the routes of the African-American musician's imagination of Africa turns on that "home." For those African Americans who desire and need to link themselves to their African origins, Africa will always be, poetically, spiritually, if not literally, home. For those who link themselves exclusively to their origins in this hemisphere, Africa can never be home. Between these extreme positions are those who move along a continuum embracing various ties to Africa.

For anyone in America, black or otherwise, interested in locating home prior to immigration to the New World, there is always the possibility of imaginatively conceiving of a historical scenario explaining how and why one's roots are other than the site where one is currently residing. So common are these imaginative scenarios explaining one's true home that it appears an archetypal quality in the American psyche, this lust to interpret authentic home, the ancient theme of "exile and return." These are the contents of the psyche which never melted down in the American melting-pot. We are longing for elsewhere, and for certain African Americans, elsewhere is inevitably some form of Africa.

So Foster's "Old Folks at Home" was a rather peculiar popular song for minstrelsy where seriousness of emotion was usually sacrificed for the quick laugh or knowing smirk. Beneath the obvious surface sentimentality and racist dehumanization of the song's narrating voice was that quintessential American nostalgia for "going back" to where one's ancestors hailed from. There is also a progression in the song's three stanzas from images in the early stanzas to sounds in the final stanza (bees humming, banjos strumming). Finally, the sounds of home, specifically the sounds of the natural world and banjo twangs, succeed in conjuring up a sharply immediate image of true home in imagination.[8] That this can occur within a song so saturated with racist condescension is never short of miraculous, but part of that miracle has to do with our intentionality as modern listeners hearing it divorced from minstrelsy's antebellum context. Further, our modern freedom to recontextualize the song through a diasporic sensibility creates deep meaning transcending easy entertainment. In Foster's day, this and other songs of this caliber were part and parcel of an entertainment structured to transform racial intolerance into musical comedy. The "Ethiopian Serenaders" who performed in black face, as their name would suggest, not only insulted the character of the blacks they portrayed, they further mocked the notion of any African civilization.

This assault upon the integrity and civilization both of

African Americans and of their African past obviously impacted upon the ways in which African Americans chose to relate to Africa. Since ragtime and early jazz (and the two terms were often used interchangeably with imprecision) were reflections of American culture, it was inevitable that ambiguous, ambivalent, but often mocking references to Africa would surface in the music. Indeed, it is safe to claim that in the early years of jazz, before the massive popularity of Duke Ellington, the majority of references to Africa in jazz were most often humorous, ironic, or mocking, about as serious as Hoagy Carmichael's adolescent dream that dancing to black jazz made him a Congolese medicine man.

From Hoagy Carmichael country, the Indiana heartland, came a white jazz band, Hitch's Harmonists, which would have been relegated to obscurity if not for the fact that the young Carmichael made his first recordings with them in 1925. But Curt Hitch's band enters the scope of this book because one of its recordings, "Ethiopian Nightmare," is one of the earliest jazz recordings with an African reference still commercially available. What an irony that an all-white band from Indiana should be remembered for this unlikely reason! When the band finds a niche in jazz histories for reasons beyond Hoagy Carmichael's recording, it has to do with the fact that the band instantly transformed its style along the lines of Bix Beiderbecke's Wolverines after hearing Bix's unit for the first time in 1924.

But Hitch's Harmonists recorded "Ethiopian Nightmare" before hearing Bix Beiderbecke, when they were a bunch of young men playing stiffly executed Dixieland. A more unlikely group of musicians dealing with an African theme could hardly be imagined, though the same could probably be said of that other white Dixieland aggregate which in the same year recorded the first jazz record with "Africa" in its title, the Original Memphis Five. (Their recording of "Africa" died an early death as a 78 and has not been resurrected in long-playing format).

Unlike the African-American musicians of the twenties, pianist Curt Hitch and his players could hardly make any serious claim that their playing derived from authentic African music or that they had any connection to an African lineage which would give them privileged access to African rhythms. But one hearing of "Ethiopian Nightmare" suggests that the "Ethiopian" in the title is suggestive of the use of the word in minstrelsy and vaudeville. As was true of a number of white Dixieland bands in the twenties, the order of the day was an ebullience, a partying mood translated into modestly syncopated dance numbers marked by primitively undeveloped hot solos. Although the term "swing" in jazz criticism is marked by numerous types of subjective judgments, it is fair to concur with critic Dick Sudhalter that most Indiana jazz of the twenties didn't so much swing as bounce.[9]

You can hear that comic bounce on "Ethiopian Nightmare," belying the hint of horror in the title, and the bounce has great impact when you hear a direct quotation from Irving Berlin's "Alexander's Ragtime Band." Whatever the shock of hearing Berlin's pseudo-rag and vaudeville hit quoted, the shock turns to amusement when another vaudeville hit, a more recent gem from a musical revue of 1922, "Yes, We Have No Bananas" enters. With that moment, it becomes clear that "Ethiopian Nightmare" is a syncopated pastiche of these popular songs, and that these songs have the humorous and/or ironic signatures of the minstrelsy and vaudeville circuits.

"Alexander's Ragtime Band" is not a rag at all; it is truly a march. It would be more accurate to define it as a mockery of military marches, a form often found in nineteenth-century minstrel shows where the military prowess of African-American soldiers was regularly ridiculed. Berlin's song had the potential to be magnificently played in authentic ragtime, as established by Eubie Blake's recordings, which injected a syncopated zest not present in Berlin's original version. So there was a hit song about a musical style overwhelmingly dominated by African Americans identified with a mythological ragtime band created by a white Eastern European Jewish composer!

But the real irony of "Alexander's Ragtime Band"—and of Curtis Hitch's use of it in "Ethiopian Nightmare"—is that Berlin's tune reaches further back to quote from Stephen Foster's "Old Folks at Home." To quote musically from "Alexander's Ragtime Band" is to reconnect with minstrelsy's mock quotation of slave songs on Southern plantations. What is nightmarish about Hitch's pastiche—though it is a nightmare we are supposed to laugh at as we would the nightmarish vaudevillian musical collages of Spike Jones—is the jazzy play on the chords and themes of two mocking traditions, minstrelsy and vaudeville. I am not assuming any conscious racism in Hitch's mind. In fact, like Hoagy Carmichael, he might very respectfully have realized how much his heavy-handed attempts to play hot jazz paled next to the music of many African Americans. Hitch just did what a young, midwestern white jazz musician could do—laugh at the pretense of being a Congolese medicine man while bouncing with the beat.

This somewhat awkward self-consciousness about Africa, occasionally leading to mockery of African themes, surfaced in both white and black jazz recordings before the emergence of Duke Ellington's band. From the 1902 song "Under the Bamboo Tree" (with preposterously Tarzanesque lyrics by the African-American poet James Weldon Johnson) to Tiny Parham's "The Head Hunter's Dream" in 1929, there were jazz records in which Africa seemed a vague ripple in the mind of the composer. Even in works with "jungle" conspicuous in the title like Jelly Roll Morton's "Jungle Blues," one wonders if the title refers only to the black section of New York City which went under that name in the early twentieth century.

A quick glance at several dozen titles of early jazz compositions (Table 1), some of which are still readily available on record, suggests that a number of works used

Table 1

Intimations of the Africa Theme in Ragtime and Early Jazz

Ragtime Compositions (dates indicate first publication):
"Sounds of Africa" (retitled "Charleston Rag," Eubie Blake, 1899)
"An African Beauty" (Sousa's Band, 1899)
"An African Reverie" (H.B. Newton, 1900)
"Under the Bamboo Tree" (B. Cole, J.R. Johnson, James Weldon Johnson, 1902)
"Africa Pas" (Maurice Kerwin, 1902)
"Africana: A Rag-Time Classic" (Leo Berliner, 1903)
"African Dreamland" (George Atwater, 1903)
"Ethiopia Rag" (Joseph Lamb, 1909)
"The African 400: An Educated Rag" (Arthur Pryor's Band, 1909)
"The Barbary Rag" (King's Military Band, 1913)
"Cleopatra Rag" (Joseph Lamb, 1913)

Early Jazz Compositions (dates indicate first recording; asterisks indicate those re-released in LP format. See discography for further information):
"Sudan," "Down the Nile (to Old Cairo)" (Art Hickman's New York London Five, 1920–1921)
"Pharoah Land" (California Ramblers, 1922)
"Zulu's Ball" (King Oliver's Creole Jazz Band, 1923)*
"Ethiopian Nightmare" (Hitch's Harmonists, 1924)*
"By the River Nile" (Jack Gardner's Orchestra, 1924)
"Africa" (Original Memphis Five, 1924)
"African Suite" (Zez Confrey, 1924)*
"African Echoes" (Parenti's Liberty Syncopators, 1925)
"Senegalese Stomp" (Clarence Williams' Blue Seven, 1926)
"Morocco Blues" (Joe Jordan's Ten Sharps and Flats, 1926)
"Jungle Blues" (Jelly Roll Morton)*
"Zulu Wail" (The Devillers, 1927)*
"African Hunch" (Richard M. Jones' Jazz Wizards, 1927)*
" 'Mid the Pyramids" (Clarence Jones and His Sock Four, 1928)*
"The Head Hunter's Dream" (Tiny Parham and His Musicians, 1928)*
"Congo Love Song" (Dixie Rhythm Kings, 1929)*
"Red Hot Hottentot" (J.C. Johnson and His Five Hot Sparks, 1929)*
"African Jungle" (Jungle Town Stompers, 1929)
"South African Blues" (Windy Rhythm Kings, 1929)*
"Back to the Jungle" (Tiny Parham and His Musicians, 1930)*
"There's Egypt in Your Dreamy Eyes" (Louisiana Rhythm Kings, 1930)
"Egyptian Ella" (Ted Weems Orchestra, 1930)*
"Shakin' The African" (Don Redman and His Band, 1931)*
"African Ripples" (Fats Waller, 1931)*
"Futuristic Jungleism" (Mills Blue Rhythm Band, 1931)*
"Jungle Fever" (Mills Brothers, 1934)*

African themes in a peripheral way. Since few jazz musicians had ever heard Egyptian music during the twenties, we should not be surprised that "Pharoah Land" by the California Ramblers does not use any Egyptian instrumentation, or that Clarence Jones' " 'Mid the Pyramids" musically uses no rhythms identifiable with music of the Nile. Yet it is remarkable, in an age when academic scholarship about ancient Egypt detached it entirely from the rest of the African continent, that the African-American pianist Jones would place his composition there, even focusing upon that symbol of Egyptian spirituality. In light of Sun Ra's Egyptian-focused jazz of the past two decades, Jones' title is prophetic.[10]

The Egyptian references in the recordings by the California Ramblers and Art Hickman's New York London Five (an English band in spite of the oxymoronic name) begin the progress toward the second significant theme in the history of jazz recordings making African references. If the first theme involved a humorous, ironic reference to Africa (often screening what was really music composed by whites), the second theme declares "Africa" as an exotic and mysterious landscape, corresponding to the ignorance of African actuality by the vast majority of music listeners in America. The title of George Atwater's ragtime composition sets the tone: "African Dreamland." In the first two decades of this century, Africa was largely the stuff of dreams, whether of Teddy Roosevelt's safaris or of midwestern church talks on bringing salvation to the savages (attended by Ernest Hemingway, who later explored Africa on his own, testing the verity of his childhood imaginings while in church).

Populating these early imaginations of Africa on jazz records were "Zulus" and "Hottentots," not signifying any real people in South Africa so much as token images of tribes whose names had gained currency in American minds through explorers' accounts or sensationalized fiction. A reference to the real South Africa occurred, perhaps for the first time, on the Windy Rhythm Kings' "South African Blues"; in 1929 American newspaper readers would have been aware of South Africa's increasing consolidation of white nationalist power and economic depression, clear reasons to have the blues.

The theme of Africa as a *romantic* dreamscape has never died, and examples abound in recorded jazz to the present. But a third theme grew out of the African dreamscape, declared in the song "Under the Bamboo Tree" in 1902. The song's locale represents it as being an ideal site for a Zulu to love his "dusky" maiden, a theme taken up three decades later in the Mills Brothers' "Jungle Fever." According to the old racist stereotype, Africans were libidinous savages, an appalling fact for the Victorian sensibility which became transvalued by the American post-Freudian sensibility. So the once negatively connotated word "Hottentot" as any person lacking a civilized capacity to communicate—old shades of Shakespeare's Caliban—became part and parcel of the newly sexually liberated "jazz age" in J.C. Johnson's "Red Hot Hottentot." The word gathered enough excitement to be taken as the name of one of Red Nichols' jazz bands, surely the first "albino" Hottentot society in history. Associated with this eroticism of an imagined Africa was "Congo Love Song" by the Dixie Rhythm Kings and "There's Egypt in Your Sleepy Eyes" by the Louisiana Rhythm Kings (with young stars on the order of Gene Krupa and the Dorseys).

But no jazz number so successfully crystallized this obsession with a sexualized Africa as a novelty number by Don Redman's band, "Shakin' the African." One of the most obscure tunes crafted by the team of Harold Arlen and Ted Koehler (part of that lineage of Eastern European Jewish composers who composed tunes that became jazz standards), it has been treated as ephemeral, when remembered at all. History remembers the Arlen/Koehler team for Cotton Club hits on the order of "Stormy Monday" and "I've Got the World on a String." As for "Shakin' the African," even the bandleader who recorded it has treated it with flip indifference. As Marshall and Jean Stearns reported:

In the thirties, Don Redman and his orchestra recorded
"Shakin' the African" in which Redman whispered an ef-
fective vocal panning other dances and stressing the popularity of this new dance in Harlem—"It's really in there,"
he sings hoarsely, which wasn't quite true. "As a matter of
fact," he said, "I never saw anybody dance it—some writer
brought in the tune, and I just recorded it."[11]

While notable as part of a tradition of American songs
about imaginary dances which reached its zenith during the
heyday of Rhythm and Blues with "Tighten Up" by Archie
Bell and the Drells, it is more significant for its suggestive
image of shaking.

The song proclaims "a brand new movement" capable of
driving "the gang loco," patent nonsense, of course, since the
lyrics suggest that this "new" movement involves shaking the
buttocks (punning on the "can" in "African," pronounced by
Redman with a deliciously long pause between the second
and third syllables of the word). Shaking buttocks in African
and American dancing is far from new. And shaking as an
explicitly sexual dance form is recalled by Jelly Roll Morton,
who remembered "The Shake" as a dance performed by nude
prostitutes in New Orleans at the turn of the century.

There are also thinly veiled references to shaking dances
among Georgia Sea Island residents, a group which has long
attracted the attention of anthropologists and musicologists
interested in tracing cultural Africanisms into the New
World. Critic Chadwick Hansen, through research into
nineteenth century newspaper accounts, has unearthed
"shake songs" from the early 1800's. He discovered that the
lyric "Jenny shake her toe at me" actually was understood to
mean "Jenny shakes her buttocks at me," *toe* serving as a coy
euphemism masking the song's erotic intent.[12]

While Jenny's shaking her bottom appears tame today,
dance decorum in the first two decades of this century was
monolithically against such Africanized movements. "Do not
shake the hips . . . Do not twist the body" ordered America's

sweethearts of social dance, Mr. and Mrs. Vernon Castle.[13] Such moves were considered by the Castles to be crudely unfashionable, that is to say, Africanized and eroticized. Quaint as this 1913 stricture might appear, it is worth remembering that this call for de-Africanized and desexualized popular dance extended into the sixties. Here is a definition from the sixties edition of *The Dance Encyclopedia:*

> *Jitterbug,* a generic term now almost obsolete for *unconventional, often formless and violent, social dances, to syncopated music.* . . The best known forms of jitterbug were the Charleston, Black Bottom, Shag, and Lindy Hop, dances of the 1920's and 1930's. (my italics)[14]

But beyond this ignorant complaining about shapeless and murderous dance activity is an implied further accusation harking back centuries to early chronicles of French racism:

> Moreau de Saint even suggested that the manner in which people danced might "serve as a way of creating a scale to know the varying degree of civilization of different peoples." His thesis was that savages had simple dance steps, whereas Europeans had complex ones.[15]

De Saint's assumption reduced African dances to demonstrations of the savage mind actualized in movements one would expect from a simpleton or simian. Hence, hip shaking, or for that matter any body movements outside of the lexicon of accepted European dance movements, were relegated by white authorities to proof of limited mental capability. Associated hand in hand with that diagnostic label were images of savage, uncivilized sexual license. The fact that many traditional African dances mimicked animal movements only offered further fodder to the racist perception, for "behaving like animals" has long implied acting sexually unrestrained.

The "Jazz Age," which Don Redman's band helped usher in, began to transvalue these racist assumptions. Shaking was identified with Africanizing and sexualizing life, as was jazz itself. But it was also part of the zeitgeist after the First World War where the earth was shaken, literally and metaphorically. Jazz, like other art forms, shook up assumptions about what "normal" life was about, or should be. In a veritable litany pivoting on the word "shake," novelist and poet Claude McKay revealed what shaking implied in all its dimensions in his novel *Banjo*. McKay ordered his reader to "shake that thing" in order to triumph over the forces of Death. McKay was not advising therapeutic music and dance so much as he was lyrically celebrating both the continuity of African musical culture throughout the diaspora and the fact that these cultural survivals were life-enhancing.

To identify a dancer's shaking buttocks with Africa was not a cheap pun to degrade Africa so much as it was a belated recognition that the physical sexual pleasures of music contributed to a heightened consciousness of what made life worth living. The exhaustion after the First World War of the old goals of life, material acquisition and brittle patriotism, made other goals seem that much more attractive. And since that war's butchery on a scale hitherto unimaginable was executed by supposedly highly civilized white men, perhaps it was no longer unthinkable to ponder and imitate the behavior of so-called "savages."

Whether "Shakin' the African" was actually danced is of less import today than the fact that it serves as a reminder of the conjunction of Africa and expressive sexuality during the Jazz Age, and that it also contextualizes early jazz as interactive dance music. Jazz inspiring dance returns jazz to its African origin where players and listeners alike realize the importance of sharing movements to music. It is not far from the tribal dance celebrations of West Africa to the scene in New York described from a dancer's memory:

> Describing an incident at the Savoy in 1937, Leon James remarks: "Dizzy Gillespie was featured in the brass section of Teddy Hill's screaming band. A lot of people

had him pegged as a clown, but we loved him. Every time he played a crazy lick, we cut a crazy step to go with it. And he dug us and blew even crazier stuff to see if we could dance to it, a kind of game, with the musicians and dancers challenging each other."[16]

The origin of this play between musicians and dancers in West Africa is delineated by African musicologist J.H. Kwabena Nketia:

> Close collaboration is always required between musicians and dancers because of the relationship between the structure of the music and the design of the dance, the latitude given for spontaneous variation which demands that both musicians and dancers pay attention to one another, and the need for observing the conventions and modes of interpretation demanded by the particular type of dance drama or its social context.[17]

While a number of jazz critics have propagated the myth that the interconnectedness of jazz to dance was eliminated by the speedy and asymmetrical improvisations of bop, evidence to the contrary can be readily found. Alvin Ailey's numerous choreographies of Ellington's extended compositions and Charles Moore's dancing to Max Roach's *Freedom Now Suite* are examples of how dance and jazz collaboration survived the heyday of bop. During my interview with John Carter, he mentioned his interest in having the Dance Theater of Harlem choreograph *Roots and Folklore*.[18]

In noting the evolution of the African theme in jazz from a romantic landscape to a sexually expressive one, it is vital to see a common thread of composers re-evaluating what was previously thought to be base and contemptible: Africa, African-American vernacular dance, and sexual mores. That process of transvaluing things identified with Africa eventually found expression in music that was overtly political, infused with an activist, populist spirit. In keeping with Duke Ellington's emphasis upon the West Indian contribution to jazz, I would direct you to a calypso singer, Wilmoth Houdini, who regularly performed with the guitarist Gerald Clark and his band of West Indian musicians in New York City. While it is stretching most definitions of jazz to call Houdini's calypsos "jazz," his recordings certainly have any number of jazz colorations due to Clark's guitar and Walter Edwards' clarinet and tenor saxophone.[19] In the deceptively titled "African Love Call," Houdini sounded the clearest note of African awareness from an African-American perspective in popular music ever heard by 1934 on record:

> Some people say give me Booker T.
> But I say give me Marcus Garvey
> They said Marcus Garvey was looking for war
> So I asked him what did Booker T. do before
> Said he gave the Negro nation a class education
> And that was Booker T.'s chief ambition
> But his honor Marcus Garvey started the fight for
> liberty universally.[20]

It was Garvey who encouraged African-American artists to look toward Africa for aesthetic as well as political inspiration. Houdini's song was a cheerleader's enthusiastic response to Garvey's call (Houdini even sings "Hip-hip-hoorah for the sons of Africa" at one point). No longer must the African motif be indirectly veiled by romantic allusions, comically, ironically satirized, identified with the secrecies of unleashed libido. Afrocentric music becomes identified with African Americans marching through Harlem streets, demanding respect and empowerment.

And though the contemporary reggae singer Burning Spear laments "no one remembers Marcus Garvey," Garvey's return to a place of honor among Afrocentric philosophers has been illuminated by numerous jazz musicians since Houdini's recording. But while Houdini's music moved to a calypso beat, it took a musician with a Duke's nobility to render the African theme with jazzy sophistication.

CHAPTER THREE

Madame Zzaj Testifies Why a Drum Is a Woman

Permit me to introduce myself, since I don't usually pop up in a book. I'm Duke Ellington's personification of jazz in *A Drum Is A Woman,* his lifelong muse, *mirror* image of his soul (hence my name), the subject of his autobiography, *Music Is My Mistress.* As befits my position, I have largely chosen to avoid public statements after my lover's death, assuming his compositions carried his intentions so clearly that any additional commentary from me was superfluous.

But imagine my anger and distress at reading how various jazz critics have slighted my showcase, *A Drum Is A Woman.* Terrible enough that his composition was twisted, but they misread the entire history of Ellington's involvement with me and with Africa. So it's time I set the record straight.

There was never any doubt about my ancestry: a true DAR lady (Daughter of the African Revolution). Ellington was lucid about this from the start:

> We must be proud of our race and our heritage, we must develop the special talents which have been handed down to us through generations, we must try to make our work express the rich background of the Negro. . . .[1]

Three decades later, in Dakar, offering his first concert in Africa, he commented:

> After writing African music for thirty-five years, here I am at last in Africa. . . . When the time for our concert comes, it is a wonderful success. . . . It is acceptance at

the highest level, and it gives us a once-in-a-lifetime feeling of having truly broken through to our brothers.[2]

I can perfectly recall our African reception, but was I surprised? That day was easy enough to foresee four decades earlier, when Ellington's Jungle Band began. The ties between the Cotton Club "jungle music" and African music, I assumed wrongly, were obvious to everyone. Instead, I read the most comical conspiracy theory about the "jungle music" days from James Lincoln Collier:

> . . . the band had to have an identifiable and consistent style that could be promoted through clever publicity. Although we have no hard evidence of it, we can imagine that he had long conversations with Mills about how this should be done. The gimmick they came up with was "jungle music." This was suggested by the fact that the Cotton Club was at one point using a lot of "jungle" skits as excuses to introduce erotic dance. . . .[3]

Collier lacked even a shard of hard evidence and more; he lacked a rudimentary understanding of what the twenties and thirties meant for African Americans in Harlem. I'll show you a swatch of that Harlem history Ellington's music reflected in a few moments. For the present, let the critic's theory that Ellington's early "jungle style" was a commercial scam be noted.

Another critic, Barry Ulanov, knew his Harlem history, but chose to interpret Ellington's jazz through a cursory psychoanalysis of the composer, diagnosed as one who "liked to indulge in fantasies all the time about himself, his associates, his music." So Ulanov used this characterization to mock Ellington's stage presentation:

> When Ellington got to theaters in the Bronx, Brooklyn, and Manhattan, he capitalized on this impression, not consciously, perhaps, but it was that which remained with his audiences. He used a "scrim," a transparent screen of gauze-like material, which obscured the band when it first appeared after the heavy outer curtains had

> been lifted. With soft blue lights giving the stage an
> eerie atmosphere and with the scrim to reduce the
> figures of the men to shadows, the first impact of the
> band was that of a group of men from a world beyond.[4]

What Ulanov and Collier had in common was an accusation:
Ellington was pretentious in even suggesting that his jazz had
anything to do with Africa. If Collier accused him of
commercial greed, Ulanov assumed he was subject to fantastic delusions. The only way I have made peace with the
delusions of these scholars is through realizing how removed
they were from the day-to-day realities of black life in
America. But recordings, books, and photographs from
Harlem in the twenties plentifully exist.

Would any critic think mention of African jungles in jazz
was a scam if he'd joined the crowd lining a Harlem street to
watch the army of Marcus Garvey's supporters pass? Caught
for eternity in James van der Zee's photographs,[5] we see
thousands of faces caught up in the intense drama of realizing
a Pan-African vision of liberation. Among the crowd would
be volunteers for Garvey's United Negro Improvement
Association, which extended not only across the country, but
to the Caribbean, Africa, and Europe. Their handbills and
pamphlets celebrated what African freedom meant to African
Americans.

This was a movement of pageantry, a march of heroes, a
cultural revolution abbreviating the geographical distance
between America and Africa into a spiritual and political
hop-skip-jump trajectory. It was a movement which freed the
African-American imagination of Africa from white racist
stereotypes of barbarity. As historian Richard B. Moore
noted, Harlem was certainly conscious of Africa prior to the
start of Garvey's movement.[6]

Garvey understood, however, how to mobilize the feelings
after the Great War of those who felt disenfranchised from
the American dream after being asked to die for it. Their
frustration, linked to repeated outbursts of racial lynchings

across the country, enabled Garvey to summon political activism from citizens enchanted by his dynamic image of a unified Africa which no white civilization could ultimately defeat. His vision was built like a mosaic, using as building-blocks earlier images of an independent Liberia and Ethiopia as well as of the high civilization of ancient Egypt.

As someone who was never far from a Garveyite gathering, let me let you in on a secret: this was a sexy, stylish, outrageous band of characters that passed through the UNIA, "larger than life" as the Hollywood cliche peddlers would say. Even a critic as sympathetic to my ways as Marshall Stearns could not believe the scope of these personalities. That is why he mocked a Cotton Club skit in which a black aviator parachuted into a jungle, rescuing a blond "queen," with an erotic dance.[7]

Most of Harlem in the twenties and thirties—had they been allowed into the Cotton Club—would have instantly recognized the object of the skit: Colonel Hubert Fauntleroy Julian, the first black aviation hero. Who could forget that day he parachuted over Harlem, saxophone in hand, playing ragged choruses of "Runnin' Wild" during his descent. He did me proud—even if not always in tune.[8]

And this Julian was much more than a stunt man; he became so intensely involved with Garvey's movement that he volunteered to serve as Aviation Director of Haile Selassie's fledgling Ethiopian Air Force just before Mussolini's invasion. And don't you think my man Ellington and his band knew all this? Listen to the portrait of the colonel (under his Ethiopian name), "Menelik (The Lion of Judah)," on an Ellington small group recording led by Rex Stewart.

There were more than heroes forgotten from these Harlem days: tragically forgotten also were the Caribbean flavors of the time. These Caribbean influences seemed to have been overlooked by those jingoistically inclined jazz writers who have wanted jazz to be a one hundred per cent American invention (allowing only for a dash of proper European folk dance influences and African drum rhythms). Thus New Orleans has been enshrined as *the* musical mecca where jazz was birthed.

Fond as I have always been of Rampart Street, let me set the record straight: I was not born there. I was the product of an extended labor. You could say that I came into this world kicking in several places at once. Ellington realized, more than any other jazz musician of this time, how much my birth was connected to the Caribbean. Here is Ellington's tribute to the Caribbean in his appreciation of trombonist Joe "Tricky Sam" Nanton:

> What he was doing was playing a highly personalized form of his West Indian heritage. When a guy comes here from the West Indies and is asked to play some jazz, he plays what *he* thinks it is, or what comes from his applying himself to the idiom. Tricky and his people were deep in the West Indian and the Marcus Garvey movement. A whole strain of West Indian musicians came up who made contributions to the so-called jazz scene, and they were all virtually descended from the true African scene.[9]

In emphasizing the Caribbean contribution to jazz, Ellington was doing far more than acting in consonance with the Garvey movement (which also underscored the African authenticity of Caribbean cultural contributions). He was reimagining the nature of the Middle Passage for its brutalized participants, participating in a current of imaginative thought picked up by Malcolm X in the sixties. Here is Malcolm X speaking to Ellington's Caribbean emphasis:

> Historians have written the fact that slaves were never brought directly from Africa to America, but rather they were first taken to the West Indies . . . where there were special persons whose job it was to break the will of the slave. Once his will was broken, his language and cultural characteristics were destroyed, then he was brought to America. So that the black people or the

> Africans, who remained in the Caribbean area, their will
> was never broken as thoroughly as the will of those
> Africans who ultimately ended up on these shores.[10]

This theory, however ultimately unprovable, had a great deal to do with my history. You can see that my transformation into "jungle music" was not a commercial ruse or escapist delusion so much as it was the product of musicians reflecting Caribbean and African musical values. The title "jungle music" was unfortunate, implying that all of the Caribbean and Africa was a vast rain forest. But listening to those earliest Ellington recordings of the twenties and thirties, you can imagine how Ellington's audience had their imaginations stimulated by the symbolic palette of African jungle sounds issuing from Nanton's muted trombone: growls, yelps, purrs, moans, cries. Listeners are still enthralled by how Ellington's horns could smear and twist and call forth my spirit—and all created during an age when African music was stereotypically identified with drums in the public's mind.

And Ellington knew how to match that horn section's jungleistic glossolalic polyphony with polyrhythms galore. And Ellington spoke with pride and pleasure of the contribution of drummer Sonny Greer:

> Every young drummer who ever saw Sonny Greer in his
> heyday was awed and inspired by his equipment. . . .
> There were chimes, gongs, tympani, cymbals it seemed
> by the dozen, tom-toms, snare drums, and bass drums,
> enough to equip the whole percussion section of a
> symphony. It was not only ornamental, for he used to
> get some crazy effects. . . . Any tune he was backing up
> had the benefit of rhythmic ornamentation that was
> sometimes unbelievable.[11]

Duke's love of drummers was manifest not only in his drum section, but also through his percussive piano attack. He played piano with a drummer's feel for the percussive possibilities of the keyboard. And in his greatest compliment to me, he identified a drum with a woman.

While I don't mind being personified by any instrument, I have been partial to the drum. That partiality has everything to do with my ongoing history as dance music. Forget those foolish jazz "experts" who claimed that jazz as dance music ended with the Swing era. Have they ever seen Alvin Ailey's productions based upon Ellington's later music? The best of jazz drummers—be they identified with Dixieland, Swing, Bop, Free, or Fusion—can inspire dance movement. And dancing, from its African roots to American manifestations, connected me to sex and religion. Do you think I mind?

I positively love to feel the rhythmic powers putting listeners into erotic and spiritual trance—West Indian drums, reflecting African heritage, even today transport Voodoo practitioners in Haiti, Shango worshippers in Trinidad, Kumina revelers in Jamaica. Trance dances sparked by drum rhythms, frequently showcase moves suggesting lovemaking—for are not the African spirits lovers of the flesh? Ellington knew this, and thought the mingling of the spiritual and the erotic needed no apology. It was not that he gained "religion" when he wrote his "Sacred Concerts" in his advanced years—he never lost his faith. His faith in me and what I represented, in all of my sexy and transcendental splendors, was never lost.

Some of you literal-minded thinkers have had difficulty not only in reconciling jazz as an erotic/spiritual art form, but in comprehending how Ellington composed and performed *A Drum Is A Woman*. A conversation with his Columbia Records producer as he was completing work on his tribute to me is revealing. To put this 1956 dialogue in context, Ellington had already honored his fascination with African-American themes in jazz in several significant ways. He performed his extended symphonic work, *Black, Brown, and Beige* at Carnegie Hall in 1943, a work which compressed in a fifty-minute suite African-American history from antebellum days to the Second World War. Four years later, again at Carnegie Hall, Ellington premiered his suite celebrating Liberia (later danced by the Alvin Ailey Dance Company).

And as mentioned earlier, he evoked various images of the African and Caribbean roots of jazz in his "jungle music" of the twenties and thirties. Now, at the Newport Jazz Festival, he's backstage with Irving Townsend:

> Duke would go on, as usual, in around a couple of minutes' time to catch the final few bars. He asked Townsend: "Did you know that a drum is a woman?"
> "Is that the first album?"
> Ellington laughed. "Man, that's not only the first album, that's the mother of all albums. That's the story of Madame Zzaj." He repeated the phrase as he rose to leave. "Madame Zzaj. She was always a lady, you know, but she was also a drum."[12]

I understood exactly why and how Ellington was announcing my birth in *A Drum Is A Woman.* He was thinking through the meaning of jazz as an imaginative image, one symbolizing the essence of his soul. The soul has been classically identified with a woman in both the East and West, thus my feminine identity. His manner of talking through this consideration of jazz as a drum and a woman was actually parallel to the thought patterns of traditional Yoruba poets:

> In Yoruba poetry we find often a cryptic juxtaposition of images; a refusal to explain and to build bridges for the reader from one part of the poem to another; coupled with an extreme power and conciseness in the images themselves.[13]

Part of the poetic power of the West African poetic image was further illuminated by the poet-statesman Leopold Senghor, whom Ellington would meet during this 1966 African tour. Senghor wrote:

> African languages . . . are essentially *concrete* languages. In them, words are always pregnant with images. Under their value as signs, their sense value shows through. . . . The African image is not then an image by equation but an image by *analogy,* a surrealist image. Africans do not

like straight lines and false *mots justes*. . . . The object
does not mean what it represents but what it suggests,
what it creates. The Elephant is Strength, the Spider is
Prudence; Horns are the Moon and the Moon is
Fecundity.[14]

From this perspective, the elliptical and occasionally cryptic
nature of *A Drum Is A Woman* is clarified. This was not the
history of jazz put into a conventional chronological history,
textbook style. It was a poetically imaginative narrative, a
musical dance drama moving from New Orleans to the
savannas of the Caribbean to the far reaches of outer space.
What cohered the action was my romantic tryst with the West
Indian drummer, Carribee Joe. By placing Joe in a jungle
setting, Ellington was not implying that I had my origins in
some savage backwater. In his commentary upon "La Fleurette Africaine" (included in his 1962 trio album, *Money
Jungle*), Ellington offered his sense of what "jungle" meant:

> "La Fleurette Africaine," I explained, is a little African
> flower. The piece should be executed from the African
> philosophical point of view, with which it is concerned.
> The jungle, to Africans, is a place deep in the forest
> where no human being has ever ventured, and this little
> flower was growing right in the middle of it, miles away
> from human eyes in the central part of the jungle that is
> God-made and untouched.[15]

Somehow, Carribee Joe could venture into the jungle in such
a sympathetic fashion that the unspoiled nature of the place
could be maintained. He could speak to the animals there,
Ellington told us in the piece, through his music, his
drumming. And through knowing how tonally to commune
with nature, he was able to achieve a harmony with his
surroundings since lost by musicians in so-called "civilized"
cities of the world.

And I, Madame Zzaj, had to fall in love with the drummer,
had to transform myself into the shape of a drum, to lure him
away from his pristine Caribbean home, seduce him into

becoming part of the jazz of New Orleans, New York, and beyond. But as the ending of *A Drum Is A Woman* demonstrated, he finally would forsake me and return to the Caribbean. No costume I wore could hold him in this country. Dressing in symphonic strings or donning be-bop affectations did not succeed. Even the spaciest sounds I could summon evoking flying saucer breezes (and this years before the "space" jazz of Sun Ra!) could not manage to hold him.

Ellington revealed in me how the Afro-Caribbean foundations of jazz have always had a slippery and shadowy relationship in the public's comprehension of the music. All too often these roots have been denied or forgotten in the name of presenting jazz as "respectable" or "sophisticated." Or, as I said earlier, "All American." So he had an agenda in composing *A Drum Is A Woman;* not surprising from the composer of *Black, Brown and Beige,* as well as suites honoring Liberia and Togo, songs heralding African flowers and the African woman.

But this agenda did not force him into the role of a dully didactic musical sermonizer. He treated me with humor, always, that was integral to his affectionate style. He even imagined Carribee Joe trying to spank me for neglecting my Afro-Caribbean heritage! And has a policeman trying to ticket me for driving too recklessly at breathtaking speeds! But I survived these gentle mockeries. He never forgot how to treat his mistress with dignity.

And I never let him forget how every instrument needed to mirror the tonal nuances of African languages, demanding that he call forth from his unforgettable hornmen like Cootie Williams, Juan Tizol, and Rex Stewart the sounds of speech translated through brass. To remind him of the talking functions of horns, I even presented him with a photograph in an African music text of side-blown trumpets carved out of wood to look like men talking.[16]

He kept his horns talking throughout his career, not just to maintain fidelity to that African image, but more importantly, to keep telling the story of his people. He used titles like

"Jungle Nights in Harlem" to suggest that African folkways had not completely disappeared from America's cities. The question that poet Countee Cullen asked during the heyday of the Harlem Renaissance, "What is Africa to me?", never faded from Ellington's musical consciousness.

Most of all, I gave Ellington a language to convey musically the sweep of African-American history, the key poetic images around which that history could be lyrically organized, sung, and danced for all times. And in return, he was faithful to me until his dying day. Found after his death were the fragmentary notes of a never completed opera, *Boola,* narrating the travails of an African slave in this hemisphere.[17] Should the fragments ever cohere, after the fashion of the Egyptian goddess Isis reassembling Osiris' skeleton, we may have yet another glimpse of his honoring of my African and Caribbean ancestry.

And I will have yet another reason to love him as madly as he loved my sound.

CHAPTER FOUR

"A Night In Tunisia": The Evolution of a Standard

Part One: 1942-1944

The tune began, like so many before it, with the composer simply experimenting at the piano. As Dizzy Gillespie relates:

> Anyway, I was sitting at the piano and after hitting this chord, a D minor, I said to myself, "Boy, that's a nice change." And the melodic line of *A Night in Tunisia* was in that chord. Sometimes you hit the E flat with it, sometimes the A-E flat and A, like a flatted fifth. I had to write a bridge for it, of course, and I didn't have a name for it till Earl Hines gave it that title. Tunisia was on everybody's mind at that stage of World War II.[1]

Plausible as this account sounds, Gillespie contradicts it in his autobiography, *To Be, or Not . . . to Bop,* disclaiming the role of Hines entirely and professing to have played it in Benny Carter's band years before joining Hines. And just to further cloud the issue, drummer Art Blakey claims to have seen Gillespie write the tune in Philadelphia using the top of a trash can as a makeshift desk, supposedly while Gillespie was with the Hines band. And, finally, when the tune is recorded in 1944 by the then nineteen-year-old Sarah Vaughan, the title is further altered to "Interlude (A Night in Tunisia)."

Faced with this towering babel of contradictory theories of origin, hard evidence arrives in the form of the Vaughan recording with Dizzy Gillespie. It does seem indisputable that news about Tunisia was constantly in the air in the States from

1942 to 1944. For myself, as for many of the post-war generation, Tunisia might simply conjure up images of an exotic Casablanca-like romance, but for the generation who lived through the war, Tunisia was the site of the culminating confrontation in 1943 between the Allies and Axis in Africa.

A year later, Sarah Vaughan was in a New York City studio making the first recordings of her career with a seven-piece band led by Dizzy Gillespie. Vaughan curiously transforms Gillespie's *A Night in Tunisia* into a blues, exactly what the tune itself does not immediately suggest. Not only is Gillespie's tune not structurally related to any traditional blues form but it is a complex tune for a young singer to follow. Its interlude passage between the tune and the choruses is tricky to execute convincingly, instrumentally, let alone vocally.

The tune's alternative title, "Interlude," seems a pun sparked by this interlude. Vaughan sings the slightly lachrymose lyrics about love being just a kind of "interlude" in a somewhat tentative style lightyears removed from her mature tone of the fifties. It is a perfectly respectable, bittersweet lament. The excitement of the recording comes from the composer's rich and anything-but-tentative trumpet solo, its brashness oddly out of sync with Vaughan's restrained vocal. One can be grateful for the control and lassitude in Vaughan's rendition. Anita O'Day recorded a blustering and crazily breakneck version of "Interlude" a decade later in which the lamentable lyrics are forced into an up-tempo showstopper, an act of utter tastelessness equivalent to Al Hirt's Dixieland Band doing an arrangement of *Verdi's Requiem*.

Punning once again on the alternative song title, "Interlude" was only an interlude in the evolving life of "A Night in Tunisia," most memorable as the entry vehicle for Sarah Vaughan accompanied by Dizzy Gillespie's solo. Rarely again in the history of recordings would the tune be taken at such a slow tempo or sung with such bluesy inflections. It was about to take on a renowned history as a cornerstone composition identified with bop.[2]

While Vaughan was willing to slow the piece to nearly a dirge, Charlie Parker accelerated it into the stratosphere. In what is arguably one of the most ornate alto saxophone improvisations ever recorded, Parker's forty-seven second break on "A Night in Tunisia" lives on as proof of the depth of his genius. Ironically, that shard from a 1946 session represented his richest interpretation of the tune, in spite of numerous other recordings, all worth hearing. Gillespie recorded "A Night in Tunisia" with Parker on several occasions and has also performed it with numerous units ranging from quartets to big bands. Bud Powell's surging piano version, energetically fueled by Max Roach's drumming, holds the place of honor as the sole version of the tune included in Martin Williams' recorded jazz anthology, *The Smithsonian Collection of Classic Jazz.* Scores of new recordings from around the world continue to surface with no end in sight. Yet the composer Gillespie is probably less identified with the tune than one drummer, an odd fate for a composition originally recorded with a vocalist and trumpeter as lead voices. But Gillespie had drums in mind when he composed it:

> Very early in my career, I realized that our music and that of our brothers in Latin America had a common source. The Latin musician was fortunate in one sense. They didn't take the drum away from him, so he was polyrhythmic. My conception was, "Why can't our music be more polyrhythmic?" In 1941, I wrote "A Night in Tunisia" where the bass says, "do-do-do-do-do-do" and "daanh-da-da-da-da-da" was being played against that. That was the sense of polyrhythm.[3]

Part Two: 1957-1960

> The melody had a very Latin, even oriental feeling, the rhythm came out of the be-bop style—the way we played with rhythmic accents—and that mixture introduced a special kind of syncopation in the bass line. In

> fact, for the first time in a jazz piece I'd heard, the bass
> line didn't go one-two-three-four-, "boom, boom,
> boom, boom." Afterward we played the tune on
> Fifty-second Street and called it "A Night in Tunisia."[4]

Sarah Vaughan's vocal on "A Night in Tunisia" did nothing
to reveal the rhythmic underpinnings, "the special kind of
syncopation" undergirding the work. Only Gillespie's terse
solo suggested the rhythmic riches, a treasure further adumbrated by Parker and Powell and countless interpreters since.
But it was drummer Art Blakey who, like Gillespie, had been
part of the legendary Billy Eckstine orchestra during the
mid-forties, who made "A Night in Tunisia" the tune most
identified with himself and his band, The Jazz Messengers.

By 1948 Gillespie and Blakey's careers took different
turns. Gillespie continued to proselytize for the new gospel of
be-bop through recordings and concerts across the U.S.
Blakey made a trip to Africa during 1948-1949, though not
ostensibly for musical reasons:

> I didn't go to Africa to study drums—somebody wrote
> that. I went to Africa because there wasn't anything else
> for me to do. I couldn't get any gigs, and I had to work
> my way over on a boat. I went over there to study
> religion and philosophy. I didn't bother with drums. I
> wasn't after that. I went over there to see what I could
> do about religion.[5]

Trusting Blakey's sincerity in making this statement, it is still
difficult to conceive of him not knowing that African religions
are practiced through drumming, dancing, singing. Yet
Blakey's disclaimer of any musical intentions informing his
African odyssey goes hand in hand with an even more
emphatic disavowal of any connections between jazz and
Africa:

> It [jazz] has nothing to do with Africa. I've had African
> drummers in my band—they've toured with me—but
> they have nothing to do with what we are doing. You

have to respect the African for what *he* is doing . . . But
you can't mix what comes out of the African culture with
what came out of our culture. I play a western made
drum.[6]

All of which brings to mind a D.H. Lawrence aphorism,
one so often applicable to jazz history as we have seen in
examining Gillespie's various versions of the origin of "A
Night in Tunisia," "Trust the tale, not the teller." A quest to
Africa to discover a viable religious identity unavoidably
brought African rhythms to the forefront of Blakey's consciousness. The first evidence of the musical impact of his trip
surfaced during his 1953 Blue Note recording, "Message
From Kenya." Albums based upon drum ensembles led by
Blakey, *Drum Suite* and *Orgy in Rhythm,* followed, culminating in a most ironic project for a musician so strongly
disinclined to identify jazz with Africa, *The African Beat.*
Blakey leads a drum choir consisting of drummers from
Nigeria, Senegal, Jamaica, and the U.S. in a program of tunes
based largely upon traditional African melodies and rhythms.
Multi-instrumentalist Yusef Lateef, who would later play with
his own ensemble comprised of largely African musicians (see
Chapter 13), contributes spritely solos on a variety of
instruments both Western (oboe, flute, tenor sax) and African
(cow horn, thumb piano).

While *The African Beat* is as musically challenging and
memorably entertaining as any jazz-African musical fusion
ever recorded, the most significant fruit of Blakey's African
trip was the solidification of one of the most unmistakable
drum styles in jazz. It is a style, like that of his fellow musical
innovator from the heyday of the forties, Max Roach, which
blends spectacular cymbal shimmers with explosive accents
bounding from the heads of snare and bass drums. This bop
approach becomes Africanized through a very sophisticated
use of cross-rhythms and by experimentation with pitch.

Blakey might have been uninfluenced by the sight of
African drummers using their elbows to vary the pitch of

talking drums (two headed goblet-shaped drums whose pitch is markedly variable depending on the arm pressure the player applies to the chords binding the top and bottom heads together). Yet he brings his elbows to his drum heads in a like exercise to alter drum sound.

Blakey's is a loud, volcanic drum sound full of explosive drum rolls and shattering cymbal crashes. Yet he possesses an uncanny sense—apparent both in drum ensembles and conventional jazz combo configurations—of knowing how to utilize well-placed silences. This awareness of what musicians would call "negative space" (often identified with the fifties and early sixties recordings of Miles Davis) might have also come from his African experiences. In what is a definitive account of a Western drummer learning African drumming, John Miller Chernoff writes of drum students:

> Apart from simply learning to maintain their rhythms, the most difficult task the student faced was learning to continue to maintain their rhythms. A rhythm which cuts and defines another rhythm must leave room for the other rhythm to be heard clearly, and *the African drummer concerns himself as much with the notes he does not play as with the accents he delivers.*[7]

While Chernoff's remarks pertain to drumming traditions among the Dagbamba people of Northern Ghana, the insight can be generalized to many West African drumming styles, and can be illuminating when applied to a jazz drummer like Blakey. Part of Blakey's artistry involves intricately playing off various cross-rhythms by fully utilizing *every* musical resource his drum kit offers, including striking the metallic and wooden or fiberglass parts of the drums. This cross-talk between rhythms (the standard 4/4 is often countered by a more Latinish rhythm) is dramatically illustrated through the various recordings of his signature tune, "A Night in Tunisia."

Two Blakey recordings of the composition are pinnacles. The 1957 recording features an edition of The Jazz Messengers spearheaded by Jackie McLean on alto sax and Johnny

Griffin on tenor sax. It is the first jazz recording that ignited my fascination with jazz, a fascination equivalent to what a madeleine meant to Proust, opening up a hitherto unimaginable world of riches. The original album graphics depicted some illustrator's romantic conception of a Tunisian city, intriguing to me since I had never heard news of Tunisia on the radio, a post-war listener far-ranging in my ignorance of Africa. I remember responding to the coolly precise fury of Blakey's drumming—an appealing thought throughout my adolescence "cool fury"—and even responding to the complex interplay between Blakey's thunderous introduction and various hand-held small percussion instruments played by the other Jazz Messengers.

In later years I have come to treasure above all other Blakey recordings the 1960 session showcasing saxophonist Wayne Shorter and trumpeter Lee Morgan. Blakey sounds absolutely possessed, his drumming wildly uptempo, his cymbal strikes apocalyptic in impact, his tom-tom reverberating seemingly from the earth's core.

While Gillespie considered "A Night in Tunisia" in terms of how it liberated bassists from a ploddingly linear and symmetrical style, I cannot recall the contributions by the bassists on either recording clearly. Blakey steals the show. It is his tour-de-force vehicle, as identified with the splendor of his technical execution as is "Sing, Sing, Sing" with Gene Krupa's. But unlike Krupa's showpiece, "A Night in Tunisia" has weathered the various stylistic periods of jazz with great vitality, as has the seventy-year old drummer himself. Perhaps he found more than music and religion in Africa. Perhaps Ponce de Leon should have looked for that fountain of youth under a Tunisian sky.

Part Three: 1962

Eighteen years after Sarah Vaughan transformed "A Night in Tunisia" into "Interlude," two further attempts were made to marry lyrics to the tune. Ella Fitzgerald recorded "A Night in Tunisia" with a piano-led quartet in the same year that Eddie Jefferson recorded his version with a large horn-driven unit.

The lyrics and singing styles are studies in contrast. Fitzgerald takes an easy-going swinging approach and renders a picture-postcard vision of Tunisia that is static. Virtually nothing happens over the course of several stanzas except the image of the moon and stars shining brightly over Tunisia. In a monumental evasion, Fitzgerald sweetly sings that this is a story "too exotic to be told."

Jefferson's version swings with greater urgency, projected through his hoarse and peppery vocals (later recorded with slight modifications on his 1974 recording, *Things Are Getting Better*). It begins with a static Tunisian snapshot, Tunisia as romantic dreamscape. But the interlude section departs from this motif by honoring the song's composer Dizzy Gillespie, and declaring that the song gives him "a lift." Just how much of a lift is apparent in the ensuing stanzas.

Jefferson's night in Tunisia is a hallucinatory odyssey, starting with the premise that "Tunisia" is where one finds love (far from the 1943 tune, composed when Tunisia meant a war zone where troops found death). Through various flights of imagination, Jefferson moves from the image of "love you've longed for under a Tunisia sky" to a tribute to Dizzy Gillespie "who swung this Tunisia with his mighty band." But the song startles most when Jefferson makes explicit in his lyrics what he sees in Tunisia:

> Lots of people may deny that they have ever seen them
> Funny little people walking around in the sky
> But I know myself I've seen a thousand little people
> Everytime I look into my baby's eye.

> I saw an eskimo climbing up a moonbeam
> Dizzy started playing Sammy Kaye
> I saw a chicken with lips, a snake with hips
> And that is why I ran away.

Faced with this mind-boggling assortment of devilments, he flees from Tunisia, or, more precisely, from this dream of Tunisia and his lady. Having escaped from this dream, the singer apparently realizes that he has to get going to find his lover beyond the dream realm.

This is a remarkable set of lyrics since the image of "Tunisia" is mainly a gate into the complexity of a lover's multiple personality if taken at the surface level. Yet the song is also about its own creator, a celebration of a Dizzy Gillespie who never sounds like Sammy Kaye. And it could also be taken, at least in some parts, as Eddie Jefferson's own autobiography, looking for the love eluding him, yet still dreaming about its possibility, in a voice, however gruff, tender.

No other instrumental or sung version of "A Night in Tunisia" so mines the far reaches of humor and hallucination, or so causes the listener to want to go there, wherever that "there" is, than Jefferson's. The vitality of his vocal dance reflected his practice as a tap dancer. He created spontaneous lyrics in the recording studio with disarming freshness, like a master hoofer with always the promise of new improvisation on an old theme a beat away.

Part IV: 1989

When working on this book, I began to hear in imagination, at times beyond control, fragments of some of the hundreds of recordings of "A Night in Tunisia" that I had listened to. This was hardly surprising, given how supersaturated my listening hours had been with every version I could locate.

What was surprising was a dream of a jukebox in Lagos, the capital of Nigeria (where I have never been). The jukebox, an old gleaming Wurlitzer, was at the rear of a smoky, ramshackle taproom. I approached the jukebox and noted that all two dozen selections were "A Night in Tunisia." In addition to the expected versions by Gillespie, Parker, Powell,

Fitzgerald and Jefferson, there were more obscure versions by musicians like pianist Mal Waldron and bassist Bob Cunningham. Wanting to bring the music to life, I fished in my pockets for a quarter without luck. Turning away in frustration, I faced the only other white in the bar, Herbie Mann.

I woke from the dream with the awareness that this "Herbie Mann" in the dream was considerably more than the commercially inclined jazz flutist. The actual Herbie Mann had led a State Department sponsored musical tour of Africa in 1960. In George Hoefer's *Down Beat* account of that tour, I discovered the following:

> Many of the concerts ended with Dizzy Gillespie's "A Night in Tunisia," which featured a five-minute drum solo by Rudy Collins. As Mann had suspected, this was what the Africans loved. If they failed to understand anything else, this they loved.[8]

There was enough ambiguity in Hoefer's account—did Mann think Africans would enjoy only five-minute drum solos or think they would love the specific force of the drums in "A Night in Tunisia"?—that I wanted to keep an open mind about Mann's intention in bringing "A Night in Tunisia" back to its imagistic motherland.

But my optimism about Mann's perspective was shattered when I read his liner notes to the *The Common Ground* album:

> "A Night in Tunisia" is one of the first Dizzy Gillespie Afro-Cuban compositions. It exerted a tremendous amount of influence on the early modern jazz movement. . . . With all due respect to Dizzy, we were in Tunisia, but we didn't hear any music that was like this.[9]

This oafish literalism fit the tone of the rest of the liner notes which included, not surprisingly, "The 'African' origin of jazz has been overstated."

My frustration with Mann's inability to interpret Africa's impact on jazz in an imaginative and metaphoric manner was converted in my dream into a "Mann" who symbolized musicians and critics dogmatically opposed to even considering the possibility of a hitherto unacknowledged link. This "Mann" recalls critics on the order of Max Harrison, who expressed contempt for Eric Dolphy's affinity for pygmy music, or James Lincoln Collier who takes Ellington's interest in Africa as pretentious puffery.

The point is not that "A Night in Tunisia" sounds like indigenous Tunisian music; it is that Gillespie's minor chord changes and syncopated rhythms have sparked the imaginations of instrumentalists and lyricists to put new life in the old standard. Gillespie's composition has also inspired at least one African jazz musician, Hugh Masekela, to invent his own instrumental version with something of the "motherland pulse."

The richness of the various interpretations of "A Night in Tunisia" suggests that jazz musicians will continue to mine Gillespie's standard for generations to come. And unlike my frustrated dream, when I lacked the coin to activate the tune, the resources in recorded form await your sampling. Let no one stop you from your appointed time in the Magreb.

A Selective Discography of "A Night in Tunisia"

There are hundreds of recorded versions of "A Night in Tunisia." Those on the following albums are distinguished in a number of ways to warrant singling out. The Masekela and Terry versions are the most Africanized, the Masekela improvising over a bed of African drumming. Terry (accompanied by Dizzy Gillespie) sings lyrics translated into Egyptian in a vocal style recalling Om Khalthoum, Tjader heavily Latinizes the piece while the Turtle Island String Quartet offers the composition without drums. As much as the composition has been transfigured by McFerrin's vocal gymnastics or Bluiett's deconstructionist reading on baritone sax, it seems to maintain a structural integrity that invites generation after generation of jazz players to make it new.

Hamiet Bluiett, *Ebu* (Soul Note SN 1068).
Clifford Brown, *The Beginning and the End* (Columbia KC 32284).
Ray Brown Trio, *Bam, Bam, Bam* (Concord CJ 375)
Michael Carvin, *First Time* (Muse MR 5352).
Bob Cunningham, *Walking Bass* (Nilva NQ 3411).
Miles Davis, *The Musings of Miles* (Fantasy/OJC 004).
Stan Getz and Albert Dailey, *Poetry* (Elektra/Musician 60370-1-E).
Dexter Gordon, *Our Man in Paris* (Blue Note CPD-46394).
Johnny Griffin, *Bush Dance* (Galaxy GXY-5126).
Bobby McFerrin, *Spontaneous Inventions* (Blue Note BT 85110).
Hugh Masekela, *I Am Not Afraid* (Blue Thumb BTS 6015).
Lee Morgan, *The Best of Lee Morgan* (Blue Note B11E 91138).
Bud Powell, *The Amazing Bud Powell, Volume One* (Blue Note BST 81503).
Sonny Rollins, *Live at the Village Vanguard, Volume One* (Blue Note B21k-46517).
Lillian Terry, *Oo Shoo Be Doo Be Oo Oo* (Soul Note SN 1147).
Cal Tjader, *Greatest Hits, Volume Two* (Fantasy 8374).
Turtle Island String Quartet (Windham Hill Jazz WH p110).
Mal Waldron, *Update* (Soul Note 121 130-1).

CHAPTER FIVE

John Coltrane: Sounding the African Cry for Paradise

> Ethiopia had a powerful hold on the imagination for yet another reason: it was here that the Nile was believed to have its source. And the exegesis of Genesis 2:10–11 established a connection between the Nile and Paradise. So the renewed interest in Ethiopia now created the possibility of locating the geographical whereabouts of Paradise.—*Henri Baudet*[1]

Where does one look in a musician's biography for the most fruitful clue to explain the flowering of musical individuality? The temptation with someone like John Coltrane is to examine a list of his former employers before he struck out on his own: Eddie "Lockjaw" Davis, Dizzy Gillespie, Miles Davis, a veritable "who's who" of the bop era. And while there is undeniable value in placing the saxophonist firmly in the context of bop at his career's start, I would like to begin a consideration of Coltrane's musical contribution by listing a non-musical ancestor.

The St. Stephen's African Episcopal Zion Church of North Carolina had as its pastor John Coltrane's grandfather. In itself, this fact appears slight, particularly since Coltrane's various biographers do not note any particular affinity between the saxophonist and his grandfather in personality or Christian commitment. The musician would not undergo a spiritual crisis and transformation until age thirty, and the form of that spiritual passage would have seemed incomprehensible to the conservative members of a Southern African-American Episcopal Church led by his grandfather.

Yet I am underscoring the fact that the black church tradition was present in Coltrane's background because his relationship to the ritualized sounds of that church sheds revealing light on the evolution of his musical style. And in studying the translation of African-American church service sonorities into jazz, consider also the play of African musical sounds and images which altered Coltrane's sound. This perspective does not exclude any of the multifarious founts of musical inspiration for Coltrane's music: blues, Indian and Far Eastern modes, bop, ballads, but offers insights into one particular strain in his work.

Table 2 (see page 62) suggests one way to interpret the evolution of Coltrane's career. The usual analysis among critics proposes that Coltrane's music moved from a conventional bop style to an exhaustion of possible elaborations on the chord changes of standard compositions, signalled by the album *Giant Steps*. The next stage in his career involved compositions based upon modes with few chord changes, with examples abounding in his first albums released on the Impulse label. The final stage represents a set of experiments leaving behind most rules of formal jazz composition so that a simple emotional catharsis through a sax could be attained.

Whatever one thinks of the plausibility of demarcating his career in this fashion, consider alternatively segmenting Coltrane's career in terms of the nature of his imaginative identification with Africa. Although Coltrane never visited Africa, it was a presence in his musical imagination at exactly the same time that he began leading his own bands in 1957. He began collecting recordings of African music during this time, and, from these recordings, began to try on various bits of African musical ornamentation for two years: the recording sessions with trumpeter Wilbur Harden are dusted with sparse African colors; a recording of Watutsi drum rhythms inspired the rhythmic underpinnings of "Dial Africa"[2];

Table 2

Three Periods of John Coltrane's Recordings
Reflecting African Interest

African Ornamentation (1957–1959)
This period reflected some tentative experimentation with borrowing African rhythms and tone colors. The following were interpreted but not composed by Coltrane:

"Dial Africa"
"Oomba"
"Gold Coast"
"Tanganyika Strut"
"Dakar"
"Bakai"

African Program Music (1960–1967)
The following are original compositions by Coltrane in which moods and events are musically created to express the nature of specific African places, persons, and events:

"Liberia"
"Dahomey Dance"
"Africa"
"Tunji"
"Kulu Se Mama"
"Ogunde"

Africanized Spiritual Music (1964–1967)
These are original compositions by Coltrane in which the musical forms and chanted texts are created to inspire spiritually transformative consciousness in listeners:

A Love Supreme
Ascension
Meditations
Om
Interstellar Space
Jupiter Variations

See the Coltrane discography for further information about these and other Coltrane recordings.

"Oomba" has horns soloing over a one-chord vamp; "Bakai's" (meaning "cry" in Arabic) horns rigorously repeat call-and-response patterns; "Dakar" uses an Eastern-sounding mode, perhaps inspired by Yusef Lateef. These initial suggestions of Africa are tentative, the titles of the compositions (not written by Coltrane) like "Tanganyika Strut" promise more than they offer musically. The land of bop (or in Dizzy Gillespie's parlance, "The Land of Oo-Bla-Dee") is more the geography to be reckoned with.

Coltrane's music of the sixties reflects a more programmatic involvement with Africa. He formed his classic quartet with pianist McCoy Tyner, bassist Jimmy Garrison, and the one-man-drum-choir, Elvin Jones, and he was playing his own music, free of bop trappings, though still linked to the modal compositions of Miles Davis. Titles of compositions were exact descriptions of African realities. "Liberia" was inspired by meeting Liberians who attended one of his New York club dates. "Dahomey Dance" reflected a serious attempt to translate a Dahomenian field recording of musicians making their voices percuss like conga drums into American jazz sounds. "Africa" translated pygmy vocals into horn chorus elaborations. "Tunji" was a tribute to the influential Nigerian musician Olatunji (who also collaborated with Randy Weston, Yusef Lateef, and Max Roach), and "Ogunde" celebrates another Nigerian musician who contributed to the preservation of the traditional musical heritage of his homeland. "Kulu Se Mama" and "Afro Blue" interpreted the African rhythms and textures implicit in Caribbean music.

If Coltrane's African program music attempted to create narrative sequences with moods and events evoking specific African places and persons, his last musical works attempted to spiritualize the African theme, largely through large-ensemble units in which each player had considerable freedom to solo. The music of Coltrane's music prior to 1964 is well illuminated by two biographies by Cuthbert Ormond Simpkins and Bill Cole.[3] The music of Coltrane's final three

years has seemed to confuse, anger, or simply baffle commen-
tators. I would offer the lens of Africa-as-spiritual-form as a
tool for clarifying and understanding this period.

The one album of this period which has proven most
accessible to critics and jazz record buyers is *A Love Supreme*.
It offers inspired Coltrane tenor sax improvisation against a
background of a chant, the mantra "A Love Supreme." Its
appearance in 1965 was in the context of a countercultural
fascination with Eastern mysticism. George Harrison of The
Beatles was learning sitar, and Timothy Leary was offering a
reinterpretation of *The Tibetan Book of the Dead* to LSD
devotees. Since Coltrane's interest in Indian musical modes
and ragas was apparent as far back as 1961 when "India" was
recorded at the Village Vanguard concerts, it was easy to hear
A Love Supreme as a composition reflecting Hindu spirituality.

Coltrane's liner notes to the album suggest the evocation of
African and African-American spirituality, specifically
through sacred song, psalm. The biblical Book of Psalms
could easily have set the tone for Coltrane's recording. Psalm
150:

> Praise Him with the sound of the trumpet: praise Him
>   with the psaltery and the harp.
> Praise Him with the timbrel and dance: praise Him with
>   stringed instruments and organs.
> Praise Him upon the loud cymbals: praise Him upon the
>   high sounding cymbals.
> Let everything that hath breath praise the Lord. . . . [4]

This hymn of praise, integral to the Judaeo-Christian tradition
in the West, also has a counterpart in indigenous African
religion. Showering praises upon divinity is paradoxical since
the Divine, who has everything, knows everything, would
seem to have little need of praise. Yet the implication
throughout the Biblical songs is that God *hears* the nature of
human spiritual devotion, that faith is made tangible through
musical embodiment. Interestingly, the four parts of Coltrane's *A Love Supreme* correspond to this perspective:

"Acknowledgement," "Resolution," "Pursuance," "Psalm." First the acknowledgement of the need for a spiritual relationship with the Divine, then willing it, seeking actively for it, and, upon attaining it, raising the voice musically in celebration of the new-found spiritual bond. Coltrane's liner notes to the album described such a progression in his life, from the recognition of the need to find God, through a crisis where he emerged resolved and purposeful, and finally into a stage of praise-song recognizing his newly-won spiritual communion.

The sung psalm as proof of spiritual conversion was the meeting ground that synthesized African and African-American religion. Both spiritual traditions emphasize the habitation of the spirit by the Divine as the crux of spiritual conversion. In a perceptive article on gospel music Morton Marks writes:

> The roots of Afro-American gospel music go back to the black Protestantism that emerged on the plantations and the cities of eighteenth century America. This was the time of the Great Awakening, when the belief system of Protestant fundamentalism came into contact with certain ritual patterns of West African religions. Protestantism was newly ritualized by them, and concepts such as salvation, conversion and baptism were reinterpreted in different terms . . . . Possession-trance played an important part in many West African religions, and it was in the related areas of musical style, trance enactment, trance induction, and cult organization that a new configuration emerged . . . . [5]

The trance state in African-American churches has been historically carried by sermonizing speech rendered in song-like cadences and by song itself. Through these church services as well as through the singing of spirituals, music becomes the vehicle through which the heavens are brought to earth, God dwells in the flesh (particularly in the vocal cords) of worshippers. The catalogs of musical metaphors which fill the Book of Psalms, those countless injunctions, of

"Hear!" (as appropriate to a jazz listener/musician as to a spiritual seeker) are a part of a process where music makes heaven happen on earth. So the singing of the spirituals, with lyrics grounded in Biblical imagery, helped blaze a path that would lead slaves to liberation, both spiritual and political.

African-American church music can never be adequately notated on sheet-music, for much of the music's beauty emerges in the spontaneous creativity of the church community "raising" a song, call and response, weaving a new musical creation through volleys of spoken and sung exchanges. The leader of the congregation can be likened to the leader of a jazz band. He literally calls forth through his elaborate phrases the possibility for new musical directions, sparks new avenues of creativity. The high-point of the service—not unlike the high point of a jazz concert—occurs when one or more members of the congregation feel "possessed."[6]

The ritualized convention of possession in revivalist African-American church services offers a socially acceptable form for an individual person possessed by the spirit. Glossolalia (speaking in tongues) and abandoned dance movements are expected behaviors greeted receptively by the community of believers.

When speaking loosely of a jazz or blues musician who appears possessed while performing in concert, conservative believers would not question the authenticity of the musician's trance state so much as query *who* is bringing about the possession. Hence, blues became identified with "the Devil's music," a stigma also placed upon jazz by fundamentalist African-American churches early in this century.

What musically links the black church service with blues and jazz is multivocal antiphony with an emphasis upon repetitive and cyclical forms. This form serves the same function as the arabesque in Islamic sacred music: conventional worldly time passage appears suspended. One senses entering the timeless realm of the spirit, making real that rapture described by composer Gustav Holst:

> Music, being identical with heaven, isn't a thing of
> momentary thrills, or even hourly ones. It's a condition
> of eternity.[7]

This quotation could be interpreted in an African and African-American light by saying that *music is identical with the realm of the ancestors whose voices are materialized through its forms.* Heaven is that locus where the ancestor's spirits (voices) dwell. Music at its best brings those voices into this imperfect world, making our world more perfect by their presence.

This emphasis upon *voices* shows the traditional African belief in polytheism, or in pluralistic emanations of one Divinity. A devotee speaking in tongues has transcended his or her individual earthly personality and can speak with as many voices as Nature itself, as the Divine. The solitary singer of praises has become, while still in one body, a choir, a person of cacophonous, symphonic musical possibilities.

John Coltrane's fascination with multiple voices of sacred song was notable at the onset of the sixties. His leaps from the low to high register on his saxophone and experimentation with overblowing create a variety of simultaneous tones within the context of trance-inducing extended compositions. In his orchestrated evocation, "Africa", Eric Dolphy's brilliant arrangements for a large horn ensemble gave Coltrane the opportunity to improvise modally in a call-and-response field of other players voicing trills reminiscent both of complicated pygmy vocal harmonies and animal cries.[8] The possibilities of evoking such a multiplicity of musical sounds engaged in spiritual celebration materialized soon after *A Love Supreme* with the *Ascension* album.

For this effort, Coltrane joined together a half dozen young lions of the reed and brass world: Freddie Hubbard, Marion Brown, Pharoah Sanders, John Tchicai, Dewey Johnson, and Archie Shepp. Shepp's explanation of the music is cogent:

> It achieves a certain kind of unity; it starts at a high level
> of intensity with the horns playing high and the other

pieces playing low. This gets a quality of like male and female voices. It builds in intensity through all the solo passages, brass and reeds, until it gets to the final section where the rhythm section takes over and brings it back down to the level it started at.[9]

Shepp proceeds to compare the recording to "action painting" (like the abstract expressionism of Jackson Pollock) where various colors through their dramatic clashes create energetic fields of aesthetic experience. What I hear is less related to abstract expressionism than connected to the African-American church. *Ascension* records the constant passage from large ensemble free-blowing cacophony (never totally free of the mooring of pianist Tyner's minor blues patterns) to solo declarations and back to a swarm of large ensemble blowing.

Translated into African-American church imagery, this composition sounds like a hubbub of worshippers, each in the throes of his or her separate musical devotion, suddenly falling away as the voice of one possessed member works through a trance-possession. That possession completed, the worshipper returns again into a sea of voices until yet another worshipper receives the call. The thirty-eight minute *Ascension* doesn't so much "progress" to a clear dramatic resolution as much as complete a circle. This sense of music completing a cycle speaks to the circle image in many traditional African religions. While the Christian symbol of the cross graphically illustrates the intersection of worldly time and eternity, the circle suggests that through experiencing the rhythmic cycles of worldly life consciously and repeatedly, we spin ourselves into a sense of the divinely eternal.[10]

While eschewing any obvious single dramatic peak or resolution, *Ascension* functions through an extremely densely layered texturing of distinctive voices. This textural density is what a listener to an African field recording might immediately note, particularly since hearing the music removed from the visual tribal context removes it from a danced religious and social spectacle. African music as realized through a phonograph, Coltrane's primary means of hearing it (along with his friendship with Nigerian drummer Olatunji), is an experience of musical voices in dense accumulation to be eventually heard strand by strand.

What can make African traditional music on record attractive to a Western listener is the way the listener's various feelings can be multiply projected into the music's various layers. Complicated emotions for which our language lacks simple vocabulary, states like "happiness/sadness" or "communion/solitude" can be projected since each part of the emotional process can be identified with a musical level. The capacity of African music to embrace such a gamut of emotional complexity and apparent contradiction through its dense textures makes it a supremely powerful music for Westerners seeking spiritually transformative experiences. In one of the clearest definitions ever offered of traditional African music, W. Komla Amoaku writes:

> To me, traditional African music is the phonic expression of psychic experiences generated within the spiritual framework of traditional institutions . . . . These psychic experiences belong to and are revered by all members of the society, a homogeneous unit with common ancestry and a shared world view. Traditional African music is symbolic, an expression and validation of psychic energy. African music is a living thing ensouled by the spiritual energy that travels through it.[11]

Amoaku's definition suggests that no Western musician can exactly play "African" music since the non-African is cut off from being part of a "a homogeneous unit . . . with a shared world view." African Americans exist in a very pluralistic society. Yet I think this offers an explanation of the tremendous spiritual longing in Coltrane's later music, representative of his attempt to imagine the solidity and understanding a living African community might offer his music:

> John wanted to take his horn with him not to perform,
> but to practice whatever he learned. John said to
> Olatunji: "Next time you go to Africa, I'm going with
> you. I gotta go over there. I want to go over there with
> someone like yourself." Olatunji assured him that they
> would certainly go together, and John spoke of "having
> to get to the source," feeling that Africa contained the
> throbbing heart from which all music came.[12]

Lest this sounds like run-of-the-mill sentimentality for
"The Motherland," note the following twist on this theme:

> John once told Elvin [Jones] of a series of notes which,
> when played, could eliminate all friction in the universe.
> The consequences of this, John explained, would be to
> cause all matter to fall away from itself, since there
> would be no friction to hold it together.[13]

This musical mysticism, musical metaphysical philosophy has
roots in both ancient and contemporary African religion, a
basis for what South African bassist Johnny Dyani describes
as "Music as Medicine."[14] Because music carries the energy-
force of the Divine, it is capable of creation/destruction on a
scale ranging from the personal to the cosmic. This places an
awesome responsibility upon the shoulders of musicians, one
that Coltrane acutely felt. Hence his statement of purpose in
a *Down Beat* article:

> . . . I think the main thing a musician would like to do is
> to give a picture to the listener of the many wonderful
> things he knows of and senses in the universe. That's
> what music is to me—it's just another way of saying this
> is a big, beautiful universe we live in, that's been given to
> us, and here's an example of just how magnificent and
> encompassing it is.[15]

Simply summarized, Coltrane identified the purpose of his
music as visionary; it made audible otherwise unseen and
unheralded splendors of divine creation. As Coltrane knew
through his life experiences, this spiritual insight could be

realized not only through making music but through prayer and meditation. Perhaps it would be more accurate to say that Coltrane achieved spiritual insight through music inducing, and reflecting, the states of prayer and meditation.

The *Meditations* composition, recorded initially for quartet and later in a better-known sextet version, consists of five sections each titled for a state of spiritual consciousness and reminiscent of *A Love Supreme.* The earlier quartet's opening section is entitled "Love." The title shifts to "The Father and the Son and the Holy Ghost" on the large ensemble recording. It is this version I would like to address since the quartet's was an initial sketch of what Coltrane realized more fully in the sextet version with Pharoah Sanders. The title shift might even reflect the rumor that Coltrane referred to Sanders as his musical "son" and Ayler as "the holy ghost."

Meditations, as its title suggests, is a ruminative work, with melodies easy for a listener to catch on a first listening. The intertwining tenor saxophones of Coltrane and Sanders assume stage-center throughout. The absence of a larger horn aggregate makes McCoy Tyner's piano parts easier to discern than on *Ascension* since his contributions are never smothered by cacophonous reed choruses. Another voice heard in high definition is bassist Jimmy Garrison's whose elegant introduction to the second movement, "Compassion," sounds like a reminder to Coltrane and Sanders that meditation requires a gradual deceleration and stilling of the soul's buzzing activity. So the exploration of musical meditation led to the search for the ultimate quiescence of the soul, symbolized by the title of Coltrane's album, *Om.*

Om opens with a droning chant recalling *A Love Supreme.* Several voices personify the ultimate state of peace, contained in a mantra. But the evocation of Hindu India falls away when the first instrumental voices come into sharp focus: an African thumb-piano, and percussion, followed by a massive groundswell of turbulent saxophones. The horns create not so much "sheets of sound," in Ira Gitner's graphic phrase, but rather veils, or scrims over Elvin Jones's drumming (recalling an image from early Ellington), as Coltrane and Pharoah Sanders take convulsively overblown solos, sounding like frenzied worshippers facing apocalypse.

A quarter of a century old, these albums still sound revolutionary, particularly for those who assume that the musical expression of prayer and meditation must be executed in a sotto voice, tranquilizing listeners into placid bliss. As critic A.B. Spellman wrote about the impact of *Ascension:* "Your nervous system has been dissected, overhauled, and reassembled."[16]

African music, through its interplay of music with dance, drama, and spiritual ritual, has never tried to do less than restructure the nervous systems of listeners. Transformed, listeners see and hear the world in radically new fashions, inhabiting a geography where paradise can be found, through music, on this earth. We who live so far from the African ancestors may need another compass to find our paradise, a sign through sound—say the highest note of a tenor saxophone in the hands of John Coltrane.

CHAPTER SIX

George Russell Teaches Us To Play the African Game

One common thread linking the musicians considered in this study is overreaching ambition, sometimes of Wagnerian proportions. After all, there is something potentially pretentious and pompous in attempting musically to synthesize two cultures as distinct as African-American and African. It is one kind of challenge to come up with an original recorded interpretation of "Body and Soul," quite another to offer musically a novel philosophical slant on cultural intermingling, with a few asides to cosmology, archeology, and the psychology of consciousness.

Presumptuous as it might be for any program music, jazz or otherwise, to scale such Olympian heights, Russell's music attempts no less. And the expansiveness of his intellectual program is matched by his compositional skills, a rare mix in any musical era.

Russell is best known for his theory of the "Lydian concept," a conceptual framework enabling musicians to establish tonal centers based upon the relationship of their pitches from any central note. I would like to focus, however, upon Russell's musical start as a drummer. His first notice in the jazz world was heralded by "Cubana Be/Cubana Bop," a key vehicle for Dizzy Gillespie's brand of Afro-Cuban jazz. As memorable as Gillespie's stamp on Russell's piece, even more riveting was the contribution of the Cuban drummer Chano Pazo, who well understood the African basis of the Cuban drumming patterns undergirding Russell's piece.

The fruition of Russell's involvement with African rhythms has slowly evolved over the decades, only to be ignored by critics as his harmonic theory paved the way for the modal improvisations of Miles Davis and John Coltrane. His most explicit African reference occurs two decades after "Cubana Be/Cubana Bop" with a complexly layered composition completed during Russell's extended stay in Scandinavia, *Electronic Sonata for Souls Loved by Nature.* It is remarkably original on several counts, primary among them is the fact that Russell utilizes taped African voices as an instrument against which his sextet improvises. The tape is comprised, in part, of the voices of a 70-year-old Ugandan and his two sons, recorded in Northern Uganda by a United Nations relief worker. African lute sounds mingle with the voices. No translation is provided so the words are offered to non-African listeners as a musical expression of language, a dreamy sound-fragment of song/speech.

The African voices are but a few minutes on the fifty-two-minute electronically treated tape that provides the counterpoint to Russell's sextet. Russell's album liner notes define the perimeter of his intention:

> The essential concepts which inspired the creation of the "Electronic Sonata for Souls Loved By Nature" lay in philosophical and socio/musical areas. Its socio/musical objective was to create a pan-stylistic electronic tape; a tape composed of fragments of many different styles of music, avant-garde jazz, ragas, blues, rock, serial music, etc., treated electronically. And to have this tape serve as a palette upon which non-electronic musical statements of a pan-stylistic nature could be projected. The wedding of non-electronic pan-stylism to electronic pan-stylism was meant to convey the cultural implosion occurring among the earth's population, their coming together. Also it meant to suggest that man, in the fact of encroaching technol-

ogy, must confront technology and attempt to humanize it. . . . [1]

This program is essentially identical to that at the heart of *The African Game*. Note that Russell considers electronic music technology as a tool in need of humanization. So African voices form a key, albeit brief, portion of an electronic tape. What is most indigenously African in the composition is that which is made manifest through the most Westernized technological form.

Sets of seeming contradictions run through Russell's extended compositions, all resolved within the music. Improvisation and formal composition, ancient African rhythms and American rock rhythms, African-American soul (as exemplified by Russell's piano playing) and Nordic soul (as exhibited by Jan Garbarek's inspired saxophone), acoustic and electronic instrumentation—these contradictions bubble at the surface of the *Electronic Sonata*. A half dozen styles are synthesized not just as musical tour de force or academic exercise, but because Russell's music reflects an expansion of global musical consciousness. So his *Sonata* parallels Ellington's *Afro-Eurasian Eclipse*.

Ellington's sly spoken introduction to that work on record ends with a cryptic: "Who is enjoying the shadow of whom?" With the maestro's masterful ambiguity, that statement can be interpreted to describe both the demise of white racial supremacy and of a monolithic musical style. Much as no style is privileged in the Afro-Eurasian musical melange, so Russell extends the boundaries of pan-African music—that music all too neatly subsumed under the umbrella label of "jazz," a tag Ellington felt uncomfortable with throughout his lifetime.

But while *Afro-Eurasian Eclipse* plays variations on the theme of the whole world "going oriental" (implicitly the white world going nonwhite), Russell extends that pan-stylistic sweep with *The African Game* nearly two decades after *Electronic Sonata*. For the first time in the history of jazz, he boldly universalizes the African experience. His lyrical liner notes read like a poetic manifesto:

> It is said that Albert Einstein once remarked, "God doesn't play dice with the universe." Perhaps he did, once, in Africa during the Miocene epoch some 5 to 20 million years ago when the African Game began.
>
> God said grace, and rolled the dice on the human race. As the cradle of humanity, Africa is our common home; white, yellow, red, brown or black. [2]

There are several levels to consider here: this is a remarkably compassionate statement for an African American, particularly one who intentionally lived and worked in exile to remove himself from expressions of racism at home. Rather than claiming the exclusivity of African roots as a way to maintain an elite identity in jazz, with the aid of archeologist Louis Leakey, he takes Africa as the mother of all humanity as an inspiring image.

But the Africa that Russell claims as cradle of humanity is not so much that locus of traditionally advanced civilizations that pan-African historians like DuBois and Cheikh Anta Diop have reanimated in their texts. Russell's is an archetypally-fashioned biogenetic and spiritual game, progressing through various evolutionary stages.

This is a heady notion to put into music. The approach he chooses is an extended composition in nine "events" for his Living Time Orchestra (twenty young musicians joined on the recording with the Olu Bata drum ensemble). In typically disconcerting fashion, Russell opens the piece not with any acoustic instrument but with the sounds of several electric pencil sharpeners. He transforms into musical voice one of the most flagrantly wasteful technologies spawned by Western consumer culture. The barely audible motors create an otherworldly hiss, symbolic of the theme of Event I: unicellular life becoming amphibious. Following the lead voice of the sharpeners are softly beating bata drums, a most ironic juxtaposition of the traditional Afro-Cuban drum and the technological toy. A menacingly staccato trumpet plays what could be taken to be a Morse-code signal for the formation of DNA chains. Other horns layer themselves into the arrangement, as does an electric guitar. The piece swells, yet never dramatically resolves. It is an oddly timeless snapshot of the prehuman world.

Note that *The African Game* begins with Africa discovered at the cellular level, making real the metaphors of Senghor and the Negritude Poets: that Africa must be understood as being in one's blood before it is analyzed intellectually.[3] The amphibian movement from liquid birth to solid ground parallels human birth. Event II, "The Paleolithic Game," offers a musical portrait of just that. It opens with a martial drum tattoo from Keith Copeland. Bata drums (double-headed drums with a goblet shape originating from various West African traditional drum designs)[4] pick up the beat. Drums and trumpets, saxes, and trombones segue into a stumbling, lurching funk figure, comically evoking the tentative movements of the first humanoids learning how to walk on the earth. The horn section bleats and brays like a pack of mastodons on the run from the extinguishing force of evolution—and as proclamation that the experiment of humanity has begun.

Event III introduces the factor that makes God's African experiment such a high-risk game: consciousness. Mark Peipman's querulous and probing trumpet solo emblematizes consciousness scanning the horizons of outer and inner space like a lighthouse beam. Russell maintains his musical proclivity of letting a trumpeter assume stage center in his music. The trumpet, as in Biblical texts, heralds a spiritual awakening.

But Event IV, "The Survival Game," moves from consciousness to depictions of the Darwinian struggle for survival of the fittest. Heavily accented funk and rock rhythms dramatize the struggle, underscored by a trio of brass and reed solos and a nervously edgy electric guitar solo by Mark White.

Respite from the struggle occurs during a lovely musical interlude sustained by Gary Joynes' searching tenor sax solo. His fifty-second solo lives up to its label: "The Human Sensing of Unity With Great Nature." Russell postulates that this awareness of a human tie to nature occurs only after a titanic struggle, in contrast to Rousseauian and other pan-African theories of African origin.

Human identification with Nature provides the foundation for the African empires (which are also depicted in works by Count Ossie and John Carter). Russell's empires are less political, social, and economic entities than they are power-centers of consciousness. Once again, Gary Joynes' sax becomes the mouthpiece for an evolving consciousness; in this case, of the interdependency of the human and the natural world.

The next transition is perhaps the hardest to follow. Event VII Russell labels "Cartesian Man." This stage represents humanity as the inventor of technology, overwhelmed by the fruits of that creativity which brings about widespread fragmentation. This sounds like an appropriate image for the postindustrial United States. The African reference here appears unclear; the musical message, however, is vivid and lucid. Helter-skelter drum rhythms mingle with horn bleats which can be heard as automobile horns on the loose during a hectic urban traffic jam. Bob Nieske's bass solo sounds like the rumbling complaining voice of an ancestor under the earth who wants this urban racket to cease so he can sleep in peace. The theme of further alienation from nature, brought about by the technological age of machines, is continued in Event VIII, "The Mega-Minimalist Age." (The title pokes fun at the mechanically repetitious rhythms found in the minimalist works of composer Philip Glass.) The most African-inspired instruments, bata drums, are paradoxically used to mimic the hammered-insistence of machines run amuck.

The final event, "The Future?" moves from a Spanish folk rhythm to an uptempo jazz finale and concludes with a fade. It leaves the listener with the unanswered question of whether humanity will overcome its destructive separation from nature and "win" the African game.

What is Russell trying to convey by so ambitious a musical program? I think he is first and foremost finding an historical foundation for his musical pan-stylism since Africa itself has been the birth site for thousands of musical styles. The American awareness of these styles and the combining of styles emerging over centuries has only evolved in the past five decades. To be a jazz composer means for Russell not only to incorporate the commonly borrowed West African drum rhythms but to take all possible tools, even including those African styles recreated through encroaching Western pop music influences (like James Brown's funk). Further, being pan-stylistic is to think nonhierarchically about various musics. One can evade that bugaboo historically aggravating so many jazz composers: are they producing high-brow "art" music or low brow musical entertainment? The distinction between "high" art and "low" entertainment is nonexistent in traditional African societies, as is the Western defined barrier between nature and culture. Russell's music is about transcending these dubious dualities.

Finally, and this was either brave or quixotic of Russell, depending on your point of view, he tries musically to praise Africa as the origin point of all races. By this stance, he proposes a theory that can fully accept the authenticity of white jazz players as innovators as well as followers of African Americans, thus confounding proponents, black and white, of Crow-Jimism. But of far greater significance is the fact that Russell establishes a philosophical vantage point whereby all music, not just jazz, is traceable back to Africa.[5]

Rather than academically arguing for this position, as past generations of anthropologists and musicologists have done, he musically persuades by creating the image of Africa as a game board in which the Divine intervened to open the game of humanity with a dice throw (confirming the French poet Mallarmé's mysterious poetic refrain: "A throw of the dice will never abolish chance"[6]). The outcome of this game is yet unknown. But contrary to the stereotype of the jazz musician as a tortured romantic driven by a philosophical nihilism, Russell takes a robustly optimistic view of the African game:

> The African Game says something of a positive nature about this. It says that God (Great Nature) is on our side. It wants to win the game it began millions of years ago. But in order to win, it needs the awareness and cooperation of each of us descendants from the Miocene epoch now inhabiting Planet Earth.[7]

Like Ellington's, Russell's instrument to raise consciousness is an orchestra, a vast change in scope and complexity from his early days as a drummer. Yet his use of the orchestra as an instrument echoes one function of the drum in traditional African music. Russell's extended compositions tackle the apparent contraries of improvisation and composition, acoustic and electronic instrumentation, and so on. An apt metaphor to describe these and all of Russell's pan-stylistic bridgings would be *weaving*. Discrete colors, rhythms and textures are continually being imaginatively synthesized.

Weaving is not associated in the Western imagination with drumming, particularly since the image of the master drummer/composer is relatively new to jazz. In a touching account of his visits with a spiritual teacher of the Dogon tribe in the Sudan, French anthropologist Marcel Griaule records this insight from his talk with the elder spiritual prophet Ogotemmeli:

> For the technique of making a drum was similar to the technique of weaving; and the bodkin with which the craftsman pierces the edge of the skins to thread the tension-cord through is a symbol of the shuttle and of the Nummo's tongue. Beating the drum is also a form of weaving. The blows of the drumstick made the sound leap from one skin to the other inside the cylinder, as the shuttle and its thread pass from one hand to the other in the warp.[8]

"Nummo" refers to divine spirits associated with water, a reminder of the medium God chose to begin the African Game.[9] Not only can listeners to *The African Game* hear the weave of drum beats within the cylinders of the double-headed bata drums, but the weave of many musics can be heard throughout the dense orchestral arrangements.

Whether or not one judges *The African Game* a musical success is probably a function of how one perceives Russell's pan-stylistic woven fabric. This listener finds it a triumph and recalls the West African proverb: "God does not weave a loose web."

Nor does George Russell, creating music which weaves various beats into a new global harmony.

CHAPTER SEVEN

John Carter: The Play of Roots and Folklore

"I'm flattered to hear my name spoken in the same breath as Duke Ellington's, but it wasn't his music that inspired me to write these suites—it was my son spending a summer in Ghana." So began my interview with clarinetist/composer John Carter about his five-suite *Roots and Folklore: Episodes in the Development of American Folk Music.*[1] I entered the interview with my overstuffed agenda of comparisons to Ellington's *Black, Brown, and Beige,* but Carter adroitly brought to the foreground the impact of immediate family upon his music: "My oldest son returned from a trip to Ghana and Nigeria in 1973 and talked about the castles of coastal Ghana where slaves were held before their passage to the New World. I was fascinated."

Hailing from Texas, Carter developed his instrumental prowess initially on tenor sax playing for local bands, studying the bluesy Louis Jordan sounds. He began a transition from saxophone to clarinet in the sixties—but never abandoned his fervor for the blues. The sixties also found him resettled in Los Angeles, along with a fellow Texan, Bobby Bradford, a cornetist with a bluesy/avant-garde bent, teaching schoolchildren in Watts about the African roots of blues and jazz. To hear Carter talk about the sixties clarifies enormously what moral and artistic obligations he feels are connected to the African-American search for roots:

> I felt during the riot period that everybody should be doing something to try to make this place right. I

thought: I'm a teacher and a musician. So I should be
involved with what I consider my strengths. So that's the
reason I was in Watts teaching and playing. That period
is not going on now—but I feel the same way. Having
the chance to do a project like *Roots and Folklore,* saying
what I wanted to say in the music, and in a few sentences
in liner notes, helps me make a contribution in the best
way I can to this society.

This integration of music with historical consciousness and
morally motivated social activism has long marked John
Carter's career. It must also infuse his teaching. Among his
students have been Julius Hemphill and Ronald Shannon
Jackson, musicians who share Carter's vision to a large
degree. Carter was also instrumental in helping to crystallize
a jazz scene in Los Angeles, recording a series of duet albums
with Bobby Bradford as well as performing regularly with
multi-reed player David Murray, drummer Stanley Crouch,
and flutist James Newton.

Part of Carter's historical mission has been his intensive
concentration upon the clarinet, too often neglected as a lead
instrument in recent years. The antecedents for his clarinet
style owe much to New Orleans players like Johnny Dodds
and George Lewis, who placed a premium on the clarinet
mirroring speech patterns and timbres: narrating, preaching,
sermonizing. Clarinet swoops and glides were part of the
New Orleans tradition, harking further back to West Africa
where the spirit's excitedly possessed voice careened through
wind instruments. For a musician like John Carter to
concentrate upon the historical origins of jazz clarinet styles
necessarily required a detailed study of the ranges of
African-American speaking voices. As John Storm Roberts
noted:

> Every time a movement in jazz turns away from the
> instrument as human voice, there is a turn back again.
> Leon Thomas recently said what Jelly Roll Morton had
> said another way forty years before: "The most profi-
> cient horns are those which do not play the regular

phrases and come close to the human voice and
screeching and crying and shouting."[2]

It was not, as the white racist nightmares of African savagery
described, that peoples of African descent proved their
barbarity by screaming when a sotto tone would do. It was
that the fullest possible vocal range was valued in African
traditions, to allow the spirit realm full expression through
human carriers.

Translating this sumptuousness of wide-ranging vocal
expression to jazz has increasingly meant a willingness to
explore the fullest spectrum of horn sounds. So it was not an
unimaginable evolution from the throaty vibrato-laden tones
of Johnny Dodds' clarinet in the twenties to Eric Dolphy's
signifying and sermonizing bass clarinet soliloquies of the
sixties. Through Dolphy's imaginative plays with atonality,
microtonal clusters summoned by frantic overblowing, and
assorted squeaks and squalls, you can hear a narrating voice
talking at you. While Dolphy's clarinet undeniably possessed
swing (that ultimate litmus test of instrumental integrity for
conservative jazz aficionados) it was in the service of
storytelling. The African griot, a people's storyteller, was
traditionally a master musician with an encyclopedic grasp of
rhythmic and melodic tools, but this musical proficiency was
totally in the service of relating a people's epic tale.

The word "epic" came to mind repeatedly during my
interview with Carter because *Roots and Folklore* is precisely
that: an epic musical narration of the consequences of the
trans-Atlantic slave trade. While epic has an established place
in the Western classical musical heritage, attaining an apotheosis in Wagner's Ring cycle, the term has rarely if ever been
used to describe jazz. The only use of epic in relation to jazz
I can ever remember seeing in print was in one of many
derogatory reviews of Ellington's *Black, Brown, and Beige,* the
critic implying that the work's "epic" length did not befit jazz.

Since early jazz was often performed for recordings capable
of holding only a few minutes of music per side, it developed

the aura of a brief entertainment, a music requiring only a few minutes of concentrated attention on the part of listeners. As jazz approached symphonic complexity and epic scope with Ellington's musical innovations in the forties, the music began to place demands upon the attention of listeners quite unparalleled in the history of American popular music. Yet these same demands for focused concentration and memory to recall repeated leitmotifs from one portion of the musical epic to another, had long been placed upon African listeners listening to griot music.

In *The Roots of the Blues,* musicologist Samuel Charters described his first hearing of the hour-long staple of the griot repertoire, "Chedo":

> . . . it describes the beginnings of the religious wars which led to the destruction of the Mandingo kingdom in the 19th Century. . . . As with all griot narratives, Jali Nyama wove his own comments, moral judgements and isolated poetic images into it.[3]

Much as that starting point for the study of Western epic poetry, the *Iliad,* this African example is a musical narrative describing a violent convulsion in history with consequences extending even into the present moment. A lengthy segment of the historical narrative was underscored instrumentally by various melodic and rhythmic inventions, and factual data was adumbrated by singular poetic images, and insertions of the composer's opinion and judgment.

While this description bears a striking fidelity to Carter's design in *Roots and Folklore,* it is also enlightening to remember differences between an African griot and an American jazz musician. Griots are born into families where their role as musical transmitters of historical and folkloric data is universally understood and appreciated; they are trained to assume that position from youth. No analogy to this exists in the New World. Jazz musicians may be totally ignorant of their histories as African Americans, and still be accounted eminently successful in their roles as musicians.

Those jazz musicians who receive formal musical training are taught technical proficiency on their instruments, not how to utilize that instrumental prowess in the service of historical and racial narration. The training that Ellington offered his band members during performances of his extended works might be among the few examples in jazz history of that historical, narrating impulse in music being linked systematically to jazz education. And I had begun my interview with the conviction that it was Ellington's sense of the musical epic that inspired Carter, only to find out that it was actually rooted in his son's trip to Africa. But what followed reflected his own pathways through music education:

> During the seventies, I came to really understand the beginnings of jazz—what came from Africa and what from Europe—and being an American, coming up through that system of education that we have, I knew about the symphony orchestra. I knew the clarinet the way symphony orchestra people played it. I knew about jazz too—but that wasn't what I was being taught. What I knew about jazz I learned from what my own culture was. Jazz was in the air in my house when I was growing up. I remember my parents having records on the Bluebird label, Fats Waller and Ellington. And I was quite a street person, was out playing the music quite early.
>
> I began to understand that symphony orchestra music is one thing, but the whole area of drum music is another thing altogether, a music that grew out of and suited the creative and functional needs of another kind of people altogether. Just coincidentally, I was part of those people [laughter]. Then you try to put these musics together. . . . I'm still trying to do that.

As Carter's *Roots and Folklore* has built bridges between classical music, Africa, and African-American musics, it has also constructed links between the notions of strict historical narration and folkloric storytelling:

> This thing is called *Roots and Folklore* because it serves my purposes well. I can go into factual material and back

> into folklore, which comes out of my head (laughter)—
> and go to and fro anytime I want to. *Dauwhe,* the first
> album of the series, came strictly out of my head. The
> idea was to say: here is a setting these people came from
> and what their lives were about.

It is a warmly sensual and harmonious Africa that Carter's
music depicts, an encapsulation of precolonial African political and spiritual unities as imagined by the composer. If the to
and fro movement between fantasy and historical fact was not
firmly established in this first suite, another equally compelling motion was modulation between hotly inspired improvisatory passages (listen to the serpentine twinings of Carter's
clarinet and Newton's flute in the closing movement, "The
Mating Ritual") and formally composed sections. That pattern
has held true for all of the recorded suites, demonstrating
Carter's commitment to reconcile the worlds of printed
scores and improvisatory spaces.

This alternation between scored sections and zones of
improvisatory free playing also connects to Carter's subtitle
for the series: *Episodes in the Development of American Folk
Music.* Although only a handful of jazz composers have
readily acknowledged their fascination with folk music
forms—Charles Mingus and Roswell Rudd come to mind[4]—
Carter recorded an entire album of solo clarinet pieces, *A
Suite of Early American Folk Pieces for Solo Clarinet.*[5] Doing his
own very modern transmutations of old African-American
dance tunes, the cakewalk and the funky butt, Carter also
offers his interpretation of a country blues. The album offers
an aural sketchbook of what was to become the five suites of
Roots and Folklore.

The vitality of folk forms have long been appropriated in
formal compositions by Western classical composers, so there
was nothing new in Carter utilizing them—except that
Carter's music maintains the air of improvisatory energy so
often missing when folk themes are formalized into classical
scores. *Dauwhe* sets the scene for the transmission of African

music onto these shores by creating a musical atmosphere where improvisation is not contradicted in any manner by the rules of normal composition; that is what is most "African" in the first suite.

As the series progressed, the historical narration became more evident. Spoken, chanted, and sung text was introduced, largely through violinist and vocalist Terry Jenoire. Two of the most striking moments during the second suite, *Castles of Ghana,* occur with surprising injections of human voices into the largely instrumental suite. Jenoire's wordless vocal on "Theme of Desperation" is a heartbreakingly poignant reminder of the sorrows of African slaves awaiting shipment to North America. And John Carter's brief historical summation spoken in a conversational tone during the last minute of the recording sets the tone for future suites to depict what followed release of the slaves from their confinement in Ghanaian coastal castles. "The journey facing these captives would prove to be arduous and truly eventful," claims Carter against the background of what sounds like a single African drum beating, "a journey which, before its completion, would interrupt and redirect the dynamics of human existence on our planet."

Andrew Cyrille's closing burst of drumming in tandem with Carter's narration foreshadows the next suite, *Dance of the Love Ghosts,* where African hand drumming and words take on ever greater significance. It was for this suite that Carter began to look rigorously into African historical accounts as well as to record with African drummers.

> When it came to working on the second section of the suite, "The Silent Drum," I wanted the factual elements to be historically correct. So I went to UCLA to meet a Dr. Posnansky, a terrific man, an anthropology professor married to an African woman. They go back to Africa every other summer, still actively involved with anthropological research. He had just reams of materials. So we talked for a long time. Gave me a lot of class outlines that had all kinds of information about when the

first slaves came, where they were from, and so on. So I learned a lot from him.[6]

And I wanted some authentic Ghanaian dialect on the record. Through a local musician I met an Ashanti master drummer. And through that guy I met the whole community of Ghanaians living in Los Angeles. We're surrounded by them. They're everywhere [laughter]. And got invited to their parties. That is how I met the three Ghanaian drummers I recorded with. We worked here in my studio. They translated my English text for "The Silent Drum" into a Ghanaian dialect, and we rehearsed the drum thing that we were going to do. Later we went to the recording studio and did all that.

That was heavy. We sat here in my studio—there were three of them. One of the guys is a play producer, one an engineer, and one a master drummer who has done some Hollywood studio work. But as I sat here that night, and they spoke their native dialect, and you know, they are probably from the general vicinity of where my people are from . . . I'm sitting here listening to them translate my English into Ghanaian, thinking: "You know, these people look like me, and we are undoubtedly from the same place—yet they were Eastern people. The difference between us culturally was very glaring. They were Africa—I was America—and there was no mistake about it."

In response to my question about how well the Ghanaian drummers, Kwai Badu, Osei Assibey William, and Osei-Tutu Felix, understood the meaning of their musical contribution to *Dance of the Love Ghosts*, Carter responded that they "academically" understood it, but doubted their feeling for the music beyond that. He continued:

We are not Africans at all. I tried to get my son to understand this before he went to Ghana and Nigeria. He was going to stay, and I said: "John, that's going to be awfully hard for you to do." So after that summer of his trip, he never did say anything about moving to Africa anymore. I think he understood the differences so well when he came back.

Regardless of how the three Ghanaian drummers understood their contribution to *Dance of the Love Ghosts,* they added
a musically thrilling interlude, dramatically heightened by
Carter's text offering the perspective of those left behind in
Ghana after their loved ones were transported into slavery.
And while this suite offers an aural sampling of some of the
oldest musical roots of jazz, it also offers a sample of the present
and future in Don Preston's synthesizer and electronic effects.

But the most chilling moment occurs when Terry Jenoire
recites a text reflecting her feelings as a slave woman facing
the prospect of rape by the slave ship's captain. Questioning
the reason fate has brought her to this juncture, she asserts
her dignity: "I'll never degrade my name for him. Only my old
man can hold me closely." The lamenting wail of resistance in
her voice finds resonance in her slashing and soaring violin
riffs counterpointing Carter's clarinet portamentos and blis-
teringly stark multiphonics.

Dance of the Love Ghosts brings Carter's epic across the
Atlantic. In a haunting poetic image, the suite closes with the
slaves on the ship watching the moon dance in a starry sky, a
dance, Carter suggests, in synchronization with their pain and
giving birth to the music of the blues.

With the fourth suite, *Fields,* the epic has focused upon the
transformation of these slaves in the United States. For that
story, Carter once again found a wellspring of inspiration in
his family: an uncle in his eighties with a penchant for
storytelling. His stories made reference to nineteenth-
century African-American rural life and offered glimpses into
slave life. Carter tape-recorded conversations with his Uncle
John in a nursing home just prior to the uncle's death a few
years ago. You can hear snippets of their conversation about
the old days in *Fields,* lovely bits of lore over which Carter
layers clarinet improvisations. Thus Carter's movement from
Dance of the Love Ghosts to *Fields* represents a progression
from distant African ancestors to one's immediate African-
American ancestor.

Fields also expanded the historical and musical range of the earlier suites by utilizing taped excerpts of his grandchildren playing traditional African-American rhyming games: vestiges of the old ancestors living on in future generations at play.

Images of life in the fields transform into life on city streets in the final suite, *Shadows on a Wall*. Carter dramatizes the lure of freedom northern cities offered southern workers, the promise of freedom still not fully materialized. The musical synthesis resulting from that northern migration serves to bring *Roots and Folklore* full circle. Traces of African roots, transfigured through southern slavery and postslavery days, are transformed once again in the development of African-American communities in New York's Harlem and Chicago's West Side. Terry Jenoire assumes the persona of the blues, a spirit with an all-knowing, all-seeing perspective, reflecting, as Ezra Pound discovered about this century, that "all ages are contemporaneous." The century's blend of historical realities brings about a dizzying sequence of evocative imagery in the composer's imagination:

> I am the Nile and the Hudson, the pyramids and the Empire State . . . the pyramids and the cotton field and Wall Street. . . . I am the Mississippi Delta and Times Square and Central Avenue and Rodeo Drive. I was at Abidjan and at the castles. . . .

The description continues listing the key locations of African-American history throughout centuries with the implacable tone of the "camera eye," the voice of the zeitgeist of John Dos Passos' *U.S.A.* trilogy. But this is no mere "march of history" broadcast—this is a tale of a fall and redemption:

> And I saw them build great monuments to their existence. Sing! Dance! Play! Paint! Artistically chronicle their time. And I saw them stray from old teachings and change the old ways. They were exploited, and became as shadows on the wall.

The gloom introduced by the image of shadows on the wall, underscored by Jenoire's plaintive vocal and Carter's elegiac playing, is a result of trying to escape from the totality of the history of one's people—choosing to remember only a portion, whether African or American. To recover the full range of history involves imaginative invention, the kind that was beautifully present as African Americans developed the blues:

> And I saw them forge a national music on Saturday night and Sunday morning. And I saw the world come to know and love that music. I am the blues.

For all the episodes depicting despair, *Roots and Folklore* ends with the image of the transformative power of music, distilled from the centuries-long agony of African peoples and offered to the world as a blessing. Music represents what of the old African ways could never be totally dissipated, in spite of times when "the old ways" were neglected. The blues has possessed a phoenix-like strength, reflective of the people who birthed it. The five suites of *Roots and Folklore* chronicle not only the enduring strength of African-American music but the growth and various elaborations (swing, bop) of African roots that continue in it. In paying tribute to old country blues and ancient West African drumming, Carter has continued the vitality and evolution these musical roots offer.

If *Shadows on a Wall* completes the epic tale of a people who are far from fully free in this supposed land of the free, it also fulfills Carter's musical mission. He has, through these five suites, virtually reinvented the clarinet's role during the past decade. Boldly playing in its upper ranges, overblowing, excitedly narrating, leaping between registers, Carter had advanced the clarinet experiments of Eric Dolphy and Anthony Braxton to the point where the instrument can no longer be thought of as a poor cousin to the saxophone in leading experimental ensembles. But this demonstration of instrumental freedom is never detached from the need to mesh with his ensemble in telling the essential tale demanded by the ancestors and the yet-to-be-born, so that someday, somehow, freedom will be realized and the agony of slavery will at last end.

With *Roots and Folklore* completed, I asked Carter about his interest in visiting the starting point of his series, Africa. "I've never been to Africa. I'd love to go over there for a few weeks, meet some local musicians, maybe get to record and perform with them. That's something I'd like to do pretty soon."

Meantime, Carter continues to compose, perform, and teach in Los Angeles at an ambitious clip. When I inquired about what kept him so ambitious and adventuresome, he admitted that there is something of the preacher in him (remember the griot interspersing moral judgments with historical accounts?). He ends our interview with this anecdote:

> I think the artists of the world—I said this to a lady at a local university one time and she just smiled—when the world is saved, it will be us and our idealistic notions that will save the whole thing.

A very African, and in some circles, very African-American notion: music can help save the world.

Postscript: On March 31, 1991, John Carter died of complications from lung cancer. He never traveled to Africa, but his music will continue to make possible an Americas-Africa transit for years to come through the force of his musical imagination.

CHAPTER EIGHT

Count Ossie and the Mystic Revelation of Rastafari: To Mozambique Via Marcus Garvey Drive

> Call was very important in that kind of music. Today, the music has grown up and become quite scholastic, but this was *au naturel,* close to the primitive, where people send messages in what they play, calling somebody or making facts and emotions known. Painting a picture, or having a story to go with what you were going to play, was of vital importance in those days.—*Duke Ellington*[1]

This is the voice of Duke Ellington reminiscing about the sound of jazz in the twenties. But perhaps it could have also been Ellington recalling his experience visiting the Jamaican band of Count Ossie and the Mystic Revelation of Rastafari in Jamaica's capital city, Kingston, decades later. That visit became the impetus for the group to do a tour crossing several continents, a spectacular flowering for a band with a rather inauspicious beginning.

This is the story of Oswald Williams, later dubbed "Count Ossie," whose obsession with drumming from his childhood days led him to become the most internationally renowned Jamaican musical star before the age of Bob Marley and reggae. Ossie's music was not jazz in any textbook definition of the term. And yet his achievement, unmatched by any Caribbean musician before or after, was to blend Afro-Jamaican drumming with jazz horns within the framework of a musical dance-drama narrative. Cohering that narrative was the theme of Jamaica's spiritual affinity with the motherland Africa.

This Caribbean interruption to a narrative of mainly U.S. jazz musicians has a distinguished precedent. On Louis Armstrong's 1926 recording of "King of the Zulus," Kid Ory's trombone solo is interrupted by Clarence Babcock who acts the part of a Jamaican mystified by the goings on at a chitlins party: "I'm just here from Jamaica," bubbles Babcock, whose hunger for exotic soul food is enough to throw a jazz concert in disarray. A more uncanny reminder of how the New Orleans creation of jazz was sharply seasoned by Caribbean musical influences would be hard to imagine. Babcock, a rude Caliban at Armstrong's musical feast, becomes later transformed into the drummer "Carribee Joe" of Ellington's *A Drum Is a Woman*. Just when Americans are most given to crow mightily about the "uniquely" American creation of jazz, comes the Caribbean man clearing his throat, talking about his jazz roots, and reminding us that jazz, like the Middle Passage, has come via the Caribbean.

To understand the evolution of Ossie's music, hold in mind a geography shaped by imaginative imperatives rather than by literal miles on maps. Like Saul Steinberg's cartoon map of how typical New Yorkers see the rest of the country, think of a graphic where the island of Jamaica is equally close to New Orleans and to Africa. The growth of the southern U.S. record industry, plus the fact of radio transmissions from New Orleans being easily received in Jamaica, makes this map all the more plausible. Historically, the movement of slaves from the West Indies to New Orleans provided yet another link of cultural closeness between the two locales. As the title of Armstrong's "King of the Zulus" suggests, that most quintessential New Orleans celebration, Mardi Gras, maintains in coded language a memory of the African roots of the city as powerfully as that music of Ossie's harking back to Ethiopia and Mozambique.

The contemporary pop musician from New Orleans, Cyril Neville, speaks of that proximity in terms congruent with Ossie's vision:

> The drum comes to me as a symbol of what I, or *we,* used to be. I can't speak on the drums, but I try to convey my feelings. I have never been so fascinated by an instrument like I was the conga drum. I started playing a set of drums with sticks, but I saw the congas as a direct thing I could play with my hands. I think about Africa when I play. To me right now, my Africa is the drums 'cause when I feel like going back to Africa, I play my drums.[2]

What Neville discovered through his musical curiosity—that playing drums could be a conduit for an imaginative journey back to Africa—Ossie discovered in the context of Jamaican lower-class society looking to Africa for spiritual salvation. His musical awakening was coterminous with the rise of the Rastafarian movement:

> Without him [Count Ossie], it is doubtful whether "Rastafarian music" would have been formulated as such. He himself explained how the original "traditional" Rastafarian music came into its own. It was shaped in the late 1940's in the slum section called the Dungle in West Kingston. In those days he often communicated with a set of Rastafarian brethren to "reason." During the course of time, "under a tree," the idea of the music that he was seeking came, and he was inspired to develop it.[3]

Ossie's desire to become a skilled drummer was so apparent before his teens that his mother signed him up to study in the drum corps. Unable to craft or afford a drum at a young age, he tapped on an empty paint can. By the late forties he was an accomplished player without a clear goal in mind. The Rastafarian movement nested his talent spiritually, providing a framework through which his musical ideas moved into the field of an ever-evolving band with multiple drummers and wind players.

The Rastafarians of Jamaica amplified the teachings of Marcus Garvey who insisted upon a spiritual—if not literal—return from exile for all peoples of African descent. Garvey's insistence upon the highly civilized status of Africa—in contrast to the proven barbarism of white European societies engaged in the wholesale butchery of World War I—was enormously appealing to Jamaica's lower classes. The upper classes had always tried to emulate European manners, language, and music. Those at the bottom, trapped in a colonial economic and political structure which gave them little hope of upward mobility, needed a faith to sustain them through their suffering. The image of Africa Garvey offered was empowering, and it gained further impact through the activities of the cult leader Leonard P. Howell, who transformed Garvey's "Back to Africa" vision into a form of crypto-messianism by claiming that the current emperor of Ethiopia, Haile Selassie, was actually God on earth, King of Kings. Selassie (known by the honorary title of Ras Tafari) had come to earth to lead all peoples of African descent back to Africa.

This was a heady and revolutionary claim during the heyday of British colonialism in Africa and the Caribbean, so Jamaican authorities promptly arrested Howell. But his movement persisted in spite of repeated government harassment. Part of his perennial appeal was his linking of Garvey's Africa to an exact African redeemer, something Garvey himself never did. (Unsubstantiated rumors over the years had put in Garvey's mouth the prophetic declaration: "Look to Africa, where a black King shall be crowned, for the day of deliverance is near.")[4] Howell's messianic fervor soon spread throughout the slums of West Kingston, taking new forms along the way among believers. Associated with their discussions of Rastafarian theology—talks leavened by the generous smoking of marijuana—would be rituals filled with drumming, chanting, and dancing, the beginnings of a cultural revival shortening the distance between Jamaica and the promised land of Africa. Into this world Ossie's music was born.

Drums were handmade affairs, wood plentifully found in barrels by the docks, or crafted from tree trunks hollowed out. Goat skin heads were held in place by metal tension rods and pegs. The Rastafarian drums were crafted in three sizes: a large bass drum, double-headed, between two and three feet in diameter; the *fundah,* a single-headed drum with a head about three quarters of a foot; and the repeater, similar to the *fundah,* but with a smaller head. The three drums have tones corresponding to bass, alto, and soprano.

They were brightly painted in the colors of the Rastafarians, taken from the Ethiopian flag: red, green, gold. Images and words attributed to Haile Selassie adorned the drums (frequently a lion symbolizing Selassie as "the Lion of Judah").[5]

The interaction of the three drums? Rastafarian drum sessions are initiated by the *fundah* drummer who establishes an uptempo rhythmic line with accents on the first and third beat of every measure. The bass drum enters on the same beats, adding a rib-shaking resonance to the music. Finally, the repeater enters introducing a high-ringing tone on the second and fourth beats, weaving an improvised line by darting through the spaces offered between the stressed beats of the *fundah* and bass drums. The repeater is considered the most difficult drum to master, and one arrives at proficiency at it only after an apprenticeship on the larger Rastafarian drums.

Count Ossie was the greatest repeater drummer in Jamaica. His ability to make the drum "talk," in relation to the spoken/sung Rastafarian chants, brought him notoriety in Jamaica's musical community. What began as a band of five drummers living in a commune was led by Ossie into a sophisticated organization of twenty musicians. It also became a band which was instrumental in the making of the hit pop record, "Oh Carolina" by the Folkes Brothers. By this time, what began as a drumming/percussion ensemble was expanding, largely through the efforts of tenor saxophonist Cedric Brooks, to encompass wind instruments. A number of the major horn players on the island, including Tommy McCook, Don Drummond, and Roland Alphonso (who would later receive international acclaim as part of The Skatalites), passed through Ossie's camp.

The musical ideas traded between Rastafarian drums and horns were solidified over time by Brooks and the Ossie organization and recorded under the moniker of "Count Ossie and The Mystic Revelation of Rastafari." Their first album *Grounation*, released in the sixties, is a three-record set of drumming, blowing, and chanting that represents a broad swatch of Rastafarian history, moving from the trans-Atlantic slave trade days through the Italian invasion of Ethiopia in 1937 to postcolonial Jamaica. It is not hyperbole to say that *Grounation* broke entirely new ground in the history of recorded Caribbean music.

No identification of musical personnel was listed on the album. Apart from Ossie on repeater and Brooks on tenor sax, the other players remain nameless. But what they created amazed jazz musicians on the order of Ellington and Randy Weston (who brought them to the 1974 Newport Jazz Festival). Their music, while sounding like Afro-Jamaican ritual music, also sounded like jazz of several stripes. The horns caught the tang of a New Orleans brass band, a heterophonous chorus of tangy whoops and bellows, occasionally marked by what sounds suspiciously like bad intonation, but in reality is a joyously roiling and rolling wave of saxes and trombones in dialogue with hand drums. "Rootsy" is the impressionistic term several American critics used in trying to describe the horn section.

But what I hear is the spirit of early New Orleans transplanted to Jamaica, a sound perfectly described by William Russell:

> All the parts are played in a sort of pseudo unison, or at least the parts are in similar rhythmic values. Of course they never are in true unison nor are they hit off rhythmically together, and naturally almost every sin known to European musical culture is committed—lack

of precision, out of tunefulness, smears, muffs—in other words, we have with us again the well known "sloppy New Orleans ensemble"—but an ensemble of whose unpredictable rhythms, vitalizing accents, and independence of parts (even when played isometrically) are more thrilling than any symphonic group.[6]

And where does the "sloppy New Orleans ensemble sound" find its origin? The rag-tag band tradition can hark back to American Civil War veterans, some of whom played in minstrel shows in the late 19th century. Robert C. Toll's *Blacking Up* offers one version of the transformation of Civil War musicianship through minstrelsy:

> Although dominated by the plantation and religious songs, black minstrelsy also evolved other distinctive features, particularly the uniformed black marching unit. . . . In 1875–1876 Callender's Minstrels closed the first part of their show with a "ludicrous military burlesque." . . . This skit proved so popular that it became the standard finale of the first part of the black minstrel show.[7]

Yet another origin point for the rag-tag brass band sound emanates from a long tradition in rural Georgia and Mississippi of African-American fife and drum music, field recorded by Alan Lomax in the forties, and more recently by blues scholar David Evans. Its leading living exponent, singer and fife player Napoleon Strickland, even performed in Manhattan in the late eighties under the auspices of the World Music Institute. Using quills to make homemade pan-pipes, and turning washtubs into drums, these musicians have created a music that sounds, at once, "primitive" and "postmodern," an ironic parody of military music, yet a sturdy set of tunes to do rural chores by. Although these informally organized bands lack any brass instruments to offer a metallic ring, their washtub drums, which they make "talk,"[8] put plenty of rambunctious metallic punch into their marches.

And if one wishes for a taste of an African origin for the

New Orleans marching band sound, there is the recorded example of the Lagos Mozart Orchestra (Calabar Brass Band) who recorded in all of their resplendent funkiness in the thirties.[9] But how many of those Nigerian recordings would have found their way into Jamaica?

What did find a way into Jamaica during the formative years of Count Ossie and the Mystic Revelation of Rastafari were Rhythm and Blues recordings, which were heard repeatedly on Louisiana AM radio. You can hear echoes of the horn section of the Mystic Revelation of Rastafari in the honking, overblown, sometimes sour but rhythmically solid efforts of studio hornmen like Lee Allen. The R & B traditions of New Orleans allowed for a relaxed but decorum-shattering saxophone sound that proved as crucial to the development of Ossie's sound as it would later be a key to the music of John Coltrane, Archie Shepp, Albert Ayler, and Ornette Coleman.

Whatever the influences—New Orleans R & B, minstrelsy's mock military band blasts, rural fife and drum songs, African brass bands—Ossie subordinated the horns to a purpose just as singly as he did the Rastafarian drums. His music was narrative at base, and what was narrated was always the epic tale of how the peoples of the African diaspora developed spiritually and the role that their culture had played in crystallizing their identity as children of Motherland Africa. Ras Michael, a popular Jamaican reggae performer now residing in Los Angeles, recounted to an interviewer the role that Ossie played in his development as a drummer:

> The patterns he played told stories. They told of suffering and indignation. But they also told of love, peace, and hope for the future. A lot of what he played was purely Africa. . . . Count Ossie didn't teach me how to play the drums like some people think. I was already playing the drums. He taught me about things to put into my music—things about life.[10]

While the drumming patterns do not exactly mimic known traditional African rhythms, ·the narrative insistence of the drumming, particularly the speech-like cadences of Ossie's repeater drum, later echoed in the repeater playing of his son Time, connects to what Ras Michael may have meant by the drumming being "purely Africa." Further, Ossie's drumming was a community-cohering activity, a spiritual source of renewal, certainly not a commodity to be hawked on the entertainment market. *Grounation* sounds like a field recording of a religious rite, not by any definition a polished studio production. Maybe the horns were not properly rehearsed before the recording was made? Perhaps some of the vocals were flat? This was cathartic ritual first—"art" second. Yet the art was everywhere apparent, and to call it amateurish musically is both inaccurate and misses the point. Yale anthropologist John Szwed said he thought the horns on *Grounation* were just horrible on a first hearing. Repeated hearings made him think of Ornette Coleman's band, Prime Time.[11]

Utterly unlike Ornette Coleman are the choices of jazz compositions recorded on *Grounation:* Charles Lloyd's "Mabrat" and the Crusaders' "Way Back Home." The later is a revelation. While the Crusaders' original recording had their patented brand of Texas funk/blues on horns set to a crisp steady-as-she-goes beat, the Count Ossie version sets rugged sax riffs against Rastafarian polyrhythms. If the Crusaders missed their "way back" Texas home after transplanting themselves to Los Angeles, the Count Ossie band longed for the home way back in an Africa that they had never set foot upon.

That longing for return from exile has traditionally been symbolized by references to Ethiopia in Rastafarian music, a tradition still maintained by reggae performers. Yet Count Ossie's second album thematically centered on Mozambique, a nation which superficially had little to do with Jamaica or the Rastafarians. Very few Jamaicans could claim symbolic allegiance to the place through traceable ancestry; no emperor who seemed to fulfill a Garveyite prophecy ever ruled there. While drumming ensembles have prospered there, and the drums can resemble the Rastafarian *fundah* and repeater drums, the rhythms and styles differ markedly. In Mozambique ensembles, it is the bass drum, in contrast to the Rastafarian ensemble, which takes the lead. Arab influences abound, particularly melismatic ornamentation in women's singing styles, while such characteristics are hardly prominent in Rastafarian music. Why then focus on Mozambique?

What captured the imaginations of the Rastafarian musicians was the heroic attempt there to counter European colonialism through cultural resistance, often musical resistance. In this, the Rastafarians could see their own struggle within Jamaica as through a mirror. As Edward A. Alpers comments:

> One of the most important popular expressions of resistance to the brutality and humiliation of colonialism in Mozambique was cultural. Of these, songs, music and dance were easily the most universal form of protest, with proverbs, stories, and wood sculpture providing other vehicles of resistance. Just as important, these cultural expressions also served the additional function of asserting the values of specific African cultures against the dehumanization of colonialism, which either attempted to reduce Africans to nameless and faceless units of labor or relegate them to obscurity.[12]

In order to finesse this identification of Jamaicans with Mozambiquans, Count Ossie's band had to organize a musical narrative in which the history of Mozambique could be retold in Rastafarian style. This meant that a mythopoetic retelling was in order. The 1975 *Tales of Mozambique* album (released in the year Mozambique became independent) opens with a recital of this re-visioned history (as stated on the liner notes) postulating a veritable Eden in Mozambique prior to Portuguese discovery by Vasco da Gama:

> Before 1492, the natives of this land enjoyed to the fullest mother nature. They had total freedom, expressing the arts, crafts and the culture.[13]

On a literal level, this is patently untrue. Such a simplification of Mozambiquan history ignores the fact that this area of Southeastern Africa was invaded by the Arabs centuries prior to the Portuguese, and that the Arabs, rather than the Portuguese, had introduced slavery (though of a gentler variety than the murderous Portuguese form). But Count Ossie's narrative is really concerned with interior spiritual freedom, including forms of artistic freedom. On that level, Mozambique was "free" prior to Portuguese colonization.

The historical revision is less startling than the musical revision present on this second recording. Largely gone are the raw horn choruses. A single flute or saxophone soloing over the drums dominates much of the music. The album opens with a single tenor sax in a call-and-response with the bass. Drums, bass, and piano join the fray. Then the historical narration begins. Unfortunately, as was true of *Grounation,* the recording identifies no musical personnel. So the tenor saxophonist who is showcased on much of this album—Alphonso Roland? Cedric Brooks?—remains anonymous. But his tone is blazingly distinctive. Whoever the saxophonist is, he has learned his lessons well from John Coltrane and Sonny Rollins. He creates a husky, sometimes hoarse, propulsively spiralling set of modal improvisations which are stunning in rhythmic impact. Even when he sounds most imitative of Coltrane of the early sixties—the solo on "Run One Mile" sounds like a slightly transfigured version of Coltrane's "Out of This World"—he maintains a Jamaican rhythmic sense all his own.

But *Tales of Mozambique* is not a sprawling jam session for sax and drums. It is a far more professionally polished recording than *Grounation,* and it is a more cohesive effort. The musical narrative, in spite of elliptical and gnomic leaps in time and space, does cohere. The opening sets the scene of Mozambique struggling for independence against European oppression. What follows are a series of superimpositions in which the Rastafarian struggles in Jamaica are constantly compared to the liberation struggles of Mozambique. "Selam

Nna Wadada (Peace and Love)" is a direct borrowing from Michael Olatunji's *Drums of Passion* album, where it surfaces as "Kiyakika." Ironically, on this Jamaican musical tribute to Mozambique is a Nigerian song by an African who now resides in the United States! But the song complains about how the fast pace of Western industrialized society is taking away the pleasures of traditional African life. This theme is dear to the hearts of Rastafarians, who in "borrowing" (uncredited since they do not believe in the legality of all music copyright laws) Olatunji's tune decided to underscore the point about conflicting speeds of African and Western lifestyles by slowing the song's tempo considerably. Olatunji's version is breakneck; Count Ossie's is a moderately paced number.

This Nigerian interlude is followed by a Rastafarian hymn of faith, appropriately laced together by thick organ chords and drums, "No Night in Zion." "I Am a Warrior," while it could be taken as a symbolic tribute to the recently triumphant liberation struggle in Mozambique, is really about being a Rastafarian spiritual warrior, longing for "that happy paradise" of Africa which they in time hope to repatriate. This paradise is contrasted in Rastafarian thinking to the world contaminated by Western materialism and politics ("polytricks") in short, the Jamaica they know as daily inferno. "Wicked Babylon" chants against the forces that keep this hell in motion, and symbolically, if read in the light of Mozambique, would surely refer to South Africa.

The album's narrative resolves with the proclaimed hope of liberation for all Africans and peoples of African descent. The cry for liberation is realized first through a majestically Coltranesque tenor sax solo in communion with Ossie's drums followed by "Lock, Stock and Barrel," in which singers offer a visionary day in the future when all peoples will "soon stop quarreling." Two solo saxophone showcases close the album.

Tales of Mozambique offers a rich fusion of musical styles. The connections between Rastafarian music and the reggae it gave rise to are clearly illustrated. Keyboards, bass, and drums offer brief ostinatos within the framework of songs that are really simple chants utilizing two or three chords. But the tenor sax majestically swoops in and out of these rhythmic textures with an unmistakable jazz feel. No longer, as in *Grounation,* does the saxophone merely underscore the messages offered by the drums. The saxophone is an independent and free ranging voice by the time of the second album, as inflamed as any church revivalist preacher in offering bombastic tonal flights and coyly hoarse seductive moans and whispers.

Above all else, as Ellington heard in Bechet's clarinet playing of the twenties, there is an element of "call" in the horn sound. Not only is that loud piercing vector of dazzling energy appropriate for playing outdoors where unamplified instruments have to carry, it is also highly appropriate for players involved with music as cultural resistance. The ears of the economic and political oppressors require high volume if any music is to get past their own static.

After Count Ossie was killed in a car accident in 1976, Jamaica's two political parties argued over who should carry the coffin of this national musical hero. Meanwhile, the Rastafarians drummed and chanted. They continue to do so today with the hope that every beat brings their imagination of Africa that much closer. As you enter Jamaica's capital city Kingston, make a turn off of Marcus Garvey Drive into Trenchtown. If the name of the drive is allegorical, so is the name of Ossie's drumming son, Time. Even the repeater drum joins the allegory, as Count Ossie's beats on it *repeated* the memory of *her,* the unforgettable Motherland Africa.

CHAPTER NINE

Randy Weston: Talking Piano Like a Drum Shouting Freedom

> I've been going through a period of heavy concentration on rhythm . . . using a lot of traditional rhythms and also playing the blues, so people can recognize that there's actually no difference in the musics. It's like I'm developing the language of the African-talking drums on piano.—*Randy Weston*[1]

You can hear intimations of Randy Weston's style in the earliest recordings by stride and ragtime pianists. It was explosively realized by Willie "The Lion" Smith and later transfigured by Ellington, most charmingly, on his piano trio recording, "Tap Dancer's Blues." Just about every Cecil Taylor session offers a showcase.

The piano keyboard as a percussion instrument is what these artists share, a style as old as jazz itself harking back to an era when a single piano had to take the place of a band or orchestra providing a full, rich, loud soundstage. In the days before electronic amplification, it was the piano which did the lion's share, providing a rhythmic bottom on recordings—the technology to accurately record drum sets arrived relatively late in the history of audio recording.

Emphasizing the piano as an instrument to pound out rhythms—lovingly encapsulated by Cecil Taylor's "an 88 key drum"—did not necessarily lead to the notion of the American piano as an African drum in disguise until Weston. Ellington's "jungle music" sounds depended heavily upon

brass growls and smears to evoke Africa. And Eubie Blake
(Will Marion Cook notwithstanding) never believed that the
addition of the word "Africa" in the title of his rags implied
that he was playing authentic African music. But hints of
something akin to African drumming do occur in a remark by
Willie "The Lion" Smith who:

> . . . described how he used competing songs with
> different rhythms in each hand: "A good pianist had to
> be able to play with both hands performing in perfect
> unison . . . we had such control that we could play a
> different song with each hand at the same time."[2]

Without making any explicit reference to Africa, Smith has
described one of the most central principles in African
drumming: the creation of multiple rhythm lines emphasizing
the independence of the motions of the right and left hands.
Although cross-rhythms may be created in African music by
multiple drummers, one drummer can play a percussive
parallel to Smith's piano pyrotechnics. Writes J.H.K. Nketia:

> Both cross-rhythms and polyrhythms may sometimes be
> handled by one and the same performer when he pits
> the left hand against the right hand. Every good
> drummer learns to handle these as he masters the
> techniques of drumming.[3]

John Miller Chernoff offers a glimpse of the consciousness of
an African drummer playing multiple rhythms:

> . . . though the rhythms are played apart, the music is
> unified by the way the separate parts fit together into a
> cross-rhythmic fabric. Only through the combined
> rhythms does the music emerge, and the only way to
> hear the music properly, to find the beat . . . is *to listen to
> at least two rhythms at once.*[4]

This as a preface to hearing Randy Weston's music—
autonomy of right and left hands in establishing different
rhythms—should be considered as one of several apparent

oppositions he resolves: synthesizing continents, generations, styles. Throughout a thirty-five year career as pianist, band leader, and composer, the constant in Weston's art has been the dynamic tension between rhythms of Africa and America. Friction between cross-continental rhythm lines surfaces in his earliest 1955 piano recordings; his original "Zulu," announced tentatively what would flower into a programmatic and lifelong exploration of the American-African musical bridge. And, as was the case with Shepp and Shannon Jackson, a father's record collection became the door to a large field of awareness of black—and African—music.

Weston's talents were nourished by Brooklyn of the late forties. He attended high school with the drummer who would later accompany him on his largest scale recording, *Uhuru Africa,* Max Roach. Like Shannon Jackson, Coltrane, and John Carter, he developed musical breadth playing Rhythm and Blues in various local clubs. Tired of the routine of a New York jazzman, he moved to the Berkshires, in Western Massachusetts, a move which two decades later would attract many of his compatriots like Roach and Yusef Lateef. There he met one of the pivotal figures building bridges between African and American music, Marshall Stearns.

Ironies abound in recounting Stearns' determination to spark Weston's involvement with African rhythms. A white academician with a doctorate in English, he was a catalyst, not only in encouraging Weston to listen to African recordings, but also in steering him toward the classic ragtime players. Reinforcing Stearns' impact was Asadata Dafora, who played a tape of music from Guinea for Weston. The tape Weston heard, rather than exotically unheard-of musical figures, was a waltz, a form familiar and dear to his heart—save for the fact that hand drummers playing waltzes are not commonplace in Western music. Completing the trinity moving Weston toward African rhythms was Duke Ellington. Ellington recorded Weston for his never-realized record company, but the tapes were released eleven years later on Arista as

Berkshire Blues. Weston's sensitive performance of "Purple Gazelle" is a reminder of Weston's fondness for Ellington's African rhythms.

It is a mystery why and how a young musician's influences solidify at a given point in his career. By 1960, Weston was handily mixing swing, blues, ragtime, the dissonant leaps of his friend and teacher Thelonious Monk, and the percussive attack of Ellington into a very personal style. Solo, trio, and quartet formats were most familiar to him. The challenge in 1960 was to create a large-scale composition for jazz orchestra with an Afrocentric theme. Enlisting the arranging talents of trombonist/arranger Melba Liston, he assembled twenty-eight musicians in a New York studio in November.

Keep in mind that Weston had not actually been to Africa at this point (his first sojourn would be a year later), but Africa was looming large in the news. During 1960 was the year seventeen nations, nearly a third of all Africa's states, achieved independence. It was a time of heady expectations; no year in this century witnessed such a sweeping proclamation of freedom from colonial rule. And simultaneously, Weston was evolving a friendship with the writer Langston Hughes. Discussions with Hughes often circled around the meaning for African Americans of a newly emergent Africa. This, then, was the context for Weston's *Uhuru Africa.*

Weston eloquently describes the origins of the music:

> So I got together with Melba Liston. I wanted to use a big band, and I wanted to use artists from Africa, and artists of African descent. Jazz musicians, cats from the Broadway shows, a classical singer, a guy from East Africa, a guy from West Africa. And all of a sudden, because a lot of the musicians said: "Uhuru Africa!," I didn't have to worry about the name. . . . I wanted to use the African language on the recording. I had never heard the African language except in stupid Tarzan movies, and in reality, the languages are so beautiful. So we used Swahili, and we asked Langston Hughes to write the texts, to try to draw a connection between all these peoples and this music. . . . [5]

This was a remarkably ambitious program: Weston set for himself the goal of portraying pan-African consciousness while recording with musicians of wildly different stylistic bents. There were two precedents for this. Ellington's recording of *A Drum Is A Woman* had successfully integrated the classical operatic soprano Margaret Tynes. And Max Roach, a month earlier in a New York Studio, had recorded the *Freedom Now Suite* with the African drummer Olatunji and an all-star African-American band. But Weston was working with a still more diverse group. Caribbean drummers Candido and Armando Peraza had to forge a cohesive sound with the Nigerian drummer Olatunji. Bassists Ron Carter and George Duvivier and drummers Max Roach and Charles Persip had to find quickly a common ground in the studio.

And then there was the issue of the large band realizing how best to complement the texts of Langston Hughes. Hughes' poems were evocations of the joys of new-found African freedom and of the archetypal woman at the heart of Africa, the feminine powers emblematized by the phrase "Mother Africa." This bold salute to African woman makes explicit what earlier works by Ellington and Roach hinted at. In *A Drum Is A Woman,* the African-inspired drum is a woman, but the garments of jazz are what she most flashily displays. The jazz metaphor in Ellington's scenario subsumes any reference to actual women of African descent. In Max Roach's *Freedom Now Suite,* Abbey Lincoln's is the voice vehemently communicating suffering and protest, yet, again, her voice is less specifically actual African woman than of all African humankind. (Lincoln would record her own unique version of the "African Woman" section of *Uhuru Africa* on her solo *Straight Ahead* album a few years later.)

Hughes' poetic texts are evocative (though general) statements of mood, unfettered joy at liberation, praise of the feminine forces. The big band had a fair degree of freedom to find ways to complement the texts. Weston and Liston worked out a four-part suite progressing through a stylistic sequence harking back to Marshall Stearns' influences a few years earlier.

Uhuru Africa opens with a classically African call-and-response: Hughes' evocation of African earth and river is echoed by Candido's drums, later joined by Olatunji, Roach, and Peraza. Weston then enters, playing a repetitive figure running up and down the scale and calling response from horns, reeds, then brass. The music evolves from the most traditional African sound to a Westernized big band arrangement. The joy of African independence is evoked in an uptempo romp with all of the band raising the cry of "Uhuru Freedom."

The mood rapidly shifts as the album segues into "African Lady" taken as a slow ballad with a ruminative bluesy feeling. Soprano Martha Flowers and baritone Brock Peters each sing a stanza of the Hughes text to a restrained musical accompaniment. Brief instrumental interludes of strong uptempo rhythmic vitality open out between the sung passages, as if relieving the pensive atmosphere created by the vocalists.

The third movement, "Bantu," utilizes Weston's old favorite, the waltz. The waltz seems as classically Western as the drummed chant African. Yet remember Weston's hearing a waltz in the Guinean tape. The waltz form is known both in African and Caribbean colorations, as John Storm Roberts has documented in his field recordings and *Black Music of Two Worlds,*[6] Weston early in his career composed jazz waltzes and inspired other musicians to follow in his footsteps. In fact, the horn arrangements in "Bantu" foreshadow the horn charts of Cannonball Adderley's enormous 1961 hit, "African Waltz."[7]

Uhuru Africa concludes with an uplifting synthesis of waltz and blues, "Kucheza Blues," the only section of the work entirely improvised in the studio. In his perceptive liner notes, Hughes comments he would have titled the movement "The Birmingham-Bamako Blues" since he hears "accents of Alabama and Africa." The composition hits with an exuberant shout of hope for Africa, in particular, and for peoples of African descent throughout the diaspora.

Within a year of the recording, Weston and Hughes would

make a trip to Africa along with a number of other African-American artists to perform at a festival of African-American and African arts in Lagos, Nigeria. They were part of a delegation formed by the American Society of African Culture (AMSAC). What occurred was astonishing, completely unpredictable. Perhaps the memory of Louis Armstrong's tumultuous reception by Ghanaians on the eve of their independence was still in the minds of the visiting African Americans, at least in Hughes' mind. A festive reception at the airport for the American guests raised their expectations of an enthusiastic reception for their artistic performance by Nigerians.

In his biography of Langston Hughes, Arnold Rampersad describes the scene:

> . . . the homecoming was a disaster. Denouncing the effort as "everything from 'badly organized' to 'an unqualified fiasco' and [a] 'downright insult' '" to African intelligence and taste, the Nigerian press heaped scorn on its organizers. The painting and sculpture were called facile and imitative, but the music drew the harshest comments. . . . Words such as "stupid," "repulsive," and "embarrassing" appeared frequently in the local press from both African and expatriate European reviewers.[8]

It is fascinating to see what Weston did with the sour reviews. Ignoring the bad press, he focused on the meaningful dialogue with African musicians during the festival, and he resolved to return. Weston explains:

> I went back in 1963, just myself and a painter, Elton Fax, and we did lectures in Nigerian universities and at various schools. I gave demonstrations on the piano and I would tape Nigerian folk music, then take the same melodies and the same rhythms and play it on the piano, and explain to them that this music that is called jazz . . . for me is really an extension of African culture.[9]

The return to Nigeria was followed by an extensive fourteen-country tour of Africa in 1967 for the U.S. State

Department.[10] At the end of that year, Weston moved to North Africa, making Tangier his home and even opening up a jazz club there appropriately named "African Rhythms Club." He remained for six years before returning to the U.S. What could have been a psychological disenchantment with Africa stemming from the disastrous Nigerian reception was transformed into a concentrated involvement with Africa.

How could Weston overcome his initially hostile reception? Remember that his earliest vision of Africa was solidified by listening to his father's record collection. Those imaginings of the African-American musical bridge were further solidified with Marshall Stearns, whose musical scholarship confirmed Weston's intuitions. Weston's initial confrontation with African actualities did not discourage him from penetrating African culture more deeply; he brought to his first African visit an already well-established musical mission. The recording of *Uhuru Africa* the year before his Nigerian trip had cemented his sense of the perennial meaningfulness of the African–African-American musical tie. His recordings and numerous concert appearances since 1960 (he performed in a 1989 revival of Ellington's *A Drum Is A Woman*)[11] have been a vivid testimony to his enduring musical power compressing the miles of the African diaspora.

One might argue that Weston's insistence upon a seamless musical unity between African and African-American music is a grandiose oversimplification. Historically, jazz did not have its inception in Morocco, and it is arguable whether contemporary African listeners recognize U.S. jazz as their "own" music. But Weston has programmatically attempted to evolve a universal Pan-African musical lingua franca through the sheer force of his musical imagination and sophisticated performances. Unlike Esperanto, Weston's hybrid synthesis does not reduce two languages to a lowest common denominator.

He has chosen to create an intercultural weave based upon a profound respect for the complexity of music East and West. It is an intergenerational weave as well; his son Azzedin has performed and recorded with him. And for all the emphasis on African rhythms at the heart of his style, it is a weave with melodies as memorably singable as Ellington's (listen to the catchy vocal arrangements by Lambert, Hendricks, and Ross)[12] and as harmonically jolting as the best of Monk's. His music possesses a chiming clarity, a honeysmooth tone, no mean achievement for a pianist who can keep rumbling New Orleans rhythms with his left hand while his right plays a North African dance figure.

Yet in writing about Weston's achievement, I kept pondering what difference his musical celebration of African freedom and womanhood has made in Africa itself. In spite of the praise of African woman—echoed in compositions by other jazz musicians honoring Cleopatra and Nefertiti—many African women are often not treated with minimal human decency or economic justice by Western standards. South Africa is as totalitarian and racist a State today as in 1960.

But in 1964, the government of South Africa banned the sales of Weston's *Uhuru Africa,* as they did the other epic jazz album of that year, Roach's *Freedom Now Suite.* The censorship board decided:

> In the future . . . it plans to examine carefully all records imported from the United States that feature Negroes and to investigate any that uses "freedom" in its title.[13]

A greater compliment to the inspirational impact of Weston's music couldn't be imagined. Music has never been known to engender an immediate political transformation (unless one takes the Biblical account of Jericho's fall literally). Yet the celebration of the beauty of slave songs offered by W.E.B. DuBois still speaks to peoples of Africa and African descent at the close of this century:

> Through all the sorrow of the Sorrow Songs, there breathes a hope—a faith in the ultimate justice of things. The minor cadences of despair change often to triumph and calm confidence. Sometimes it is a faith in life,

sometimes a faith in death, sometimes assurance of
boundless justice in some fair world beyond. But
whichever it is, the meaning is always clear: that
sometime, somewhere, men will judge men by their
souls and not by their skins.[14]

Weston's response to DuBois' magnificent rhetoric has
been to accept a moral responsibility to educate to keep hope
alive. Weston responded to the misunderstandings at the
1961 Lagos Festival by writing a report (really a manifesto and
call-to-action) for the *Nigerian Music Review*. While a number
of Weston's proposals to increase musical communication
between the continents seem tame and conventional (more
conferences and music libraries) one suggestion reveals the
richness of Weston's vision. He imagines:

> The establishment of a series of interrelated "cultural
> villages" in Africa—designed in the style of traditional
> African architecture—as centers for creative artists in all
> areas of the African cultural heritage. . . . What I
> envision is a congenial setting, with travel and living
> accommodations to be subsidized by the participating
> countries as well as the host country, where artists
> throughout the black world can come for a few weeks or
> months to rest, think, study, perform, teach and lecture
> . . . .[15]

This dream of an Afrocentric counter-academy and
chautauqua rolled into one, has been attempted in the U.S.
with varying degrees of success, attracting musicians on the
order of Sun Ra and Albert Ayler. But Weston's is the only
proposal I have found by an American musician to build a
cultural community in Africa open to artists of the diaspora.
There have been individual migrations of musicians. Marcus
Garvey's musical director, Arnold J. Ford, unsuccessfully
attempted to establish a new life in Africa as did clarinetist
Edmond Hall.[16] A handful of U.S. and Jamaican musicians
have attempted to singularly transplant themselves to various
regions of Africa.

But Weston's dream involves establishing villages, communities. He proposes a radically different circumstance than jazz musicians traditionally find themselves in—an alternative to individually competing on the nightclub and concert circuit. It is a wish for a transcultural musical community the likes of which the world has never known. And he is surely not singular among jazz artists in wishing for a continent-spanning communitas to ease the heartbreak of being part of a small band playing for the scattered remnants.

CHAPTER TEN

Max Roach: Drumming the Tales of African and African-American Liberation

> It is my duty, the purpose of the artist to mirror his times and its effects on his fellow man. We American jazz musicians of African descent have proved beyond all doubt that we're master musicians of our instruments. Now, what we have to do is employ our skill to tell the dramatic story of our people and what we've been through.—*Max Roach*[1]

What is the central theme of jazz composers who share Max Roach's desire to be "a mirror of the times" and tell the story of African Americans? Beginning with Ellington's *Black, Brown and Beige* and continuing through the extended musical narratives of Roach, Weston, Count Ossie, and John Carter, the unifying thread linking these vastly different multisuite or concept albums together has been the theme of liberation. (See Table 3 on page 119.) "Liberation" for these composers is from political oppression, economic depression, spiritual and psychological bondage dictated by the white world, and even freedom from traditional European-based musical conventions. Remember that Ellington's *Black, Brown and Beige* premiered as the first large-scale symphonic jazz composition composed by an African American to be showcased in the respectable arena of Carnegie Hall. Jazz of such symphonic richness was unimaginable until Ellington.

The odd aspect of writing about "liberation" at the start of the nineties is the impulse to frame it in quotation marks, as

Table 3

Afrocentric Extended Musical Works: Variations on the Theme of Gradual Liberation

	Ellington *Black, Brown and Beige*	Roach *Freedom Now Suite*	Weston *Uburu Africa*	Ossie *Tales of Mozambique*	Carter *Roots & Folklore*
African Peoples Before Colonization				"Tales of Mozambique"	*Danwbe*
The Age of Colonization & Slavery	"Black"	"Driva' Man"		"I Am a Warrior"	*Castles of Ghana & Dance of the Love Ghosts*
First Vision of Liberation	"Brown"	"Freedom Day"	"Uhuru Kwanza," "African Wo-man," "Bantu"	"Let Freedom Reign"	*Fields*
Long Road to Freedom	"Beige"	"Prayer/Protest/Peace" & "Tears for Johannesburg"	"Kucheza Blues"	"Lock, Stock and Barrel"	*Shadows on a Wall*

if the word were an antiquarianism of the sixties, shop-worn into a cliche by the seventies, and largely forgotten in the neoconservative political climate of the eighties. Yet, I would suggest that the significance of the word for African-American cultural studies is perennial, that the word has a phoenix-life as regenerative as the theme of separation/ assimilation, that the word symbolizes an archetype at the center of both the African and African-American collective consciousness. Not only have five major jazz composers narrated liberation sagas—hundreds more have touched upon the idea of liberation as a wellspring for musical inspiration.

It is not a coincidence that Roach joins the ranks of a number of other drummer/composers in reformulating this musical theme. Like Milford Graves, Andrew Cyrille, Sunny Murray, and Count Ossie, Roach has contributed to the evolution of the role of the drummer as band leader, composer, and storyteller, the Africanization of the jazz drummer. The history of the drum in jazz has been a slow ascent from providing a discreet rhythmic backdrop, so horn voices could maintain primary focus, to becoming a front-line voice. One of Roach's chief sources of inspiration, Jo Jones from the Count Basie Band, brought spectacular hi-hat cymbal work and irregular accents on bass drum (two trademarks of Roach's style) to the forefront of the Basie style. Roach belongs to that lineage of drummers (including bop musicians Kenny Clarke and Art Blakey) who explore the possibility of drums stepping out from their background role as foundation for improvisations by other instruments.

It does not require a massive leap of imagination to draw a metaphoric parallel between the ascent of the drum as an independent and distinctive jazz ensemble voice and the ascent of the African Americans in a white-ruled society. African Americans, like Africans under colonial rule, learned to exist in the background, their rhythms as common laborers supporting society, yet rarely were allowed to assume "stage center." This metaphor offers a plausible way to understand Roach's increasingly intensive political statements in music beginning with the *Freedom Now Suite*. Cynical music critics have accused Roach (as they did Ellington before him) of embracing racial politics in order to gain publicity for his music, or of latching onto a new musical trend for the sake of seeming "new" (what art critic Wyndham Lewis jeeringly referred to as "Aheadofism").

But these criticisms become trivial when pitted against even a cursory examination of the liberation struggles of the late fifties in the U.S. and Africa. When Max Roach and his band entered the recording studio in the Fall of 1960, to record the *Freedom Now Suite,* they had witnessed, through newspaper and television news over the past nine months, a series of events profoundly reflecting liberation struggles in Africa and the U.S.

The sit-in movement to integrate restaurants, which was inaugurated by four college students in North Carolina, spread to fifteen cities in five states and involved thousands. Civil rights protests occurred in Montgomery, Alabama. Race riots broke out in Tennessee, Mississippi, and Florida. The home of an attorney representing sit-in demonstrators was bombed. The Civil Rights Act was enforced so that black Tennessee voters could freely practice their democratic rights. Two New Orleans black schoolchildren integrated a public school with the help of U.S. marshals. These are merely samples of the depth and breadth of racial conflict in the U.S.[2]

The news reports from South Africa that year were also tumultuous. The year began with riots in the white-created townships of Durban and Pondoland East, which left numbers of police and villagers killed or wounded. In March, thousands of Africans gathered in a peaceful protest against the notorious passbook laws (which severely restricted travel by black South Africans within their own country). The demonstrators were met in Sharpesville by armed troops who fired into the crowd, killing 67 and wounding 186, mostly unarmed women and children. A special session of the United Nations Security Council voted unanimously to condemn South

Africa's apartheid policies and demanded that it abide by the
U.N. charter. Boycotts of South African goods were initiated
internationally, privately in the U.S., through governments in
Ghana and the Caribbean.

This, then, was in the air when Max Roach entered the New
York recording studio. What musical response would be
appropriate to these American and African struggles? One
response might have been music unrelated to the news
assuming that it is made for entertainment and could not
directly change the course of history. Further, there would be
no reason to link jazz with African problems thematically
since jazz is quintessentially an American invention. One
could heed the statement by pianist Lennie Tristano:

> There are Negroes and/or slaves all over the world, but
> nothing like jazz ever happened anywhere but here in
> this country. There is nothing African about jazz. Jewish
> cantors and gypsies sound more like it than anything
> from Africa.[3]

Or one could choose to create jazz to make a statement in
support of African-American and African struggles, a statement linking the two continents with a shared musical
heritage. Roach and associates chose that path.

Roach's ensemble for the recording spanned the continents. The Nigerian drummer Olatunji (who a mere month
later would again be in the studio celebrating African
liberation with Randy Weston) brought his command of
traditional West African drumming and chanting. Vocalist
Abbey Lincoln (who would later travel to Africa and receive
the African name of Aminata Moseka from Guinea's Presi-
dent) brought her newly won musical individuality. The
veteran saxophonist Coleman Hawkins brought the spirit of
inventive swing. The young trumpeter Booker Little brought
a searing and searching tone underscoring Lincoln's delivery
of lyrics by Oscar Brown Jr. Trombonist Julian Priester,
bassist James Schenck, tenor saxophonist Walter Benton, and
Afro-Cuban percussionists Mantillo and Du Vall (embodying

Roach's long fascination with Afro-Caribbean, particularly Cuban and Haitian, drumming traditions) helped flesh out the sound.

It should be emphasized from the onset that the recorded version of the *Freedom Now Suite* represents only a portion of the total work. Differences in opinion between Roach and singer/songwriter Oscar Brown, Jr., resulted in the recorded work representing a compromised portion of a larger work-in-progress. Further, it has been presented as a dance-drama on several occasions (linking it to Ellington's *A Drum Is A Woman*). Thousands witnessed *Freedom Now Suite* on stage in New York and at the 1961 NAACP convention in Philadelphia. Narration was offered by baritone Brock Peters (who, like Olatunji, also recorded with Weston on *Uhuru Africa*). Among the dancers was Charles Moore, who distinguished himself in the next two decades as one of the major innovators of African-American dance grounded in traditional African movements.[4]

But even now with Roach's composition available only in audio format,[5] one can be swept up by the spell of the music and the power of the images, struck by the fact that the killing and maiming created by South African apartheid is no less now than it was in 1960. And the struggle for racial equality in the U.S.—threatened by the ascendancy of the New Right with its rolling back of affirmative action programs—is far from finally won.

The recorded work moves swiftly through five sections: "Driva' Man," "Freedom Day," "Prayer/Protest/Peace," "All Africa" and "Tears for Johannesburg." Oscar Brown's straightforward lyrics reflecting the rhythms of a slave laboring are eloquently delivered by Abbey Lincoln. Lincoln's vocal and a tambourine open the recording mournfully, ruminatively, accenting a sledgehammer's repetitive fall. Then the rest of the band follows, horns solemnly leading the way into a developing dirge. The antebellum South is transformed into a new land of possibility through an uptempo vocal with Lincoln proclaiming "Freedom Day." But the joy of liberation from slavery is short-lived (as was also the case in the "Brown" movement of Ellington's *Black, Brown, and Beige*) since more subtle forms of slavery take the place of the old shackle and chains.

The denial of equal opportunity for African Americans is protested through the burgeoning civil rights movement. In the centerpiece of *Freedom Now Suite*, "Prayer/Protest/Peace," Lincoln and Roach engage in one of the most astonishing dialogues in recorded jazz. The sympathy between the musicians (who would be married two years after this recording) is nothing short of telepathic and torrential in emotional force. Roach begins the dialogue with short sequences of melodic drumming, suggesting Lincoln's vocal patterns which will follow. Lincoln's wordless vocal builds from a softly modulated prayer hum to a shatteringly cathartic scream sequence (manifesting the frustrated screams of protestors in the U.S. and African in one cry). The piercing cry finally winds into a soft and peaceful strain. Roach doesn't miss a beat, constantly interacting with the arc of Lincoln's song. His efforts to express conversational dialogue through the drums, tonally between speech and song, foretells his 1980 interactive drum solo with a tape of Martin Luther King, Jr.'s March on Washington Speech, "The Dream/It's Time," on the *Chattahoochee Red* album.

In "All Africa," Roach moves out of his stage center role to allow African drummer Olatunji to engage in a call-and-response exchange with Lincoln. Lincoln chants the names of various African tribes while Olatunji answers with drum rhythms and chanted Yoruba maxims about freedom, forging an explicit link between American and African liberation struggles. The full ensemble, including Roach, returns on the lament, "Tears for Johannesburg," in which Booker Little injects his trumpet solo with as much of the sound of heartbreak as Lincoln's vocal on "Protest," testifying to the continuity of the struggle for liberation.

These mark the first of Roach's compositions engaged with liberation struggles, compositions which would earn him a five-year censorship by white-owned recording studios. Following *Freedom Now Suite* came *Percussion Bittersweet* (with its tribute to Marcus Garvey); two further compositions protesting South African racial injustice, performed with Archie Shepp; an album length evocation of racist injustice, *Scott Free*, the musical elaboration of Rev. King's "I Have a Dream" speech, and the soundtrack for a King documentary.

That impulse to keep narrating the freedom saga of peoples of African descent was furthered as Roach assumed a teaching position at the University of Massachusetts, Amherst, in the seventies. The financial security of that teaching post enabled him to spend time in Africa:

> I got a grant from the university and spent one summer in Africa for a course I proposed, called History of African Music and Musicians, and I did a lot of research over there. I brought back a lot of material and taught a course in that particular subject. The university bought some wonderful instruments for that course. We had an African drum choir, with the balaphons and the whole thing.[6]

This opportunity to connect jazz with the serious study of African and African-American history and culture, on a campus whose faculty would also include Archie Shepp and Yusef Lateef, provided Roach the opportunity to keep a heritage alive. Like his fellow jazz faculty members, Roach continues to work in a dazzlingly broad range of musical ensembles—percussion bands, jazz quartets supplemented by electronics and/or strings, and rap vocalists—in a continuing quest to expand the range of African-American music.

But the constant in Roach's music is that need to testify, to tell the tale of his people's freedom-in-process. His drumbeats are constantly shortening the distance between South Africa and South Carolina. "What we could not say openly we said in music," Ellington commented.[7] What Roach says on drums continues to expand the ranges of what peoples of African descent can say to the world. By constantly striving to broaden the field of African-American political musical statements, Roach steps firmly into the role of Tiv musicians of Nigeria. In his *Tiv Song,* ethnomusicologist Charles Keil movingly concludes his study of traditional Nigerian musicians by moving his focus to the U.S.:

> So to survive we need to make songs of our own that are like Tiv songs, in both quantity and quality. We need to make songs like Aita Anwuna's that can frustrate the big men into bad health. We need songs like Anande Amende's that can persuade people to shift their political loyalties. We need song makers like Gari Kwaghbo to combat planned obsolescence. . . . We need songs with what the ancient Greeks called *ethos,* the power to define values, to shape character, and to challenge what only seems to be our fate.[8]

Max Roach's musical career is one long answer to these needs.

CHAPTER ELEVEN

Pierre Dørge: Travelling Through a New World Jungle Armed With Guitar and Orchestra

Pierre Dørge's New Jungle Orchestra, formed in 1980, is not an African garage band or an Ellington revival band playing hits from the Cotton Club's heyday. It is, unabashedly, one of Europe's most sophisticated jazz bands, with a penchant for transforming various world music elements, particularly those from West Africa and the Middle East. The ensemble of twelve to fourteen players is led by a young Danish jazz guitarist and composer. And it is the story of the development of his musical style that demands a shift in focus to the music of West Africa.

Dørge's earliest formal music training was centered upon the upright bass in school. Mandolin and guitar playing were self-taught. Radio programs and eclectic record purchases fed his appreciation of mainstream American jazz. Concerts in Denmark by John Coltrane and Eric Dolphy expanded his horizons. But one concert in 1967 proved a turning point in his development. Frank Zappa opened for John Tchicai's Big Band. Zappa's music offered Dørge permission to break down barriers between jazz and rock, a desire stirred by his discontent with traditional jazz guitar. As Dørge informed *Down Beat* writer Mitchell Feldman:

> From the beginning, I never liked the sound of jazz guitar—I thought it was boring. I like it a little better today, but back then the tone always sounded the same—there was no real expression there. . . . I always

> wanted the guitar to sound like a horn. . . . I've always
> been resisting and fighting the guitar's sound and trying
> to make it smoother than it is. At the same time, I have
> a problem, because I attack the guitar with a pick very
> hard. . . .[1]

The hard-picked attack on electric guitar strings creates clearly etched individual notes of brief duration—unless the guitar sound is electronically altered through various pedal attachments or modified through intentional feedback by holding the guitar close to an amplifier. When Dørge was musically coming of age in the sixties, rock guitarists rather than jazz guitarists were leading the way in experimenting with the far reaches of electric guitar sound, including the creation of strikingly long-sustained notes with horn-like cadences. In the most memorable single performance of the much-heralded Woodstock Festival, Jimi Hendrix concluded the event with an electric guitar transformation of the "Star Spangled Banner" in which its "bombs bursting in air" were turned into glissandos on guitar strings, sustained into smoldering bursts of effervescent feedback. Along with Hendrix, Frank Zappa was the other major rock guitar innovator, although his contributions were overshadowed by his scatological lyrics with the Mothers of Invention. Zappa and Hendrix also shared a similar musical history, both beginning their careers as rhythm and blues guitarists whose personal vision led them to break out of the boundaries of that style.

Zappa's *Shut Up N Play Yer Guitar* suggests what Dørge found attractive in Zappa's style. Not only does Zappa create long horn wails on numbers like "Heavy Duty Judy" where his guitar sound creates an equivalent to R & B sax "honking," but he also mimics sounds like soprano sax vibrato on "Gee, I Like Your Pants." And Zappa's guitar takes on these various jazz horn sounds and styles, with a singing tone, exactly that vocal-based sound that Dørge was after. "I've always been working to get the guitar to sing," Dørge informed Feldman.

John Tchicai's influence on Dørge has been more ongoing than Zappa's. After joining Tchicai's Big Band in 1969, Dørge had the opportunity to explore guitar textures which would work in a multiple horn ensemble with a large percussion emphasis. Tchicai first made his mark on the jazz scene with alto sax playing on Coltrane's *Ascension,* making his voice heard within the uproarious surge of the seven-horn, eleven-piece band. Tchicai (whose father was from Zaire and mother Danish) also contributed his tart and angular sax sounds to recordings by Archie Shepp. His playing covers not only free jazz and European New Music approaches, but embraces a number of African and African-American styles utilizing passionate vocalisms. In the early seventies, Tchicai temporarily abandoned playing to spend time in spiritual reflection in a Danish ashram.

Dørge handled this break with Tchicai as musical colleague and teacher by pursuing workshop studies and participating in several rock bands. The eighties marked the crystallization of Dørge's identity as a guitarist and band leader as he formed the New Jungle Orchestra, sixteen members strong, and also studied with African musician Foday Musa Suso.

Suso was an ideal influence since he was master of an African stringed instrument, the *kora,* which sounds simultaneously both like and unlike a guitar. The *kora* is a harp lute, usually strung with twenty-one nylon strings, which creates a sound Westerners frequently identify with classical guitarists on the one hand and Mississippi Delta blues guitarists on the other. Yet if the tone and hepatonic scales of the instrument can resemble a guitar, its West African music bears little resemblance to classical or blues guitar literature. Samuel Charters, who searched for the roots of African-American blues in the Mandingo tribal areas of Senegal and The Gambia, describes his first impression of *kora* playing by Nyama Suso:

> He played a long, highly ornamented introduction; then began singing. The music was strongly expressive, a mixture of recitation and song. At times he told part of

a story, then intermingled the narrative with comments
and praises for the great men mentioned in the song.
The accompaniment he played on the kora was a
repetitive, highly rhythmic figure that was light in
texture and contrasted brilliantly with the dark tone of
the voice.[2]

What Charters heard during the sixties, and what Dørge
heard in 1980 from that other member of the musical Suso
clan, was a performance based on the role of *kora* musician as
tribal historian, as *griot*. In this tradition, the *kora* accompanies
the singing/chanting voice of the griot, whose function is to
regenerate the memory of listeners so they can commemorate
and praise ancestors. Four topics repeatedly noted in
Mandingo griot songs by ethnomusicologist Roderic Knight
are death, bravery, religion, and animal imagery.[3]

Without knowing exactly what Suso taught Dørge, it is
probably safe to assume that Suso acquainted the guitarist
with the role of *kora* player as griot, as a narrator. And Suso
also encouraged Dørge to visit his home town of Brikama in
The Gambia, where other remarkable *kora* players could offer
Dørge instruction and inspiration. But Suso could also offer
Dørge an imaginative recasting of traditional *kora* music: Suso
had left his homeland years prior to meeting Dørge and had
settled in Chicago where his band, the Mandingo Griot
Society, in spite of its pure-sounding name, experimented
with synthesizing blues, jazz, funk, and Mandingo music.
Once again, Dørge found in Suso permission to imagine a
new form of music which could blend late twentieth-century
electronic technology (synthesizers, drum machines,
echoplex) with traditional African instrumentation. The
album cover to Suso's *Watto Sitta* has a *kora* floating in the sky
adjacent to an electronic printed circuit board.

Dørge made repeated trips to Brikama in The Gambia
where he studied *kora* with Alhaji Bai Konte and Malamin
Fobareth, but interestingly, this study in no way dissuaded
him from maintaining the electric guitar as his primary
performance instrument. The African studies further en-

hanced his incorporation of West African rhythms and a deepening sense of musical narration. While in no way simply imitating griot narratives, nonsensical at a literal level for a Danish musician, Dørge's compositions seem to present narratives squarely within those traditional griot categories of death, bravery, religion, and animal imagery.

The first New Jungle Orchestra recording in 1982 (*Pierre Dørge and the New Jungle Orchestra*) begins to develop these themes. There, his animal portraits include a hilariously dissonant take of "Tiger Rag" implying that "Hold That Tiger!" carries a different dynamic in Africa than elsewhere. That first album includes a musical/spiritual portrait of Foday Suso, his *kora* teacher, as the next album, *Brikama,* would contain a portrait of his other *kora* instructor, Alhaji Bai Konte. There are landscapes infused with religious significance, "Jungle Rituals" and "Fullmoon in Brikama (Africa)." But the high point of the record is a portrait, the praise song of a Brikaman tailor, Bo Bo Sanneh. Percussion and chanting voices are the bedrock of the composition. Dørge's guitar along with various horns enter as the tempo picks up and the composition moves into an ecstatically swinging romp, concluding with shouting horns. (The form of this piece is repeated in subsequent New Jungle Orchestra albums.) This was an extremely accomplished first album for a new band, but what follows reflects a leap in musical sophistication.

Brikama, released two years later, marks the appearance of South African bassist Johnny Mbizo Dyani with the ensemble. Dyani had established his reputation over a decade before joining the New Jungle Orchestra, playing with Steve Lacy, David Murray, Archie Shepp, and a number of distinguished South African musicians who, like himself, were living in exile throughout Europe. Dyani was an extremely physically forceful player who loved the loud snap of upright bass strings, the powerhouse wooden tones felt first in the feet then in chest. His bass playing was often accompanied by chanting and dancing on stage. Dyani became Dørge's link to the world of South African folk

music. And Dyani brought a hotly cathartic emotional cast to
the group sound. As Dyani told an interviewer:

> . . . playing to me is like a medicine. . . . I'm like a
> psychiatrist. I've seen people in the clubs and at concerts
> who get drunk with the music. They get so excited and
> drunk because of the music that I sometimes get very
> angry. But sometimes they also keep very quiet or they
> even get scared! I have to understand that this all is in
> the music when people come after the playing and tell
> me what they've experienced.[4]

By adding Dyani to the ensemble, Dørge added a shaman's
touch to a unit already embodying the griot's spirit of
storytelling. One composition on *Brikama* truly spotlights
Dyani's unique contributions: "A Rainbow Over the Bamboo
Forest."

American jazz vocalist Bobby McFerrin has accompanied
his wildly expressive vocal pyrotechnics with chest thumping,
but McFerrin can't hold a candle to Dyani's thunderous slaps
on "A Rainbow Over the Bamboo Forest." The eight-minute
work builds gradually from a mysterious passage on the nasal
sounding Egyptian bamboo ney flute. Dyani's body beats are
mixed with Irene Becker's synthesizer riffs and a gathering
swarm of saxophones and trombones. Then, suddenly, the
band members chant: "Johnny Dyani, what do you see?" and
without missing a (chest) beat Dyani answers: "I see a
rain-bow over the bam-boo forest!" After this enchanting
call-and-response is relayed several more times, let me assure
you, your heartbeat is quickened as you, too, see the rainbow.
The question voiced by the band falls away as Dyani repeats
what he sees, eventually shifting into a series of interjections
("wow, come look!"). There are few listening experiences in
the history of contemporary recorded jazz as full of unfettered awe and ecstasy, pure cathartic joy at the beauty of an
alive earth. It is a first cousin to Ellington's "Virgin Jungle"
and "Thanks for the Beautiful Land of the Delta," musical
landscapes saturated with spiritual illumination.

If "A Rainbow Over the Bamboo Forest" is the triumph of *Brikama* (as well as the band's most fully realized recorded number), it is by no means the only composition full of delightfully surprising blendings of the old and new, Western and African. *Brikama* opens with "Monk in Africa," described in Dørge's liner notes as a fantasy of what it would have been like if Thelonious Monk had been born and brought up in Africa and had played guitar. Dørge opens the work with a rhythmically careening West African-style guitar workout, spinning whimsical tales off slippery sounding single strings. Tenor and alto saxes soon join the fray. "Monk in Africa" welcomes you to round about midnight south of the Sahara.

The band's next album, *Even the Moon Is Dancing,* appeared a year later. This work connects the "jungle" in the band's name with Duke Ellington's "jungle" music period (which was not Dørge's original inspiration for naming the group). Ellington's "The Mooch," a classic from the Cotton Club days, opens and closes the album. Yet Dørge and band don't simply reverently imitate the Ellington jungle sound but, ironically and humorously, carry that sound to its logical musical conclusion. Growling reeds evoke the Ellington use of brassy animal sounds from the twenties, but the album's closing number, "Even the Moon Is Dancing," ricochets back to "The Mooch" and growling brasses are traded for African horns. This was the step that Ellington's musical Africanization never took. Dørge and colleagues recontextualize early Ellington by underscoring, more than ever, the affinities between early American jazz and African music. Shared also with Ellington are musical tributes to the dead ancestors and a celebration of nature and animal life.

Totally unexpected was Dyani's death in 1986 in Berlin while Dørge was touring with his quartet in North America.[5] The band's 1987 album, *Johnny Lives,* reflects the scope of that loss, both in its title (playing on the "Bird Lives" graffiti trailing Charlie Parker into eternity) and through a twelve-minute work, "Mbizo Mbizo," in which volcanic chant and percussive frenzy evoke the spirit and form of "A Rainbow

Over the Bamboo Forest." While the album contains the usual mix of portraits of humans and animals ("Waltz for Two Camels," "Lilli Goes to Town") a new facet is revealed: a happy/sad blues atmosphere permeates "Flying Home With SAS," as if Dyani's death left the group with a new blues to wail, a loss not easily overcome.

Dørge continues to record and tour with a quartet as well as with the ever-changing New Jungle Orchestra. While emphasizing his African (South and West) influences, I don't want to neglect other roots of his music. There is an enormous amount of dadaist whimsy in his music ("Bambla Jolifanti" was sparked by dadaism's founder Hugo Ball), the kind of humor that turns Monk into an African guitarist or composes a waltz for camels. The horn chants are in debt to the arrangements of Ellington and Mingus, as is the insistence upon a musical narrative focus. And there is the irreducible fact that Dørge is an individualist with his own sturdy distinctive musical vision.

His imaginative play with African styles and instrumentation is unparalleled by any other musicians not of African descent. Perhaps being free from ideological strictures imposed by black nationalism or a search for personal roots enabled him to work with African ideas from a fresh and original perspective. Yet his music does pay homage to his African spiritual ancestors, African musicians all, from Gambian *kora* players to a South African bassist.

The young Dørge, through his study of African music, succeeded in turning his guitar into something that sounded like a horn. He further learned how to make it sound like a tiger, camel, rhino, songbird, or more miraculously, like a human voice that would have been at home in Ellington's band on the staged jungle of the Cotton Club. And he learned how to make that guitar call the spirits of the ancestors forth, from Brikama to his Nordic home.

CHAPTER TWELVE

Archie Shepp: Magical Portraits for the Diaspora

> And I believe this, that if we migrated to Africa culturally, philosophically and psychologically, while remaining here physically, the spiritual bond that would develop between us and Africa through this cultural, philosophical and psychological migration, so-called migration, would enhance our position here, because we would have our contacts with them acting as roots or foundations behind us.—*Malcolm X*[1]

Marcus Garvey's dream of a mass migration of African Americans back to Africa was long forsaken by the time saxophonist-composer Archie Shepp came of age in the early sixties. The fleet of Black Star Liners bearing Garvey banners and hordes of Harlemites returning to the Motherland never materialized. But Shepp's early adulthood saw Garvey's dream of Pan-African unity realized by another black prophet, Malcolm X, whose father had been a deeply involved Garvey activist. It was Malcolm X who bypassed the physical migration of Americans back to Africa in favor of a psychological and spiritual reconnection and communion. And as a participant in the revolution of black consciousness of the sixties, it was this vision that informed Shepp's musical contributions.

The temptation when looking at Shepp's career is to buy into that cliche of "the angry young man of the avant-garde" which Shepp's own public statements seemed to reinforce. Such labeling neglects the obvious: Shepp has been concerned from the earliest days of his career with the fullest

135

possible musical expression of the history of the black diaspora. Central to this lifelong mission have been imaginative evocations of the African foundations in African-American music.

Finding permission for this Afrocentric musical vision through two of his key musical mentors, Duke Ellington and John Coltrane, Shepp first demonstrated his imagination of Africa through *The Magic of Ju-Ju*. The eighteen-minute-long title cut is essentially a percussion display not unlike Art Blakey's percussion albums, particularly *The African Beat*. Against a choir of five drummers (combining the traditional African talking drum and rhythm logs with the Western drum kit), Shepp on tenor sax joins with trumpeter Martin Banks and trumpeter/trombonist Michael Zwerin in improvising over this dense percussive layer. Shepp's tone, characteristic of his mid-to-late sixties recordings, is full of short jabbing phrases in the mid-to-upper registers, a volcanic mix of later Coltrane and early Rollins, intensely wrathful. The listener is left with the impression of an exorcism in process. Shepp blasts away any and all resistance in this racist society which would prevent him from connecting to the vital force, African roots, and from attaining full liberation as an African American. The work's thickly layered rhythms represent, like ju-ju, a magical accumulation of spiritual power to help propel souls toward liberation.

Logically enough, the next album with an African feel is an in-concert recording of Shepp and band at the 1969 Pan-African Festival in Algeria. In contrast to *The Magic of Ju-Ju*, in which American drummers provided an *African-like* percussive texture (with no attempt to accurately replicate traditional African drum rhythms per se),[2] in the 1969 concert Shepp is accompanied by a battery of *traditional* North African percussion and *raita* (an oboe-like double-reeded instrument) players as well as his own band and the poets Don L. Lee and Ted Joans. This was a brave experiment on several counts. While most attempts to mix jazz with African music have incorporated West or South African musics, Shepp looked toward the Arabic flavor of the North. The complication of such a focus is suggested by Gunther Schuller:

> It should be noted that African music, unlike Arabic, is basically not microtonal in structure. By contrast, Arabic (North African and Spanish) music is basically a homophonic, variational, microtonal music, and does not feature the solo-to-ensemble juxtaposition.[3]

Not only are the musical rules very different in North African music, but the clear majority of African Americans do not trace their racial heritage in any *specific* fashion to that part of the continent. So there is something preposterous, on a literal level, when the half-hour centerpiece of this concert opens with poet Don L. Lee chanting: "We have come back"; it is dubious that Lee's people ever were in Algeria before.

But this is a symbolic gesture, clearly fashioned for a Pan-African Festival where musical differences between Northern and Western Africa were to be set aside for the sake of the aesthetically unifying event. What is harder to grasp is how Lee's poem proceeds to identify jazz as an African music in the context of Algerian and Tuareg musics which sound quite unrelated. This is Shepp's attempt to forge an alchemical marriage; on the surface it appears as unlikely as any lead-into-gold experiment ever conducted.

The quixotic experiment of blending avant-garde jazz with North African musics was further colored by the poor recording technology used at the site. The musicians are nearly indistinguishable on the poorly differentiated sound-stage. Shepp's drummer, the ever-inventive Sunny Murray, is often inaudible over the intense round of African drumming. The jazz hornmen also suffer from being overwhelmed by the *raitas*. More seriously, the American players sound out of synchronization with the North African players when the recording balance permits all to be clearly heard. While the nasal-sounding *raitas* snake through exquisitely executed microtonal trance dances, creating sonic bee-dances of nervous vitality, Shepp and company sound as if they are playing outtakes from *The Magic of Ju-Ju.*

Transcultural jam sessions like this are often inevitably plagued by little to no rehearsal time and inadequate recording conditions (similar charges would be leveled against Shannon Jackson's jam with the Nigerian band led by Twins Seven Seven). But Shepp's courageous attempt to integrate the North African sound is significant in *Live at the Pan-African Festival.* Further, the exposure Shepp and his band members had to traditional African musicians would have lasting consequences upon every member of his group: Murray would produce *Homage to Africa;* cornetist Clifford Thornton's ambitious *The Gardens of Harlem* would trace African musical influences throughout the diaspora; Grachan Moncur would, like Thornton, compose and record his *Echoes of Prayer,* which evokes Marcus Garvey, for large jazz orchestra; Alan Silva would record a small group work, *Ashanti,* centered upon West African themes. Shepp, as Table 4 indicates (see page 139), would evolve from the Pan-African Festival experience with a three-tiered program tracing the movements of African music throughout the diaspora.

The "Afrocentric Statements" in this chart collect Shepp's most explicit album references. "Thematic Oratorios" consist of extended compositions for large ensemble which combine dramatizations of African themes with a range of other styles. "Modular Explorations" offer reinterpretations of spirituals, blues, and bop, each a self-contained showcase spotlighting Shepp in a duet context. Looking at this three-tiered display suggests that in addition to the dominant thread evoking Africa through Shepp's recordings, there are two parallel paths tracing the movements of black music through the diaspora.

The Cry of My People and *There's A Trumpet in My Soul* hark back to the ambitious Ellington tradition of *Black, Brown and Beige* and *A Drum Is A Woman* in the mythopoetic narrations (out of the conventional linear sequences of Western history). *The Cry of My People* opens with a gospel-flavored "Rest Enough (Song to Mother)," with the lyrics carried by the

Table 4

Archie Shepp's Portraits of the Diaspora

THEMATIC ORATORIOS
The Cry of My People (1972)
There's A Trumpet in My Soul (1975)

AFROCENTRIC STATEMENTS
The Magic of Ju-Ju (1967)
Live at the Pan-African Festival
"Yasima" (*Yasima, A Black Woman,* 1969)
"Tuareg" (*Blase,* 1969)
"Song for Mozambique" (*A Sea of Faces,* 1975)
"South Africa 76" (*Force,* with Max Roach, 1976)
"South Africa Goddamn" (*The Long March,* 1979)
Here Comes the Family (with Family of Percussion, 1980)
Duets (with Dollar Brand, 1982)
"Poem for Mama Rose" and "Things Have Got to Change" (*Things Have Got to Change,* with Cheikh Tidiane Fall, 1979)
"My Heart Cries Out to Africa" (*Jazz A Confronto,* 1975)

MODULAR EXPLORATIONS OF TRADITIONAL MUSICAL STYLES
Goin' Home (1977)
Trouble in Mind (1980)
Looking at Bird (1980)

woman's gospel quintet, the Patterson Singers. Strains of the
Southern Baptist and Holiness Church gospel music combine
with a jazzy R & B arrangement in what is a characteristic of
Shepp's extended compositions, a praise-song to the archetypal female. This heroic figure of the black mother opens
The Cry of My People, as the black woman as lover establishes
the center-focus of *Blase. Yasima* embodies the rhythmic
vitality of the spirit of the black woman. Semenya McCord's
silky vocal opens Shepp's Afro-Brazilian opus, *There's a
Trumpet in My Soul;* she rhapsodizes, sounding like the voice
of jazz, a new reincarnation of Madame Zzaj.

From the celebration of the black woman, *The Cry of My
People* shifts into jazz performed by a large ensemble which
maintains a strong hint of the traditional African-American
church. "A Prayer" (by the neglected composer Cal Massey)[4]
and "All God's Children Got a Home in the Universe," then
seque into a tribute to Billie Holiday, that most secular of
black vocalists. Yet this apparent programmatic discontinuity
is really not a gaffe since Shepp identities black church music
with the black mother, perhaps even with that lovely black
concept of "mother wit." Black women have historically made
a unique contribution to the Southern Baptist and Holiness
church traditions, both musically and spiritually.[5] So Billie
Holiday's jazz/blues cry mingles with the sung cries of
generations of women raising their voices on Sunday in the
black church, and the composition presents a narrative in
which all ages are contemporaneous.

So it is not contradictory that this musical history moves
from Holiday of the thirties through fifties back to a
celebration of African drums, "African Drum Suite." Holiday's soulful cry is an American invention, like jazz itself,
having roots in a continent where African rhythms are carried
by drums. The work concludes majestically with Joe Lee
Wilson singing "Come Sunday," adding even greater coherence to the composition. "Come Sunday" was the culminating
moment in the first section, "Black," of Ellington's own
extended composition tracing African roots into the flower-

ing of the diaspora in the U.S. While Shepp's tenor sax solo cannot begin to achieve the majestic statement of Johnny Hodges' horn on the 1943 live Carnegie Hall recording of *Black, Brown, and Beige,* Shepp and ensemble do convey a tremendous amount of bittersweet spiritual longing, the feeling at the heart of the diasporic consciousness. And of course "Sunday" had traditionally meant freedom from the bondage of wage-slavery, if only for a brief respite. In that sense, Sundays are rhythmic punctuations of the calendar encouraging spiritual (and/or political) transcendence.

Shepp's manner of narrating black history in *The Cry of My People* treats historical events not so much as points on a timeline but as a dynamically moving constellation. Events are subject to eternal recurrence; the Western definition of "progress" is irrelevant. Billie Holiday's suave ballads of the thirties are not a musical improvement upon the drumming choruses of traditional African drummers, but simply part of an African continuum that includes the unknown composers of Holiness church spirituals and Duke Ellington. This music is not only Afrocentric in historical reference, it is Afrocentric in its construction to the extent that a narrative is offered in which historical events move in a circular dance.[6] A similar narrative method informs *There's a Trumpet In My Soul.* The evocation of the old African deities during carnival ("Down in Brazil") is strikingly juxtaposed with Shepp's poetic autobiography, which moves from a Southern Highway 8 in Florida to New England, where he currently resides and teaches.

In contrast to these large scale works weaving multiple black styles and cultures are a trilogy of tributes to three key African-American music genres: spirituals, blues, and bop. Each of these three recordings freshly reinterprets style in a duet format, heightening the sense that Shepp is in conversation with a musical ancestor about the ongoing evolution of the style. Pianist Horace Parlan was a fine choice of accompanist for the spirituals set, *Goin' Home,* and for the blues collection, *Trouble in Mind.* Parlan's own interest in the roots of African-American music are strikingly evident on his

Happy State of Mind album, which opens with Ronnie Boykin's piece, "Africa Is My Home," and closes with a spirited interpretation of Randy Weston's "Kucheza Blues" (from Weston's *Uhuru Africa*). The bop set, a tribute to Charles Parker, was recorded with the highly versatile Danish bassist Niels-Henning Ørsted Pedersen.

These recordings offer Shepp in a regal, meditative, refined and rather Apollonian state. They are not nostalgic exercises in neo-conservatism but are polished statements declaring that jazz ancestors are alive in the present. Mining spirituals, blues, and bop as sources can offer a lifetime quest of adventure. Instead of simply creating version ten thousand and one of "Body and Soul," this is ancestor tribute in the African sense: the ancestors are vividly alive as sources of guidance for every musician who approaches them reverently and imaginatively.

While the extended compositions blend African sources with jazz, and this trilogy of duets illuminates the stylistic building blocks of the diaspora, Shepp has also created a number of compositions with *specific* African references, generally for small ensembles. A direct consequence of playing with the Tuareg musicians at the 1969 Pan-African Festival was "Tuareg," a tribute to the nomadic desert players. The piece concludes the album *Blase,* and offers emotionally wide ranging, passionately executed sax solos by Shepp, exquisitely matched with rhythmic inventiveness on trap drums by veteran bop player Philly Joe Jones. (Jones had also stepped quite a ways out of his traditional drumming style to contribute, along with co-drummer Sunny Murray, to the rhythmic explosiveness of *Yasima.*) While Jones doesn't literally recreate the patterns of Tuareg drummers, he does convey a hypnotic rhythmic groove, potentially trance-inducing, which is what Shepp apparently heard in the Tuareg music.[7]

I find the single most moving Shepp composition of Afrocentric vision the "Song for Mozambique" on *A Sea of Faces.* Propelled initially by Shepp's soprano sax stating the theme, Bunny Fox's vocal declares "There's a beautiful sound that is heard/It begins with an African word." The word, as earlier set to music by Randy Weston, is "Uhuru," Swahili for "freedom." Cameron Brown's driving bass sets in motion the melody line as Shepp recites the poem "A Sea of Faces." The text describes in seven brief stanzas his 1975 performance in Perugia, Italy; his past as a child wanting to be a musician growing up in Florida and Philadelphia; and tributes to his parents and to his spiritual father, John Coltrane. The seven-piece band plays with anthemic insistence following Shepp's poetic recitative, and Bunny Fox once again offers her hymn to "Uhuru" in an uptempo version answered by the players chanting "Africa." The chant is transformed to "Africa . . . Freedom." Shepp's multi-tracked voice on the recording once again recites his autobiographical poem which is now counterpointed by the sung chant of "Africa . . . Freedom." His sax returns to close the poem as Bunny Fox's "Uhuru . . . Africa" fades. It is a triumphant musical celebration of the intersection of the personal and political. The song is dedicated to Mozambique, which declared independence from Portuguese colonial rule a mere two months before the recording was made.

Shepp's duet with drummer/composer Max Roach on "South Africa Goddamn" four years later is quite the opposite in spirit and form to the uplifting anthem of "Song For Mozambique." Roach and Shepp exchange furious sounding improvisatory phrases in this piece from the 1979 Willmar Jazz Festival, a time where the promise of a liberated South Africa appeared no more possible than at the present. The composition is Roach's noteworthy successor to his "Tears for Johannesburg," but the sadness and fury is equally Shepp's.

Shepp's desire to play with an African musician is realized on his duet album with South African pianist and composer Abdullah Ibrahim (Dollar Brand). Both men are somewhat controlled to avoid a clash between their distinctive personalities—a situation similar to the Ellington/Coltrane recorded collaboration—and the set is involving although neither musician attains new heights.

One of the most intriguing of Shepp's Afrocentric projects resulted in a recording session with four drummers who called themselves "Family of Percussion." The session was originally planned to include Ti Roro, one of Haiti's most significant traditional drummers, but he died just before the recording session. In spite of a format similar to *The Magic of Ju-Ju,* the mode of this recording is less cathartic and manic, more playful and exploratory. The drummers are well placed on the recorded soundstage so their individual contributions can be sensitively discerned. Shepp opens with a funny rap, playing on the name of the percussion ensemble, "Here Comes the Family." The variety of rhythmic drum and percussion styles is far broader than on Shepp's earlier album: Trilok Gurtu (who would later gain fame as percussionist with the jazz/world music quartet, Oregon) contributes Indian tabla drums; Peter Giger plays Caribbean steel drums; Doug Hammond adds the traditional African balaphon (a xylophone with gourd resonators); Tim Nicholas adds timbales and congas from the Latin musical world. No one sounds manic; each player has plenty of breathing space. The wide percussive palette working off a broad range of African, Afro-Caribbean, and jazz rhythms frees Shepp to express a wide range of emotion; note his tender flute playing on "Street Song."

Whatever context Shepp has created for his music—large jazz orchestra, duets, or percussion ensembles—he constantly desires to tell the story of the struggle of black humanity through the diaspora. The tension in his music is the result of the difficulty of building those cultural, philosophical, and psychological bridges between African Americans and Africans that Malcolm X spoke of so movingly. That Promethean task makes Garvey's original dream of transporting African Americans en masse by steamship seem simplistic by comparison, but Shepp launches his work with the fervor of a driven minister, reminding his congregation that however many rivers they have already crossed, the image of their true homeland can keep them keeping on.

CHAPTER THIRTEEN

Yusef Lateef: Re-Visioning the Geography of the Blues

"Blues. A troublesome emotion."—*The New Harvard Dictionary of Music*[1]

Highway 61 stretches across two hundred miles of rich black land known as the Mississippi Delta where mile-long rows of cotton and soybeans spread out from its pavement and surround occasional towns. . . . The flat Delta land extends from Memphis, Tennessee, to Vicksburg, Mississippi, and is defined by loess bluffs on its eastern edge and the Mississippi River on its west. For centuries the river has overflowed its banks each spring, and deposits of alluvial soil are thirty feet deep in some areas.—*William Ferris*[2]

William Ferris' definition of the blues begins by actually putting you in the Delta, gazing upon luxuriously fertile land, feeling the seasonal strength of the Mississippi River as it changes the shape of the earth every spring. Ferris offers a type of prose-poetry linking the rhythms of a place with the form of its music. Not only is a metaphoric link between the rich agricultural soil and the musical fecundity of the Delta created, but a sense of time moving cyclically, with a river's sense of obedience to nature's rhythms, is sustained. Although the origins of the blues may be forever unknowable with finality, there is a compelling possibility that the music was created out of a perception of life localized in a particular geography. As John Lee Hooker stated about his great-grandparents in Mississippi: "On the fields they'd be working and humming songs." The musical forms of work songs were not only conditioned by the kind of work practiced (the rhythms of chopping wood, hoeing a field) but by the work environment (the extreme heat and humidity of the Delta). Innovative blues singer Robert Pete Williams even registers atmospheric changes over Louisiana as a factor in his musical evolution:

> The sound of the atmosphere, the weather changed my style. . . . The air came in different with a different sound of music. Well, the atmosphere, when the wind blowing carries music along. I don't know if it's affect you or not but it's a sounding that's in the air, you see? And I don't know where it come from—it could come from the airplanes, or the moaning of automobiles, but anyhow it leaves an air current in the air, you see. That gets in the wind, makes a sounding, you know? And that sounding works up to be a blues.[3]

In an age when music is increasingly made by musicians in recording studios, sealed off from the teeming profusion of rhythms and colors of the world-at-large, it is all the more vital to emphasize what music-making in the world outside the recording studio means. Yet this obvious tie between the impact of one's habitual environment and the forms of music needs to be carried a step further. Actual lived experience of a place need not be the only requisite for musical impact; the imagination of a place, or the images developed from experience amplified and modified by imagination, can also be a powerful impetus for musical composition.

Of the thirteen musicians profiled here, Yusef Lateef and Randy Weston were the only ones who spent years actually living a daily routine in Africa. Pierre Dørge, Ronald Shannon Jackson, and Max Roach took research trips to Africa in order to enrich their musical background. Archie Shepp, Sunny Murray, Art Blakey, and Duke Ellington were invited to Africa to perform and/or record. But for all of these thirteen, regardless of the nature of their actual African contact, images of Africa were very much in their consciousness. Note on "A Jazz Map of Africa" (Table 5, see page 148) the range of musical connections to Africa established through their recordings.

This, by way of introduction to the richly complex relationship Yusef Lateef has had to Africa, a tie culminating in the recording *Yusef Lateef in Nigeria* in 1985. But Lateef's involvement with Africa could be considered to have begun with his conversion to Islam in 1948. Although Lateef has never programmatically explained his music in terms of Islamic influence, there are a few characteristics which very much fit the mold of Islamic music, particularly African Islamic music.

While Lateef's music is vigorously programmatic, and informed by various places and people the composer has experienced (contradicting the orthodox Islamic notion that music should be absolutely abstract, nonprogrammatic), his music has several of the key characteristics identified with what Lois Faruqi calls *Handasah Al Sawt* ("The Art of Sound"). One such characteristic is the use of the arabesque:

> Through manipulation of pitches and durations, the musical progression seeks to convey to the listener an impression of an unfolding pattern that never ends. This creation in tones and durations can also be designated as an arabesque. It is analogous to the similarly named creations in lines, colors, and forms of the visual arts of Islamic culture.[4]

Other core characteristics of the Islamic musical tradition include creation of extended compositions through the linkage of modular musical units: motifs to form phrases, phrases to generate refrains or new sections, new sections inspiring composition or improvisation, and these, in turn, spawning suites in a given melodic mode. Motifs are often manipulated for short durations, and musical forms rarely move toward a single dramatic conclusion. Instruments most

Table 5

A Jazz Map of Africa

Each of the musicians identified with an African nation has recorded one or
more compositions either evoking this locale or in collaboration with a
musician from this location. See the chapters about each musician for
complete details and discography.

ALGERIA:
Archie Shepp

DAHOMEY:
John Coltrane

EGYPT:
Duke Ellington
Yusef Lateef

ETHIOPIA:
Duke Ellington
Count Ossie

THE GAMBIA:
Pierre Dørge

GHANA:
John Carter

KENYA:
Dizzy Gillespie
Max Roach
Art Blakey
George Russell

LIBERIA:
Duke Ellington
John Coltrane

MOROCCO:
Randy Weston

MOZAMBIQUE:
Archie Shepp
Count Ossie

NIGERIA:
Yusef Lateef
John Coltrane
R. Shannon Jackson

SENEGAL:
Sunny Murray
Archie Shepp

SOUTH AFRICA:
Max Roach
Archie Shepp

TANGANYIKA:
John Coltrane

TOGO:
Duke Ellington

TUNISIA:
Dizzy Gillespie
Art Blakey

closely identified with the Islamic musical tradition in Africa include an oboe-like double-reed aerophone called the *algaita* (heard to great effect on Lateef's Nigerian recording), a variety of end-blown flutes, and single and double-headed drums.

Regardless of what the 28-year old Bill Evans was thinking on the day he signalled his Islamic conversion with his new name of Yusef Lateef, what is notable is how his music began evolving from a straightforward mix of bop and blues to a form embracing characteristics of *Handasah Al Sawt*. Jazz critics noted his growing penchant for "the exotic East," evident in his use of authentic African and Asian instrumentation, melodic modes, and folk rhythms.

This orientalization of Lateef's musical direction (celebrated in his own way by Ellington in *Afro-Eurasian Eclipse*) was as remarkable for what it retained of his African-American roots as for what it would accrue of the Third World. Born in 1921 in Chattanooga, Tennessee, Lateef migrated to Detroit, a place where he not only spent his youth but where he would later complete graduate studies in midlife at Wayne State University. Detroit has long held a significant place in blues history as well as for jazz highly colored by blues. While Lateef in a recent interview in *Cadence* lists tenor sax players Lester Young and Dick Williams (of the Andy Kirk Band) as major musical influences upon his sax style, Lateef's opening critique of *Cadence* magazine's masthead is likewise illuminating in revealing his musical ancestry. Noting that *Cadence* calls itself "The American Review of Jazz and Blues," Lateef informs editor and interviewer Bob Rusch:

> I've written and performed blues so I'm familiar with blues form. But jazz, I'm not acquainted with the term, it's an ambiguous term. So if you should ask me something about jazz, I wouldn't really know what you mean.[5]

Lateef is far from alone in rejecting the hegemony of the term "jazz." At various times, Ellington, Roach, Weston, and

Shepp have taken strong exception to it in public statements for a variety of reasons often linked to racism and the white commercial exploitation of black music. But more telling than Lateef's rejection of the word is his immediate claim of his identity as a blues player. The centrality of his blues playing cannot only be established through a careful examination of his recordings from three decades, but it can be further confirmed listening to recordings by Detroit jazz performers of the forties and fifties. A collection like *Tough Jazz From Detroit* offers an ideal starting point. The rude, loud, wailing sax work of Sax Kari, Wild Bill Moore, and T.J. Taylor—all impossibly obscure names now—was in Detroit's air during Lateef's formative years. And while Lateef would never record jazz sax solos so totally drenched in the atmospherics of late night R & B clubs, he would maintain a rich, thick, and full-bodied horn tone found among these players, linking them to their Southern counterparts, Texas tenor players like Buddy Tate. There is a blues wail at the core of Lateef's playing, whether he is facing his youthful musical Mecca of Detroit or the actual Mecca of his spiritual aspirations.

What occurs in the musical imagination of a blues-based American jazzman as he becomes Islamic and orientalizes his vision? First, he participates in two of the most innovative recordings synthesizing jazz and African themes, Art Blakey's *The African Beat* and Randy Weston's *Uhuru Africa*. *Uhuru Africa* brought him in contact with the drummer Olatunji, whose ensemble he joined for a brief time. Like other African Americans devoted to Islam, he wanted to witness Islam as practiced in Africa. So in 1966 Lateef visited Egypt:

> I was in the Nile Valley, just as a traveller. I identified the blues with that valley. It's so rich agriculturally. The cauliflowers that grow there, for example, are so much bigger than the ones we see here. And so I felt a parallel between that valley and the richness of the blues form.[6]

This delightful preface is to the mesmerizing "Nile Valley Blues" heard in his album from the sixties, *A Flat, G Flat and*

C. While some, like the musicologists Paul Oliver and Samuel Charters, have intentionally traveled to Africa in search of American blues, Lateef, without a conscious program, discovered a metaphoric link between Africa and the blues. That Afrocentric sense of the blues veers away from treating the blues psychologically as a feeling-tone and views it as a generative ground, fecund as Nile Valley soil. Lateef's description of the valley, reminiscent of William Ferris' evocation of the Mississippi Delta, suggests a locale dramatically reshaped seasonally by the rhythms of earth, water, and air. The valley image suggests the dynamic play of natural energies constructing, destroying, rebuilding new patterns (arabesques?). Lateef's description harks back to the rhapsodic praises of African earth found in the renowned eighteenth century slave narrative, *The Life of Olaudah Equiano*.[7]

It is one matter to say that the blues is like fecund African soil—and quite another to translate that view through a musical style. The blues traditionally have consisted of a twelve-bar statement connected to an AAB couplet in four-bar phrases. How does one develop images of African earth through this form? Lateef's "Nile Valley Blues" is a hybrid: Lateef's flute as lead instrument, plays at the edges of the twelve-bar blues form while a bass plays long meter and drums double time. Lateef's performance is outstanding; his highly aerated flute tone is occasionally marked by actually singing into the flute, a technique subsequently borrowed and modified by multiinstrumentalist Rahsaan Roland Kirk. This innovative vocalization has an African precedent noted by ethnomusicologist Alan P. Merriam. Zairian players of an end-blown flute, the *mulizi,* bring two sounds into play when they perform:

> . . . good and bad mulizi players are differentiated on the basis of their ability to produce a larynx tone conterminously with the flute tone. This tone, while akin to humming, is considerably more forceful and much rougher than the normal humming sound.[8]

Lateef's approach, by which he creates two sound layers simultaneously, is technologically duplicated through recording studio overdubbing (which marks his recordings from the seventies to the present). Note that in "Nile Valley Blues," Lateef suggests the inspiring fertility of the African earth can be expressed musically through a performance communicating simultaneity of tones in a single instrument. It is as though on African earth all things are happening at once because all time is contained in the moment of perceiving the place. The piece successfully conveys the same sense of timeless unfolding of eternal patterns described in the Islamic tradition as the essence of music. Lateef's perky flute dance ends in much the same fashion as it began, as much a rondo as the Nile Valley itself.

"Nile Valley Blues" is essentially an uptempo tour de force with blues elements coming in and out of focus through Lateef's vocalizing flute, an instrument not conventionally identified with the blues. In a little under four minutes, it announces the fact that the blues can manifest a vision of African agricultural splendor. Lateef's next recorded blues experiment, *Suite 16,* is a far more ambitious foray stretching the limits of the blues, a symphonic blues suite for Lateef's quartet and the Cologne Radio Orchestra. While the seven-movement work is not programmatically connected to Africa, it does reveal an intriguing connection to Islamic musical aesthetics.

Three of *Suite 16*'s movements are essentially conventional jazz slants on the blues (the third, sixth, and concluding seventh movements). These blues interludes in modular form are framed by a very modernist sounding atonal minuet and a very Bachian passacaglia and chorale. Yet the seven movements in no manner suggest a musical evolution from Bach or classical modernism to the blues, nor do the classical and neoclassical movements merge with the blues in order to create a "third stream" synthesis à la Gunther Schuller or George Gershwin. What emerges is an oddly timeless floating quality, sometimes bluesy, sometimes classical, that is exquisitely described in Islamic aesthetic terms, a perspective known first hand by Africans who are devout Moslems:

> The unit of Islamic art in general, and of *handasah al sawt* in particular. . . . One cannot describe it by citing a single theme; by detailing the features of a single person, object, or theme; or by singing one well-remembered theme. Instead, the participant must experience the art work as an open-ended and indefinitely expandable structure. The listener must move with it through some of its constituent segments, savoring each one in succession, thrilling at the release of gradually mounting tension near the end of each module, marvelling at the ingeniousness and creativity of the organization of visual or aural motifs.[9]

Faruqi's description of an Islamic aesthetic offers not only an ideal listener's guide to appreciating Lateef's symphonic blues form but also serves as a preface to his Nigerian recording and the symphonic works which followed. It is the art of the Islamic arabesque, the art of intricately decorated melodic lines, known in African-American terms as "worrying the line." The blues, as much as any Islamic music, can be considered an open-ended and infinitely expandable structure, and the idiosyncratically constructed blues of Robert Pete Williams and Guitar Shorty (John Henry Fortescue) suggest just how asymmetrical and full of arabesques contemporary blues can be.[10]

While the blues traditionally arose out of secular concerns (hence it was historically saddled with the label of "Devil's music" as opposed to gospel music), Islamic music arose out of an involvement with spiritual concerns, the realm of the invisible beyond this tangible earth. The listener is offered musical patterns designed to encourage contemplation of the divine ordering of the universe. By marrying the blues to an Islamic musical consciousness, Lateef has joined the passionate African-American self-expression with the Islamic-African love for transpersonal patterns revealing the divine presence in the everyday world.

Lateef's African sojourn was focused at the Center for Nigerian Cultural Studies in Zaria, in the predominantly Moslem sector of northern Nigeria. As he informs interviewer Bob Rusch:

> I was a Senior Research Fellow, that was my position. I had three obligations. First, I did research into the Nigerian flute which is called Sarewa. And this was invented by Fulani herdsmen well over three hundred years ago. . . . My second obligation was to teach research methodology to Nigerian cultural students. . . . My third duty was to interact with the performing arts group there at the center which consisted of African musicians and which included drama and dance. . . .[11]

This four-year position brought together strands from Lateef's earlier musical career. "Research" is not often a term found in jazz literature to describe the activities of a musician, yet it fits Lateef's career perfectly. He has relentlessly pursued musical knowledge from global sources. Nigeria provided the opportunity for him to research intensively African music at the source and within a community of African artists working in other media. This had to be most attractive to Lateef, given his involvements with poetry and painting as well as music.

Yusef Lateef in Nigeria, the recording resulting from his Nigerian research, is a unique document in the history of Afrocentric jazz. It is essentially two recordings: blues suite superimposed upon Nigerian rhythm tracks. Unlike other jazz recordings incorporating African rhythms, it is easily plausible to imagine these jazz or African tracks actually standing by themselves as complete musical statements. The power of this recording has much to do with the musical fullness and depth Lateef and the Nigerians achieve without compromising their respective styles.

Like his symphonic blues suite, this album evolves through seven parts, the middle section of which is an uncompromisingly direct blues statement. But in contrast to the blues suite which uses the resources of a symphony orchestra along with a jazz quartet, the instrumentation on this African effort is sparse. Lateef focuses upon tenor sax, the *algaita* (a North African oboe-like horn), and a host of flutes ranging from his Western C-flute to African flutes constructed from ceramic, wood, or rubber. The five Nigerian musicians accompanying Lateef perform on a variety of drums (identified with the Tiv, Hausa, and Yoruba peoples), shakers, and occasionally on *algaita* and *shuti* box (a harmonium-like drone instrument).

The album opens, surprisingly, with a tune sounding more Caribbean than African. Lateef in his album liner notes calls the rhythm of "Mu'Omi" "a synthesis of African and Jamaican sources"; the second and fourth beats in the syncopated pattern are emphasized as they would be in reggae and Caribbean ritual music like Kumina. His tenor sax flights soaring over the enthusiastic drumming evoke the gruff buoyancy of Sonny Rollins' ur-calypsos. Yet his tone has a calming, free-floating quality (shades of Lester Young?) that sets it apart from Rollins' heated and angular Caribbean romp tone. The coolness of Lateef's sax is in dramatic contrast to the heated drum volleys, punctuated by Lateef's cries in an African language (Yoruba scatting?).

As the album deals with the tensions between a blues suite and a series of Nigerian folk pieces (often dances), it also plays with different aspects of Lateef's musicianship. Through multiple tracks put down in the recording studio, Lateef constantly moves between performing on sax and flute. Few times in his recorded career has he done so as successfully as in the second movement, "Drama Village." Lateef describes the piece as pure program music, an attempt to evoke through music the sight of an African theatre constructed out of mud and straw located on the campus where he was teaching. Translate the nature of mud into tenor sax sounds and straw into C-flute tones, and you have the idea of how Lateef musically constructs the building. Against the background of Nigerian drummers, Lateef engages in the dialogue between an assertive, brawny, masculine energy declaring itself boastfully through sax and a daringly subtle, lyrical force shadowing the sax and defining itself through a breathy flute play. This call-and-response dynamic is theatric play as well as evocative of a theater site.

"Akima," a Nigerian word for "birth," returns Lateef to his first instrumental voice, tenor sax, as well as to the more vigorously uptempo mood which began the album. The fourth movement, "Blues in the Adaji" (*adaji* translates as "bush") is the centerpiece of the recording. It consists of a slow, ruminative and very bluesy sax solo set off by the constantly dropping pitches of a double-headed "talking drum." An odd empathy exists between Lateef and the drummer; a conventional jazz or blues drummer would have chosen to play rhythms to complement the lead of the saxophonist; here the drummer seems to modulate between complementing Lateef's playing and contrasting himself. Yet the falling-away drum tones are the African percussive equivalent to the "bent" blues notes Lateef executes on horn. The indeterminate pitch of the American blues player finds confirmation in the slippery and sliding drum tone.

"Lalit" (meaning "Lover's separation"—hints of Guy Warren's "Mystery of Love"?) offers one of Lateef's most majestic flute solos, while "Curved Spacetime," like "Drama Village," offers a witty interplay of Lateef moving between sax and flute. The piece is once again program music, evoking the life of the identical twins postulated by Einstein, where one traveling through outer space would age less than the earthbound sibling. This might seem amazingly far afield from Nigeria—though it is worth remembering Ellington's fascination with outer space coterminous with his African interest—but the Negritude poet Leopold Senghor reminds us of a tie. As Lilyan Kesteloot writes in *Black Writers in French: A Literary History of Negritude:*

> If rhythm is of such importance to the Negro poet, Senghor has often repeated, it is because through his incantations it "permits access to the truth of essential things: the forces of the Cosmos." . . . These forces,

> Africans believe, are propagated in the form of *waves*.
> And Senghor added: "And, since contemporary physics
> has discovered the energy contained in matter, the
> waves and radiations, this is no simple metaphor."[12]

Senghor suggests that Einstein's Theory of Relativity might
have had an African antecedent. If so, Lateef has discovered
and expressed the musical tie between traditional Africa and
Einsteinian relativity.

The final section of the recording, "Ruwa Water," connects
the end of the suite with its beginning, again in a fashion
reminiscent of *Suite 16*. The Nigerian album opens with
"Mu'omi" a term which translates as "Drink Water." The
piece closes with a meditation on deep water created through
the interplay of drummer Salisu I. Mashi on water drums and
Lateef on rhythmically flowing sax.

Water as a metaphor runs through all sections of the
Nigerian recording: it is water binding earth and straw into
solid architecture, and water present at the birth of any life
form; there is a watery quality to the dropping, talking drum
tone, and the separation of lovers, or twins, is often marked
by tears. Water, in its transparency as well as opaqueness,
becomes a lens through which invisible forces beyond us
manifest themselves in constant rhythmic waves of transformative energy. African religions have long celebrated water-
spirits by not only suggesting that water is life, a literal truth
throughout much of the continent, but that water also
symbolizes speech, communication, which also comes at us in
[sound] waves.[13]

Lateef was not the first jazz composer to celebrate the
spiritually and aesthetically enlivening dynamic of water.
Duke Ellington taps the theme throughout his career, from
"Stompy Jones" to the dance suite *The River*. Another
example is Sam Rivers' concept album, *Waves*. But Lateef is
unique in capturing the African perspective on water,
working with African musicians in producing an innovative
musical form.

The final section of the Nigerian album Lateef identifies as a dance piece. How can the inner meanings of water be danced? Once again, Senghor comes to our aid:

> In Black Africa, any work of art is at the same time a magic operation. The aim is to enclose a vital force in a tangible casing and, at the appropriate moment, release this force by means of dance or prayer.[14]

The force of deep water is evoked by sax, flute, drums and voices. The moment was in a recording studio in Nigeria. The dance is for those who know, as do countless Africans, that water is holy.

CHAPTER FOURTEEN

Sunny Murray and the Creation of Time

Give thanks—but also give sympathy—to the drum, denied a fair hearing ever since its African version entered this hemisphere. So suspect were its powers that Louisiana had to pass an edict against its musical-cum-political use by slaves as early as 1740. No longer treated like a Pandora's box by the time jazz was born in the early decades of this century, it still suffered indignities in recording studios, where its resonances were so hard for early microphones to record that Chinese wood blocks replaced it.

But if the drum in this hemisphere went from being a suspect and suppressed tool of political revolution to a commonplace of jazz bands within a century and a half, its status *continues* to be compromised by listeners unable to hear the full range and subtlety produced by masterful drummers. The state of audio technology can no longer be blamed for this variety of unfair hearing. Connect the problem to the fact that many jazz listeners possess a sensibility similar to that of Richard Ligon, author of *A True and Exact History of the Island of Barbados* (London, 1657). Here is Ligon on slave drumming:

> The drum all men know, has but one tone; and therefore varietie of tones have little to do in this African musick, and yet so strangely they varie their time, as 'tis a pleasure to the most curious eares, and it was to me one of the strangest noyses that ever I heard made of one tone . . . for time without tone, is not an eighth part of the science of Musick.[1]

I would like to imagine seeing Sunny Murray laughing while perusing Ligon's text, or better yet, imagining him at his drum kit, responding with a barrage of "the strangest noyses." After all, Murray has been victimized throughout his career by critics whose critical hearing losses were no less profound than Ligon's. And much of that critical misapprehension has translated into a lack of lucrative gigs and a paucity of record contracts. At the heart of that misapprehension of Murray's contribution is a failure to comprehend just how deeply Murray has extended the spirit of traditional African drumming into the far reaches of experimental jazz.

There is an orthodox party line assumed by most Murray critics, a half-truth that allows him to occupy a little idiosyncratic niche in jazz drumming history: that Murray invented a style in which timekeeping was no longer a primary feature; multidirectional and metrically irregular pulses were utilized to generate a constant flow of coloristic effects. These irregularly shaped and timed percussive explosions perfectly meshed with the music of figures like Albert Ayler and Cecil Taylor.

Critics most sympathetic to Murray's playing, Valerie Wilmer and Amiri Baraka, add to this general description an emotional dimension. Wilmer emphasizes the sheer majestic strength and intensity of Murray's drumming. Baraka underscores these points while painting Murray as a Bobby Seale of the traps, some Superfly gonna blow your white house down.

Murray's worst critics wondered why he couldn't just sometimes—pretty please?—play some semblance of time keeping as he did early in his career with Red Allen and Willie "The Lion" Smith.

Putting aside stereotypes about drums and drummers that have clouded an appreciation of Murray's art, it is a salutary act to spend hours listening to a single recording of Murray's. The one that has most engaged me, and incidentally Murray's own favorite as he revealed in a *Cadence* interview, is *Homage to Africa*.[2] The title might evoke caution. One can imagine a replay of a confused and confusing Third World jam session a la Archie Shepp's *Live at the Pan-African Festival:* a musical stew with a killing dose of unintegrated African sounding drums, vying for space with a bevy of reeds entering multiphonic nirvana. *Homage to Africa* is nothing of the sort. The title cut, occupying side one, immediately established Murray as the most *gentle* of drummers and composers (remember that this is the man who tapped drums with knitting needles, and played so softly on Ayler's terribly engineered ESP albums that he can barely be heard). The piece is a melodically simple, though utterly hypnotic, threnody based upon a three-note vamp, a densely textured fabric of largely percussion, reed, and vocal (wordless) sounds not wholly unlike many of Pharoah Sanders' extended compositions on the Impulse label also during the sixties. Unlike Sanders, Murray maintains an atmosphere of constant and refined coolness and gentleness throughout the recording. The impact is like that of viewing an exquisitely woven expanse of African kente cloth for the first time: dazzling bold colors softly modulate in and out of attention, as the stripes of color seem to float in a rhythmically pulsing paradise.[3]

This variety of lush and serene musical romanticism is not generally associated with drummers and composers at the music's cutting edge, let alone those concerned with African roots. Yet Murray's homage to the African sources of jazz pays devout tribute to precisely that side of African music most often neglected by American musicians and audiences. Counter to the racist stereotype of savage African slaves *beating* drums, Robert Ferris Thompson quotes an Afro-Cuban priest who describes a silent drum, an instrument of significant silence, "not a drum as the whites understand such instruments."[4] While Murray never goes that far in order to become a musical Mallarmé of drums, he does significantly play at the edges of the barely audible, so adroitly feathery his touch.

The *Homage to Africa* album includes three dirges, and no drummer or composer in jazz puts as much delicate sweetness as well as muscular torque into dirges. While most jazz histories trace the dirge form to New Orleans, it is again fascinating to trace Murray's understanding of the form back to Africa. In *Funeral Dirges of the Akan People,* musicologist J.H. Nketia writes:

> Because the rhythm of the dirge is free, there is no handclapping or percussion of any kind accompanying the singing. The dirge is not intended for dancing to, though this does not exclude the use of bodily movements or gestures, independent of the rhythms of the melodies. The usual way of performing dirges at funerals is for each individual mourner to perform on her own, singing dirges of her choice when and where she likes. . . . She does not have to use the same "key" or be with others or wait for a cue from another person to start. . . . In the dirge, however, the mourner is herself the soloist and the chorus and must, therefore, rely on her own resources.[5]

Substitute "drummer" in place of "mourner/vocalist," and here is a cogent summary of how Murray's art draws nourishment from traditional African music. What better summary of Murray's contribution to drumming history than to reinforce the fact that he established the primacy of the drummer as simultaneously soloist and chorus, relying upon the player's own resources? This Murray accomplished by maintaining a free sense of time, not "timekeeping," but time as Claudia Zaslavsky describes it in *Africa Counts:*

> In western or technological society, time is a commodity which must be utilized, sold and bought; but in traditional African life, time has to be created or produced. Man is not a slave of time; instead he "makes" as much time as he wants.[6]

How does Murray "make" his time, cementing the claim on his first album as a leader, *Sonny's Time Now?* He radically rethinks the role of the drum kit, sees the kit as a kinetic sculpture (a vision reinforced by his Calder-like cymbal stand handcrafted for his first album). The drums are a sculpture he dances around, giving the drum kit a numinosity like African drums utilized for ritual purposes. By dancing about the drums, not merely alertly sitting before them, he maximizes the force of his contact with all surfaces, not just skins but metal and wood as well. The sheer physicality of his approach assures a broader spectrum of timbres than those usually achieved by players utilizing conventional posture. Murray's dance in fast motion—or through the jump-cutting of stills as seen in John Jeremy's film using Val Wilmer's photographs, *Jazz Is Our Religion*—creates the illusion of several drummers performing simultaneously, a stuttering strobe effect akin to how Duchamp caused his nude to trip the light fantastic down a staircase.

If his dance around the drums produces a unique sensation of time, so do his cymbal and drum interactions. While Murray is hailed or damned by critics for freeing the drums from keeping time, I would praise Murray specifically for freeing the cymbal from its shady past as a regulator of the march steps of Turkish troopers. Murray's performance on Dave Burrell's "East Side Story" (*High Won—High Two*) is a shattering and encyclopedic demonstration of how many sounds cymbals can generate (including many varieties of white noise we assume only electronic instruments can sound). The angular post-bop twists and turns of Jimmy Lyons' alto sax are lovingly complemented by Murray's cymbal shows on the essential *Jump Up—What to Do About.* Add to the Lyons/Murray alchemy the essential ingredient of Cecil Taylor, and you have one of the classic trio recordings of our time, "D Trad That's What." For yet another demonstration in a classic trio format demonstrating how much symbolic coloration Murray can create cymballically, hear him on Ayler's *Spiritual Unity,* a spiritually attuned trio the gods rejoice in hearing.

Speaking of the gods (who probably "keep" time better than any mortal drummer), one of the drummer's functions in traditional African drumming is to maintain dialogue with the gods. Not only are the African gods fond of stretches of improvisation (providing that the improviser remembers "God does not weave a loose web"), they also expect the drummer to chant, sing, moan, shout while he drums. Murray goes as far as to please the American gods (part of his family background is Choctaw, from those tribes displaced from Mississippi to Oklahoma) as well as the African deities by performing a lengthy composition showcasing his singing/ chanting as well as drumming skills. His "Encounter" on the first volume of the *New American Music* series on Folkways is as fetching a synthesis of Native American and African-American musical styles as you'll ever hear, a tad less glossy than Jim Pepper's (Murray hits some painfully flat notes vocally; his enthusiastic performance makes these slips forgettable). You never know when he'll break into a Choctaw chant during one of his live performances, a reminder that jazz is a most *American* creation, a fact not contradicted by a full celebration of its African underpinnings.

The richness of Murray's cymbal crashes and vocals is beautifully reinforced by his drum attacks, particularly his sonorous tattoos on the bass drum. He has an astute gift for playing off extreme tonal contrasts, high-pitched cymbals ringing in counterpoint to earth-moaning bass drum tones. That sense of dramatic contrast between extreme upper and lower registers lacing his best realized dirges—like "Complete Affection" on *An Even Break (Never Give a Sucker)*—is also demonstrated in his taste as a leader of trios and quintets. His sensitivity to lower register sounds has led him to pick bassists as punchy as Malachi Favors and as lyrically piercing as Alan Silva. Not enough has been said about Murray's savvy as a leader, a fact not helped by the fact that most of his albums as a leader are long out-of-print.

In one of his most unusual projects as a leader, Murray has collaborated with the African percussionist Cheik Tidiane Fall and bassist Malachi Favors on the *African Magic* album. If *Homage to Africa* evokes the coloristic densities of kente cloth, *African Magic* brings to mind infinitely sparser cosmograms, ritual diagrams drawn on the earth's surface by traditionally observant Central Africans. *African Magic* demonstrates a minimalist approach toward fusing African-American with African music. Short bursts of sounds from Murray's drums are answered by Fall's short and sharply punctuated percussive phrases, performed on a variety of hand drums and percussive devices. Favors provides a melodic frame of reference for the Murray/Fall call-and-response, particularly on the fifteen-minute "I Am a Solider—African American Spiritual" so that the whole work hangs loosely together. It is not easy listening, since relatively long stretches of silence interrupt various percussive bursts, making Favors' bass runs the sole guiding thread for a listener seeking to find coherence in a loosely spun web of sound.

There is a sense in all of Murray's recorded works that his tie to Africa is best realized as an intensively lyrical romanticism, a romanticism linking him to John Coltrane. History (though not recording tape) records the fact that they performed on stage together (under Elvin Jones' possessive and ever watchful eye). What supercharged *Jupiter Variations* we might have been treated to if Murray rather than Rashied Ali had worked with Coltrane in the studio! Without that actual Coltrane collaboration, we are left with one recorded example of Murray's simpatico with Coltrane, "Motif of Expression" on Murray's *Aigu-Grave*. French tenor saxophonist Richard Raux is no more a winner in the Coltrane sound-alike sweepstakes than Dave Liebman, but Murray conducts himself admirably, arranging the Coltrane tune to showcase his churning sensitivity to Coltrane's lyricism. There are no explicit references to Africa in Murray's arrangement. He simply creates a sense of time which might be appreciated by a tradition-minded African, not time measured by Timex, not shaped by a cymbal's metronomic insistences, but time as the poet Blake understood it, found in the pulsation of an artery.

CHAPTER FIFTEEN

Ronald Shannon Jackson: Journey to Africa Without End

> This music is a reflection of a person who went on a journey, a soul searching historical perspective, an identification, and who found those things.—*Ronald Shannon Jackson*[1]

It was a journey through West Africa that Jackson refers to in these liner notes to his album *When Colors Play*. Yet during my interview with him, I sensed that his African journey was a thread that ran through his lifetime, one that is still ongoing. So by simply asking him about the origins of his interest in African music, I was treated to the drummer's musical autobiography in all its fullness.

The desire to interview Jackson was propelled by my appreciation of his drumming with Ornette Coleman and Cecil Taylor. Also intriguing was a recording matching drum accompaniment to poems by Sterling Brown, Robert Hayden, and Michael Harper. A recorded jam session with the Nigerian drummer Twins Seven Seven had caught my attention as well. But his place in this book was clarified when I interviewed his former music teacher, John Carter, who spoke with a teacher's pride about Jackson's achievement, and who led me to ponder how both Texas jazzmen had found their way to Africa in their recordings of the eighties. Shortly after the Carter interview, I secured a copy of Jackson's most programmatically Afrocentric work, *When Colors Play*. Reading his brief paragraph about the impact of his African travels, I wanted to know more about what led up to this African involvement.

I never had anyone show me anything about drums. I think I was about four years old when my mother took me with her to a church conference in Houston, Texas. A bunch of kids and myself were walking through the basement of a church there and I saw this drumkit. Nobody had said anything to me about drums. But I dropped out of the line of kids and just looked at them. Somehow I knew the drums had something to do with me—*totally.*

I also remember dancing in a ray of sunlight in the red clay dirt of my driveway in Fort Worth. When I was two years old, we were driving somewhere through East Texas, and my parents stopped somewhere and left me in the car, and I was fascinated by the red clay. I didn't know what it had to do with me—it never left my consciousness. And when I got to Africa, it was verified; my deep red clay. You go into the back country in Chad, and when it rains, everyone has red feet.

What I was dancing to in my driveway as a child were all these rhythms and sounds from the nearby Holiness Church. I was about six years old at the time. It never went away. Some of the rhythms and sounds periodically came back. So even as a teenager, I could hear pop songs—by Frank Sinatra and Kay Starr then—in terms of those same African rhythms. I didn't know that Holiness Church music used African rhythms when I was that young. But I knew I was hearing something coming *from* my life as opposed to *outside* my life.

In this church, any instrument that was available was being played. So it wasn't a matter of instruments per se. No one said: "I'm going to use this instrument to make the music sound this way." The purpose of the instrument was to let the spirit come through. You could hear a combination of tambourine, trombone, guitar, bass drum, snare drum, cymbal. And the rhythms . . . you could be doing one thing, but the rhythms were so powerful that if you were anywhere near them, you'd be totally affected by it.

Fortunately, Jackson's childhood obsessions about drums and African-American rhythms were greeted warmly by his musically engaged parents. His mother sang in church while his father was a record supplier for area jukeboxes. Equally fortunate was the musical variety that permeated Jackson's life in Fort Worth during the forties and fifties. As Jackson told critic Gary Giddins:

> In the morning you'd wake up and hear hillbilly music on the radio, in school we'd play *Lohengrin,* and at night we'd hear Bo Diddley or Bobby "Blue" Bland. On Sunday we'd hear gospel. It was a total black community, and the music wasn't categorized as jazz or pop—nobody told you you weren't supposed to like something.[2]

By the ripe old age of fifteen, Jackson had established his presence in the Fort Worth scene as a professional drummer, the product of self-education and a seemingly boundless passion for all musical styles. Yet more remarkable than his youthful auto-didacticism and pan-stylistics was his early intuition about the relationship of drumming to spiritual experience:

> Even as a child and teenager, I became aware of playing the drums. It wasn't about playing time and playing the standards which I had to do when I was doing rhythm and blues sets as a teenager. When I was about eighteen, I went to Texas Southern University in Houston, and I was fooling around one night after some local musicians and I had played a gig—and it happened! Everything that came to mind musically came off perfectly without me having constantly to think about it. I wasn't aware of doing it. So I had floated to the back of the room and was on the ceiling watching myself play, and listening and enjoying it. So I knew it could happen on a bandstand. But I had no control over how to get to that point.

Jackson's desire to attain control over that elevated moment of inspirational improvisation led to a move to New York during the sixties. Within a few weeks of his arrival, he met one of his chief musical exemplars, avant-garde saxophonist Albert Ayler:

> I didn't know who Albert Ayler was or what he was
> about. I'd never heard him play before. It was just the
> first gig opportunity I had. Soon I realized that with
> Ayler I was able to play the way I played back home
> when I wasn't playing for people at a nightclub. I could
> play as the people at the Holiness Church did—through
> the instrument. To Ayler, his instrument wasn't being a
> saxophone where you play "Body and Soul." Coleman
> Hawkins and Ben Webster had already mastered that.
> Ayler was the kind of person who recognized that there
> was a spiritual reality—and music was just a vehicle for
> what was trying to be expressed spiritually.

Jackson's intermingling of jazz and religion—and linking
the synthesis to intuited African rhythms—has a history
Jackson may or may not have been aware of. Janheinz Jahn's
Muntu, a sensationally popular book about Africa in U.S.
countercultural circles from the time of its publication in the
early sixties, offered an extremely generalized view of African
religion as sound, specifically word mysticism. Jahn's flair for
interpreting the West African religious concept of *nommo* led
to a rhapsodic logocentricism of this order:

> All magic is word magic, incantation and exorcism,
> blessing and curse. Through Nommo, the word, man
> establishes his mastery over things. . . . For the word
> holds the course of things in train and changes and
> transforms them. And since the word has this power,
> every word is an effective word, every word is binding.[3]

In one of several daring leaps, Jahn extends this word
mysticism to the realm of talking drums, and suggests that the
early attempts to suppress drumming by slaves in the New
World caused the slaves to lose their African polytheism.

What Jahn has confused is illuminating, particularly when
returning to Jackson's identification of Africa, music, and
spirituality. While music often accompanies various forms of
religious experience throughout Africa, this does not necessarily make music, sound, or "the word" the actual power
focused through such spirituality. What Jahn is doing is

aestheticizing the concept of African religious experience, an act comprehensible within the analysis offered by French sociologist Roger Bastide, one of the major European scholars of the African diaspora in the New World:

> At first Africa survived in America as a physical reality, mingling lovingly with other cultures, of which the Negro, as opposed to the white, gave it a fresh lease of life and vitality. Later, however, this reality began to dissolve into a mass of ambiguous, contradictory images: ideologies for the intellectuals, messianism for the masses, and more politics than mysticism.[4]

This proliferation of imaginative images of Africa eventually fed into the Western modernist position of art as mystical salvation. In parts of the African-American community, that art which was most reverential and deferential to African roots began to be seen as source of spiritual salvation and redemption. Thus, a poet and African-American community activist like Amiri Baraka (then LeRoi Jones) in the sixties articulated mystically cast Marxism intimately related to his activities as an astute blues and jazz critic with vigorous poetic imagination. It does no good to criticize the verity of an African popularizer like Jahn since what matters is how his imagination of African spirituality became embodied and lived out in various lives. As Bastide wrote about this mass of "ambiguous, contradictory images": "Now like every super-structure, these transformations are the expression of an objective reality."[5]

In Jackson's case, this identity of Africa with jazz and spirituality has led to the development of a significant body of recordings. And it was through the medium of records, as was true for Coltrane and a number of other jazz figures, that his first acquaintance with actual African music occurred.

> During the period when I was working with Cecil Taylor, he used to work a lot of colleges. And one of the most interesting to me was Dartmouth where they have a fantastic music library. It was a treasure house of music

for me. They had all of the UNESCO series. What happened was that we were snowed in during a storm and couldn't fly out, couldn't drive out. This was about 1978. I had a big cassette tape recorder with me which I was using to record what I was hearing in my head, music for flutes and drums. So I took the recorder into one of those little listening rooms and went back and forth between the listening room and the archives, playing and taping a cut from each record. I wouldn't even listen to what I was recording—there wasn't time to—I just selected a record from a brief look at the cover to see what country it was from.

So I wound up with a couple of compilation tapes that were as varied as you could possibly think of, and in some mysterious way, it fell into an order which was very mystifying. You'd be listening to Africa, then you'd go to the whirling dervishes, then you'd go to a Tibetan monastery. It covered all the music that one wouldn't normally be in contact with. When I got home, I listened to the two tapes. Then I knew I had to go to Africa. I had come upon a lot of music from Chad, from equatorial Africa and the pygmies.

The path to Africa was delayed and circuitous. Jackson had been tapped by the U.S. State Department to do an African tour with his band, The Decoding Society. By the early eighties, Jackson was on a major record label, Island, bringing his music out of the rarified clime of avant-garde jazz record companies and into a very broad market through the release of *Mandance*. His music increasingly utilized electric basses and guitars (often paired) along with varied saxophones (Jackson's fondness for pairing reeds and basses was, at the same time, being duplicated in Denmark by Pierre Dørge and his New Jungle Orchestra). While never straying far from blues modes and jazz swing, Jackson's sound on *Mandance* was a fusion of rock rhythms with jazz. It was possible that Jackson's embrace of rock made him an ideal choice for State Department tour operators wanting to reach African youth.

Bizarrely, when a State Department official sent several African host governments a record company publicity photo

of Jackson with a luxuriant head of what appeared to be
Rastafarian dreadlocks, cancellations immediately poured in.
Bob Marley had recently given concerts in Africa which were
perceived by conservative governments there as politically
subversive, so no chances were being taken. Jackson's tour
was rerouted through Asia.

> A few years later, I received a few grants from private
> foundations so I would have the money to go to Africa
> and be financially free of worries. So I packed one small
> suitcase with two flutes, two tape recorders, some
> tee-shirts and jeans, and bought a ticket to the furthest
> place I could go, which interestingly enough was Zaire.
> It was a place you might get in and not get out.
> I knew I had chosen the most dangerous situation for
> me to go into by myself. I had no reservations for hotels,
> and didn't know anybody except in one country out of
> the eight I visited. I wrote "Sweet Orange" [on *When
> Colors Play*] a day before leaving for Africa. I went into
> my studio, and it was a time in the evening when the sun
> is going down and so many plays of color are in the air.
> And, basically, it was written for fear of not knowing
> whether I was going to return. I just had to go. It wasn't
> a matter of choice. I've never been a safe player. So I left
> with the attitude, "If I don't come back, I'll leave behind
> this music." I liked what I had written.

Jackson's conversion of horizon colors into music has its
roots in earlier jazz composers, particularly Ellington, whose
compositions named after colors run into the dozens.[6]
Connecting coloristic play with both spirituality and music has
been present among the peoples of the lower Congo, as
documented by anthropologist Anita Jacobson-Widding.[7]
How conscious Jackson was of this fact I don't know, but he
did visit the area where Jacobson-Widding did her research.

What Jackson experienced in Africa quickly dispelled his
concern about his method of travel and inspired him to
imagine future compositions touched by African colors:

> What I saw and heard was unbelievable. I saw clay
> drums, drums that only women use. I ran into shapes

and sizes of drum I never knew existed. There were drums as tall as ten feet, impossible to carry, which were used just for rituals. There were drums made virtually like canoes.

One Saturday morning, some friends I had met by chance took me on a long drive through the back country of Zaire where I heard some of the most fantastic drumming I ever heard in my life, performed by a secret drum society. I also had the opportunity to attend an all-day pygmy tribal ceremony and listened to a field recording of tribal music from places researchers had never been before. Most of the time I was like a sponge soaking up new experiences, but I did play a few times. One place I played was Bamako in Mali, and someone in the crowd came up to me, laid a shirt down right in front of my drums, and started piling up money on it.

"I wrote . . . compositions during my wanderings in West Africa," writes Jackson in his liner notes to *When Colors Play,* "from Benin to Kinshasa in Zaire; to Yaounde in Cameroon; to Nigeria; to the seaport city of Cotonou in Benin; to Abidjan; to Bamako in Mali where the people are very poor, but where the music is more pure than in other places. The musical centers I found were Kinshasa, Yaounde and Bamako." And yet, from the testimony of my own repeated listenings to *When Colors Play,* no compostion sounds literally beholden to any of these sites. No African instrumentation is used, drums don't replay Zairian rhythms, nor do horns embody any recognizable African style. What is happening?

"All the melodies and harmonies grow out of my own rhythm, 'mantra,' interacting with the rhythms I experienced in Africa," continues Jackson in his liner notes. What impresses is the drummer's characteristic honesty. His own rhythms as an African American are to a degree inescapable, much as any anthropologist's ethnocentricism on an African research trip. What the creative musician is able to do—in contrast to the anthropologist—is to permit a dynamic friction between self-rhythms and African rhythms to catalyze an imaginative musical fusion. So Jackson's trip was not a matter of stealing African drum skills so much as it was an opportunity to confirm his earliest intuitions about African rhythms:

> The African trip didn't change my way of drumming—it just verified a lot of things I intuited, and, truthfully, I knew, but had no verification in reality until then. When I went to public school in Fort Worth, not only was Africa never mentioned, black people in the course of American history were not even noted. But I've always had a certain bent toward finding out about these facets of life.

Struck by the mystical bent in Jackson's talk—mentions of intuitions and synchronicities abound—I asked him about the dilemma of linguistic communication in performance with African musicians. His response is startling:

> Most of the countries I went to, the people who did speak any Western language spoke French. And I don't speak French or any African language. Certain places you go you're on a certain communications level where you don't have to use words. We communicated through the music. That's it.

His answer triggered my memory of interviewing John Carter about his interactions in the recording studio with Ghanaian drummers in Los Angeles. Carter heavily underscored his awareness of the cultural differences between the Ghanaian musicians and himself, which prevented perfect cross-cultural understanding during the recording of *Dance of the Love Ghosts*. Jackson's response to Carter's perception?

> That had to do with the area he was dealing with . . . he's talking about people from Ghana. He might have communicated without even opening his mouth with people from Gambia.

So there is a curious paradox in Jackson's thinking about Africa. While maintaining absolutely the distinctiveness of his own musical style throughout his African journey and after, he posits music as a lingua franca opening doors to nonverbal communication across Africa, an experience not universally shared by other American jazz artists who have travelled there.[8] And conversely, John Carter, who maintains his belief in cross-cultural barriers between African-American and African musicians, incorporated pure examples of African drumming into his music.

Whatever the linguistic and musical links between the cultures, Jackson has kept searching for ways to build musical bridges. A live recording of a spontaneous jam session with Jackson and the Decoding Society, along with Nigerian drummer and composer Twins Seven Seven was released in the eighties. Though it received mixed reviews due to poor sound engineering and raggedy performances, Jackson defends its documentary importance:

> I was more concerned about how profound it was for an American musician to meet an African musician for the first time and play some original compositions by the American, with the African totally improvising, with no rehearsal.

Profound or not to various ears, the album marked another moment in the evolution of Jackson and his electric, electrifying band. The Decoding Society presents layers of music—funk, blues, rock, jazz, permutations of West African pop—in an appealing mix fuelled centrally by Jackson's precise polyrhythmic drumming, full of sizzling surprises. Every recording marks an unexpected turn in a musical journey, with Jackson sounding supremely confident as leader. The source for that confidence? Call it the remembrance of an African spiritual legacy:

> A couple of times in my life I just quit playing and sold my drums. I wasn't spiritually ready to play music anymore. I wasn't playing what I wanted to play. But I never lost the awareness of the rhythms I was hearing, I was dancing to, from church nearby when I was a kid. Those rhythms were never lost.

CHAPTER SIXTEEN

Beyond the Americanization of Ooga Booga: Charting the Pathways of Afrocentric Imagination

> Nature has no Tune, but Imagination has.—*William Blake*[1]

> Outside this bookstore Africans are going about their business, transplanting Africa before it vanishes. The edges are crumbling away, slowly, gradually, but there's no panic. People go about their business, inventing new ways of carrying boxes on their heads, and building giant dams, and working on a new handwriting. . . . I said it was high time to return to the source. In a way, my old bush jacket is my source. It has four bulky pockets containing the gold ornaments. The jacket fed my imagination before I ever set foot on the continent.—*Walter Abish*[2]

In the preface to an anthology of Negritude poetry, Jean-Paul Sartre used the telling phrase: "Africa, the imaginary continent."[3] But as this study has suggested, there are a multitude of imaginary Africas, existing in various relationships to the actual continent. This reading of jazz history presents a sampling of these imaginary Africas, interpretations for jazz aficionados as well as students of African-American culture.

Like the magic mirror in fairy tales, these images of Africa have offered reflections revealing the nature of the perceiver. When Ellington envisioned Africa, he saw landscapes untainted by the pollutions of Western industrialized society.

John Carter thought of Africa as the birthplace for the unique creation of African-American civilization. Randy Weston, Archie Shepp, and Max Roach perceived Africa as the land of a revolutionary spirit, one that could inspire a political and spiritual revolution throughout the diaspora. Africa as the land of advanced spirituality was glimpsed by John Coltrane, Count Ossie, Sunny Murray, Yusef Lateef, and Ronald Shannon Jackson. For Dizzy Gillespie, George Russell, and Pierre Dørge, Africa was the place where musicians could receive inspiration and permission to synthesize new styles.

But just why are all of these various projections of Africa by non-African musicians of importance? Critic Frances Davis questions the meaningfulness of these African fantasies:

> Western musicians have been infatuated with the musics of the Third World at least since the Great Mystical Awakening of the 1960's, and few have been able to resist the urge to conquer and colonize.[4]

Davis' overheated rhetoric, a surprising excess from one of the music's most knowledgeable and balanced critics, stems from a questionable assumption. Davis assumes artistic neocolonialism is afoot, as if the process of diverse musical cultures colliding involved only the West stealing from the East. Davis neglects to mention that as non-African jazz artists have eagerly looked to the Third World for inspiration, Third World musicians have looked toward Western musical traditions and technology with equal interest.

The picture of ruthlessly colonial Western musicians exploiting Third World musicians simply pales in the face of Ellington's responses to playing in Dakar, or Lateef's and Weston's responses to living and learning about traditional African music in Africa.

The mutuality of this musical relationship between Africa and the African diaspora is poignantly captured on the film sequence of Louis Armstrong playing for Kwame Nkrumah and a crowd of one hundred thousand on the eve of Ghana's independence. Nkrumah brought to the job of prime minister impeccable credentials as a jazz fan, a love cultivated during his college student days in Philadelphia. That feel for jazz he brought into designing Ghana's independence day celebrations, capped by Armstrong performing (in what the trumpeter described as "the second happiest moment of my life," second only to playing in the King Oliver band).

Louis Armstrong's Second Happiest Moment

Nkrumah asked the trumpeter for & receives
"my only sin is in
the color of my skin"
at Ghana's birth an
unexpected anthem
"Black & Blue"
as Armstrong arcs his notes over
a stadium of 100,000
Nkrumah races through imagination's
coruscating corridor
& arrives as a too-bright college
boy in Philadelphia where
"Black & Blue" is what streets
do to your skin
& now Prime Minister becomes then
outsider's outsider
with blues for a bodyguard
dippermouth keeping polite palaver flowing
nerve flair walking dangerous Race Street
mean drum rolls rollick up spine
& trumpet in his soul squeezes caged breath
out
Shango's bopping instrument up all night looking
for Ghana not yet
born
reverie deadends as dawn wakes a filthy Delaware
Armstrong's bright finale catches Nkrumah
tears streaking cheeks filling frontpage daily mug
shot
between two Africas
Armstrong
Nkrumah

at birth of both
funeral brass bray
"didn't he ramble"
homeland - note bent enough out of shape
to boomerang &
lots of Philadelphia ancestors are hauling ass
right this minute stomping
to get on a Black Star liner
so please   please   my man
blow blues to bring their ship
to port[5]

If an invisible spirit seemed tangibly present at the moment of Armstrong's performance before Nkrumah, it had to be Marcus Garvey. Nkrumah had been an avid reader of Garvey's books in his youth, and it is easy to imagine a commingling of Garveyism and jazz in Nkrumah's consciousness, both symbolizing self-determination, fierce racial pride, an unstoppable passion for liberation.

There are charged moments in imagination—and Armstrong's "second happiest moment" in Ghana is one—where the distances between Africa and the nations of the African diaspora seem to shrink. When James Baldwin was asked for a spontaneous response to a centuries old staff created by a Zairian artisan he responded to the figures crowning it:

> I recognize the women; I met them in Harlem. But it's another time and place. They're the women who live in Harlem . . . if they are not mowed down by a machine gun, they will get to where they are going, out from wherever white people condemn them. . . . I would not know the details of the culture, but I see this on Lenox Avenue: the style, the determination.[6]

That same sense of a similar style linking Africa and the diaspora is described by Cheryll Weston in her liner notes to Randy Weston's *Blues to Africa:*

> Randy was struck by the similarity of Black people; that he could travel all over the world from Brooklyn and

> still see a face which reminded him of someone he knew
> or had seen before. The feeling was the same—that
> warmth, that soulful magic and drama re-enacted all
> over the world. So "African Village/Bedford Stuy-
> vesant" is that smiling, soulful, woman in Dakar or
> Bedford Stuyvesant saying "Good morning," no matter
> who you are. . . .[7]

The reality of this transcultural continuity surfaces whenever
someone chooses to see penetratingly through the daily veil
of culturally reinforced inattention. For the composers
examined in A Night in Tunisia, their love of jazz and
curiosity about their historical origins called forth penetrating
artistic imagination.

Associated with this curiosity about racial origins is the
search for an authentic home, a driving force behind so much
significant African-American art. Whether the artist takes the
position of Ralph Ellison, insisting his home is more Oklahoma than Africa could ever be, or assumes Don Lee's
Afrocentric vision, there is constantly in African-American
thought a hunt, complex and ambivalent, for "roots." Not
only among artists do scholars find evidence for how much
African-American thought pivots on this single word, home. In
his interviews with citizens from all walks of life outside of
academia and artistic communities, anthropologist John Langston Gwaltney heard Hannah Nelson say:

> This ground we have buried our dead in for so long is
> the only ground most of us have ever stood upon. Africa
> is mercifully remote to most of us and that is a good
> thing too. Most of our people are remarkably merciful
> to Africa, when you consider how Africa used us.[8]

Echoing through Nelson's comment is a steadfast vision of the
essential difference between Africans and who they have
become during the past four centuries, a point underscored
by John Carter in his remarks about the Ghanaian drummers
at his recording session:

> You know these people look like me, and we are
> undoubtedly from the same place—yet they were
> Eastern people. The difference between us was very
> glaring. They were Africa—I was America—and there
> was no mistake about it.[9]

But when I confronted Carter's former student, drummer Ronald Shannon Jackson, with this comment, he responded:

> He might have communicated more successfully, with-
> out ever opening his mouth, with people from Gambia.
> Certain places you go you're on a certain communica-
> tions level where you don't have to use words.[10]

Behind these two, earlier generations debated the meanings
of homeland and roots, a debate typified in the polarized
stances of DuBois and Garvey. For much of his life, it was
DuBois who insisted upon the distinctive difference between
African Americans and Africans and who thought Garvey's
Pan-Africanism a mad delusion. And yet it was DuBois who
ended his life a disillusioned American calling Ghana his
home. And it was Garvey, for all his grandiose African vision,
who never in his lifetime set foot in Africa. So they and their
followers have battled over the most authentic home of black
humanity. Home may be where we have long buried our
dead, but that could be any continent, depending upon where
one draws a point of origin.

Whether one claims immediate ancestry from the United
States or Africa, a common theme prevails. The wisdom of
one's tribe is transmitted through the lore and spirit of
ancestors. In a poem that echoes the sentiments of the
African Negritude poet Leopold Senghor, Charles Olson
wrote:

> what we do not know of ourselves
> of who they are who lie
> coiled or unflown
> in the marrow of the bone

one sd:

> of rhythm is image
> of image is knowing
> of knowing there is
> a construct[11]

The actual words spoken by slave ancestors—the televised version of *Roots* notwithstanding—can probably never be recovered. The passage of four centuries shields us from direct and lucid verbal transmissions. But what did survive from the Middle Passage were the rhythms of speech and music. And from these rhythms, transfigured and restyled by jazz musicians, the search for roots continues, through images, imagination sparked by rhythms. Rather than glibly summarizing the soul searching of the sixties as part of a "Great Mystical Awakening," composer Clifford Thornton notes the meaning of the time in light of this search:

> During the 60's, the prevailing opinion seemed to be that free playing was a return to African roots, a rejection of Western criteria. But while we were busy feeling that we were returning to the roots, it would have been better to say that we were *looking* for the roots. In fact, we're just now learning what African music is all about and how to perform it.[12]

One strain of jazz history has involved repeated searches to discover the relation of Africa to jazz. In Ellington's "Jungle Music" days, hot swing with plentiful brass smears was identified as most "African," just as surely as Josephine Baker was associated with Nefertiti. Bop and neo-bop revisionism by Art Blakey, Max Roach, and Randy Weston represented yet another episode in identifying a jazz style with Africanisms. Thornton's statement well defines the African connection felt by Sunny Murray and Archie Shepp. It is not a question of deciding which jazz style is not truly "African" as much as recognizing that all of these musical styles have represented movements of Afrocentric imagination. They were musical experiments in conceiving of Africa from distant shores.

Further, they were attempts to recover ancestral voices. If you listen to any of the recordings celebrated in these pages, using their rhythms to feed your imagination, you might begin to see a dynamically complex sequences of images of Africa, vanishing then reappearing, second by second. These are kaleidoscopic images of a continent subject to waves of influence from the rest of the earth, but also persistently pressing its influences globally. These multiple images are like filters placed over a camera lens, constantly bringing what was thought to be a known object into novel and mysterious perspectives. Past all imaginative images, actual Africa remains a still largely unknown world requiring a search, though never again that of the colonizers.

African ancestors are speaking to us through restylings of their original rhythms. And unlike the Ooga Booga Hollywood version of African talk, certain jazz rhythms might unlock the meanings encoded in their faraway voices. Why not begin with a peculiar set of polyrhythms, pulsing on bass and drums, sparked by trumpet, a tune you heard on record that was unforgettable. "A Night in Tunisia" will suffice.

Chapter Notes

I: Opening Night in Tunisia: An Introduction

1. Ishmael Reed, *Mumbo Jumbo* (New York: Avon Books, 1972), p. 94.
2. "American Jazz Is Not African," *New York Times,* 19 September 1926, p. 8. An updated version of this story, "African Disclaims Africa As Influence on Jazz" appeared in *Down Beat,* 21 June 1962, p. 12.
3. Richard A. Waterman, "On Flogging a Dead Horse: Lessons Learned From the Africanisms Controversy," *Ethnomusicology* 7, No. 2 (1963), pp. 83–87.
4. Joseph Bodkin, *Sambo* (New York: Oxford University Press, 1986), p. 222. An amplification of this joke, connecting to Dr. Louis Leakey's discovery of humanity's African origin, is offered on Richard Pryor's *Live on the Sunset Strip* album (Warner Bros. BSK-3660).
5. Harold B. Isaacs, *The New World of Negro Americans* (New York: Viking Press, 1964), p. 105.
6. Al Rose, *Eubie Blake* (New York: Schirmer Books, 1979), p. 43.
7. Clifford Geertz, ed., *Myth, Symbol and Culture* (New York: W.W. Norton & Co., 1974), p. 23.
8. Frank M. Snowden, *Blacks in Antiquity: Ethiopians In The Greco-Roman Experience* (Cambridge, Mass.: Harvard University Press, 1970) p. 106. See Paul Bowles' *Points in Time* (New York: Ecco Press, 1982) for a modern recasting of Hanno's account.
9. Michael Maren, "A Walk on the White Side," *The Village Voice Literary Supplement* 73 (April 1989), p. 15.
10. Molefi Kete Asante, *The Afrocentric Idea* (Philadelphia: Temple University Press, 1987), pp. 3, 6.
11. Colette Gaudin, trans., *On Poetic Imagination and Reverie: Selections From the Works of Gaston Bachelard* (Indianapolis: Bobbs Merrill Publishers, 1971), p. XXVI.
12. Asante, p. 154. See also Samuel Charters, *The Roots of the Blues:*

An African Search (Boston: Marion Boyars, 1981), p. 148, for more on Africa as metaphor.

13. Gaudin, p. XXVI.

14. Composer Olly Wilson's statement of musical purpose resonates with my definition of the liberation motif. See David N. Baker, Lida M. Belt, Herman C. Hudson, eds., *The Black Composer Speaks* (Metuchen, N.J.: Scarecrow Press, 1978), p. 383.

15. See the introductory essay in Stephen Henderson's *Understanding The New Black Poetry: Black Speech and Black Music As Poetic References* (New York: William Morrow & Co., 1973), pp. XI—69. A provocative critique of Henderson's theory of black imagination is offered in Houston A. Baker, Jr., *Blues, Ideology, and Afro-American Literature* (Chicago: University of Chicago Press, 1984), p. 81.

16. Allison Blakely, *Russia And The Negro* (Washington, D.C.: Howard University Press, 1986), p. 148.

17. Imanuel Geiss, *The Pan-African Movement* (New York: Africana Publishing Co., 1974), p. 8.

18. James Olney, *Tell Me Africa: An Approach to African Literature* (Princeton, N.J.: Princeton University Press, 1973), p. 57.

19. David Lamb, review of *How Can Africa Survive?* by Jennifer Seymour Whitaker, *The New York Times Book Review*, 24 July 1988, p. 18.

II: Earliest Intimations of a Return to the Motherland

1. Hoagy Carmichael with Stephen Longstreet, *Sometimes I Wonder* (New York: Farrar, Straus and Giroux, 1965), p. 57.

2. Sir William A. Craigie and James R. Hulbert, eds., *A Dictionary of American English,* Volume II, (Chicago: University of Chicago Press, 1940), p. 900.

3. John Tasker Howard, *Stephen Foster, America's Troubadour* (New York: Thomas Y. Crowell Co., 1953), p. 195. Also see the illustration to "Ethiopian Melodies" in Robert C. Toll, *Blacking Up* (New York: Oxford University Press, 1974), p. 35.

4. Frank M. Snowden, *Blacks In Antiquity: Ethiopians In The Greco-Roman Experience* (Cambridge, Mass.: Harvard University Press, 1970), p. 179.

5. Eldred D. Jones, *The Elizabethan Image of Africa* (Charlottesville: University Press of Virginia, 1971), p. 45.

6. Felix N. Okoye, *The American Image of Africa: Myth and Reality* (Buffalo, N.Y.: Black Academy Press, 1971), pp. 122–124.

7. John Tasker Howard, p. 195.

8. For a valuable explanation of the African inspiration for the banjo see Michael Theodore Coolen, "Senegambian Archetypes for the American Folk Banjo," *Western Folklore* XLIII, No. 2 (April 1984), pp. 117–132.

9. Dick Sudhalter, liner notes to *Curtis Hitch and Hoagy Carmichael* (Fountain FJ-109).

10. Sun Ra's incorporation of the symbols of ancient Egypt into his music is graphically dramatized in a film by Robert Mugge, *Sun Ra: A Joyful Noise* available on videotape (Rhapsody Films, 1986).

11. Marshall Stearns and Jean Stearns, *Jazz Dance* (New York: Macmillan Co., 1968), p. 113.

12. Chadwick Hansen, "Jenny's Toe Revisited: White Responses to Afro-American Shaking Dances," *American Music* (Spring 1987), pp. 1–19.

13. Quoted in Ishmael Reed, *Mumbo Jumbo* (New York: Avon Books, 1972), p. 106.

14. Anatole Chinjoy and P.W. Mancester, eds., *The Dance Encyclopedia* (New York: Simon and Schuster, 1967), p. 503.

15. William B. Cohen, *The French Encounter With Africans* (Bloomington: Indiana University Press, 1980), p. 78.

16. Stearns and Stearns, p. 325. Also see Ron Welburn "Dance and the New Black Music" in *Black Review #2* (New York: William Morrow & Co., 1972), pp. 55–65.

17. J.H. Kwabena Nketia, *The Music of Africa* (New York: W.W. Norton & Co., 1974), p. 228.

18. John Carter, personal interview, May 10, 1988.

19. Gerald Clark's guitar can be heard on *Jazz and Hot Dance in Trinidad* (Harlequin HQ 2016) and *Calypso Pioneers* (Rounder 1039).

20. Lyrics were transcribed by the author from the album *Wilmoth Houdini* (Folklyric 9040).

III: Madame Zzaj Testifies Why A Drum Is A Woman

1. Barry Ulanov, *Duke Ellington* (New York: Da Capo Press, 1975), p. 190.

2. Duke Ellington, *Music Is My Mistress* (New York: Da Capo Press, 1973), p. 337.

3. James Lincoln Collier, *Duke Ellington* (New York: Oxford University Press, 1987), p. 92.

4. Ulanov, p. 73.

5. Several of Van Der Zee's photographs of the UNIA on parade are available in Studio Museum in Harlem, *Harlem Renaissance: Art of Black America* (New York: Harry N. Abrams, Inc., 1987). See p. 98 for the key images I had in mind when writing this chapter.

6. Peter I. Rose, ed. *Americans From Africa: Old Memories, New Moods* (New York: Atherton Press, Inc., 1970), pp. 385–403. Also see John Henrick Clarke, ed., *Marcus Garvey and the Vision of Africa* (New York: Vintage Books, 1974), pp. 14–28.

7. Collier, p. 92.

8. See John Peer Nugent, *The Black Eagle* (New York: Stein & Day, 1971) for a comprehensive biography of Hubert Fauntleroy Julian.

9. Ellington, pp. 108–109. Also see John Storm Roberts, *The Latin Tinge* (New York: Oxford University Press, 1979).

10. Amy Garvey, *Garvey and Garveyism* (New York: Macmillan Publishing Co., 1970), pp. 305–306.

11. Ellington, p. 53. For insight into how Greer's drumming suggested African imagery, see Jim Haskins, *The Cotton Club* (New York: New American Library, 1984), p. 50.

12. Derek Jewell, *Duke: A Portrait of Duke Ellington* (New York: W.W. Norton & Co., 1977), p. 121.

13. Ulli Beier, ed., *Introduction to African Literature* (Evanston, Ill.: Northwestern University Press, 1967), p. 107.

14. Jerome Rothenberg and Diane Rothenberg, eds., *Symposium of the Whole* (Berkeley: University of California Press, 1983), p. 120.

15. Ellington, p. 243.

16. J.H. Kwabena Nketia, *The Music of Africa* (New York: W.W. Norton & Co., 1974), p. 96. I am imagining that Ellington might have seen this image (or one like it) sometime during his travels. Even if this is not so, it is intriguing to conceive of his talking brass section as an American parallel to these trumpet choirs from Zaire.

17. Angus, Paul, "Collection Holds Clues to Genius of Duke Ellington," *The Chronicle of Higher Education,* 12 October 1988, p. A-5.

IV: "A Night in Tunisia": The Evolution of a Standard

1. Stanley Dance, *The World of Earl Hines* (New York: Scribner Book Co., 1977), p. 260.
2. Dizzy Gillespie with Wilmot Alfred Fraser, *To Be, Or Not . . . To Bop* (New York: Doubleday & Company, Inc., 1979), p. 171.
3. Ibid., p. 490.
4. Ibid., p. 171.
5. Herb Nolan, "New Message From Art Blakey," *Down Beat,* 16 (November 1979), p. 20.
6. Ibid., p. 20.
7. John Miller Chernoff, *African Rhythms and African Sensibility* (Chicago: University of Chicago Press, 1979), p. 60.
8. George Hoefer, "Mann in Africa," *Down Beat,* July 7 1969, p. 17.
9. Herbie Mann, *The Common Ground,* Atlantic 1343.

V: John Coltrane: Sounding the African Cry for Paradise

1. Henri Baudet, *Paradise on Earth: Some Thoughts on European Images of Non-European Man,* trans. by Elizabeth Wentholt. (Westport, Conn.: Greenwood Press, 1965), p. 15.
2. See Robert Palmer's important liner notes for the *Dial Africa* (Savoy SL 1110) and *Countdown* (Savoy 2203) albums by John Coltrane and Wilbur Harden.
3. Cuthbert Ormond Simpkins, M.D., *Coltrane: A Biography* (Brooklyn, N.Y.: Herndon House Publishers, 1975). Bill Cole, *John Coltrane* (New York: Schirmer Books, 1976).
4. *Holy Bible,* King James version.
5. Simon Ottenberg, ed., *African Religious Groups and Beliefs* (Meerut, India: Archana Publications for the Folklore Institute, 1982), pp. 305–331.
6. Morton distinguishes between the pantheon of deities in African religions who can possess a devotee with the single choice in African-American Christianity by theorizing that various gospel music styles in the African-American church represent symbolic stand-ins for African deities. See Ottenberg, p. 330.
7. John Burke, *Musical Landscapes* (Exeter, England: Webb & Bower, 1983), p. 10.

8. Listen to *The Pygmies of the Ituri Forest,* recorded by Colin M. Turnbull and Francis S. Chapman (Ethnic Folkways FE 4457), for a sense of the music which impressed Coltrane and Eric Dolphy.

9. Quoted in A.B. Spellman's liner notes to *Ascension* (Impulse A-95).

10. For more on the theory of the cyclical nature of African art and religion, see Robert Ferris Thompson, *Flash of the Spirit: African and Afro-American Art and Philosophy* (New York: Random House, 1983), pp. 103–159; and Sterling Stuckey, *Slave Culture: Nationalist Theory & The Foundations of Black America* (New York: Oxford University Press, 1987), pp. 3–97.

11. Irene V. Jackson, ed., *More Than Drumming: Essays on African and Afro-Latin American Music and Musicians* (Westport, Conn.: Greenwood Press, 1985), p. 37.

12. Simpkins, p. 232.

13. Simpkins, p. 179.

14. Jurg Solothurnmann, "Johnny Dyani: Music Is Like Medicine," *Jazz Forum,* Issue 87 (1984), pp. 43–47.

15. Don De Micheal, "John Coltrane and Eric Dolphy Answer the Jazz Critics," *Down Beat,* April 12, 1962, p. 22.

16. Spellman, *Ascension* liner notes.

VI: George Russell Teaches Us To Play The African Game

1. George Russell, liner notes to *Electronic Sonata for Souls Loved by Nature* (Flying Dutchman FD 10124).

2. George Russell, liner notes to *The African Game* (Blue Note BT-85103).

3. See Ellen Conroy Kennedy, ed., *The Negritude Poets* (New York: The Viking Press, 1975), pp. 121–146, for a brief essay about Senghor and a selection of his poetry in English translation. An essay of Senghor's available in translation, "The Living Values of Negritude," is available in Jacob Drachler, ed., *Black Homeland/Black Diaspora: Cross Currents of the African Relationship* (Port Washington, N.Y.: National University Publications/Kennikat Press, 1975), pp. 240–244. A negative critique of Senghor's image of "African blood" is offered in Imanuel Geiss, *The Pan-African Movement* (New York: Africana Publishing Co., 1974).

4. Robert Nodal, "The Social Evolution Of The Afro-Cuban Drum," *The Black Perspective In Music* 11, no. 2 (Fall 1983), pp. 157–177.

5. A similar position is taken by pianist and composer Cecil Taylor. See J.B. Figi, "Cecil Taylor: African Code, Black Methodology," *Down Beat,* 10 April 1975, pp. 12–14, 31.

6. The French text of Mallarmé's poem with this line, along with an English prose translation, is in Anthony Hartley, ed., *Mallarme* (Baltimore: Penguin Books, 1965), pp. 209–233. A comparison of Mallarmé's poetics to Afro-Brazilian musical dance events is found in Roger Bastide, *African Civilizations in the New World,* trans. by Peter Green (London: C. Hurst & Co., 1971), p. 176.

7. Russell, liner notes to *The African Game.*

8. Marcel Griaule, *Conversations With Ogotemmeli: An Introduction to Dogon Religious Ideas* (Oxford: Oxford University Press, 1965), p. 65.

9. Listen to the musical celebration of the divine spirit residing in African-American waters in Duke Ellington's *The River* (LMR Records LMRCD-83004). For comprehending the spirit of the water as a metaphor, see Vincent Harding, *There Is a River* (New York: Harcourt, 1981).

VII: John Carter: The Play of Roots and Folklore

1. My interview with John Carter was tape recorded May 10, 1988, at the Wind College in Los Angeles. Excerpts from this interview were first published in *Jazziz* 5, No. 5 (October/November 1988), p. 69.

2. John Storm Roberts, *Black Music of Two Worlds* (New York: William Morrow & Co., 1974), p. 215.

3. Samuel Charters, *The Roots Of The Blues: An African Search* (Boston, Mass.: Marion Boyars, 1981), pp. 16–17.

4. Trombonist Roswell Rudd's research with folklorist Alan Lomax is summarized in Roswell Rudd, "The Universality of the Blues," *Down Beat,* 25 January 1968, pp. 23–26.

5. John Carter, *A Suite of Early American Folk Pieces for Solo Clarinet* (Moers Music 02014). This album is unfortunately difficult to obtain in this country. Episodes of Carter's solo clarinet playing are heard on the various Clarinet Summit albums which are readily obtainable.

6. Merrick Posnansky's most easily available publication, edited with Christopher Ehret, is *The Archaeological and Linguistic Reconstruction of African History* (Berkeley: University of California Press, 1982).

VIII: Count Ossie and the Mystic Revelation of Rastafari: To Mozambique Via Marcus Garvey Drive

1. Duke Ellington, *Music Is My Mistress* (New York: Da Capo Press, 1975), p. 47.
2. Jason Berry, Jonathan Foose, Tad Jones, *Up From the Cradle of Jazz: New Orleans Music Since World War II* (Athens: University of Georgia Press, 1986), p. 232.
3. Yoshiko S. Nagashima, *Rastafarian Music in Contemporary Jamaica: A Study of Socioreligious Music of the Rastafarian Movement of Jamaica* (Tokyo: Institute for the Study of Language and Culture of Asia & Africa, 1984), p. 89.
4. The evolution of Rastafarianism from Garvey to Howell and beyond is comprehensively and sympathetically mapped in Joseph Owens, *Dread: The Rastafarians of Jamaica* (Kingston, Jamaica: Sangster, 1976).
5. Photographs and detailed descriptions of the drums are found in Vera Reckord, "Rastafarian Music: An Introductory Study," *Jamaica Journal* 11, Nos. 1 & 2: pp. 2–13.
6. Nat Hentoff and Albert McCarthy, eds., *Jazz* (New York: Rinehart & Co., 1959), p. 29.
7. Robert C. Toll, *Blacking Up* (New York: Oxford University Press, 1974), pp. 276–277.
8. See liner notes by blues scholar David Evans to *Traveling Through the Jungle: Negro Fife and Drum Band Music for the Deep South* (Testament T-2223).
9. This selection is offered on the album *Juju Roots 1930s–1950s* (Rounder 5017). A more contemporary example of an African brass band, Nyakrom Brass Band, appears on an instructional audiocassette accompanying Jeff Todd Titon, ed., *Worlds of Music: An Introduction to the Music of the World's Peoples* (New York: Schirmer Books, 1984).
10. Robert Santelli, "Ras Michael: The Roots of Reggae," *Modern Drummer* (August 1986), p. 32.
11. Personal conversation on April 16, 1989.
12. Edward A. Alpers, *The Role of Culture in the Liberation of*

Mozambique (Washington, D.C.: Embassy of the People's Republic of Mozambique, n.d.), p. 143. Also see Stephanie Urdang, *And Still They Dance: Women, War, and the Struggle for Change in Mozambique* (New York: Monthly Review Press, 1989), pp. 42–45.

13. Liner notes to Count Ossie and the Mystic Revelation of Rastafari, *Tales of Mozambique* (Dynamic Sound DY 3358).

IX. Randy Weston: Talking Piano Like a Drum Shouting Freedom

1. Robert Palmer, "The Musical Roots of Randy Weston," *Rolling Stone,* 30 October 1980, p. 25.

2. Kathy I. Ogrew, *The Jazz Revolution* (New York: Oxford University Press, 1989, p. 16.

3. J.H. Kwabena Nketia, *The Music of Africa* (New York: W.W. Norton & Co., 1974), pp. 135–136.

4. John Miller Chernoff, *African Rhythm and African Sensibility* (Chicago: University of Chicago Press, 1979), p. 51.

5. Laurent Goddet, "Interview With Randy Weston," *Coda,* Issue 159 (February 1978), p. 9.

6. John Storm Roberts, *Black Music of Two Worlds* (New York: Praeger Publishers, Inc., 1972), pp. 54–55.

7. Cannonball Adderley and His Orchestra, *African Waltz* (OJC-258). The Nigerian drummer Olatunji, accompanist to Randy Weston, Max Roach, and John Coltrane, is part of Adderley's ensemble.

8. Arnold Rampersad, *The Life of Langston Hughes,* Volume II: *1941-1967* (New York: Oxford University Press, 1988), p. 348.

9. Goddet, p. 9.

10. An account of this trip is found in Georgia Griggs, "With Randy Weston in Africa," *Down Beat,* 13 July 1967: pp. 16–17; 38–39.

11. The Westside Cultural Center of New York presented a performance of *A Drum Is A Woman* as part of "A 90th Birthday Gala Tribute to Duke Ellington" on April 28, 1989.

12. Lambert, Hendricks, and Ross, *The Swingers* (Pacific Jazz CD 7468492). The album includes vocal arrangements for Weston's "Little Niles," "Babe's Blues," and "Where."

13. "South Africa Bans Records by Lena Horne, Randy Weston," *Down Beat,* 24 September 1964, p. 14.

14. W.E.B. DuBois, *The Souls of Black Folk* (New York: The New American Library, 1969), p. 274.

15. Randy Weston, "Report on FESTAC for Nigerian Music Review," *Quilt #1* (1981), pp. 137–148.

16. An interview with clarinetist Edmond Hall following his unsuccessful attempt to establish himself in Ghana is found in Max Jones' "Ghana Plans Didn't Work," *Melody Maker,* 2 January 1960, p. 11. An interesting sketch of Cleveland Luca, a nineteenth-century African-American musician who met a premature death in Africa, is included in James M. Trotter, *Music and Some Highly Musical People* (New York: Johnson Reprint Co., 1968), pp. 88–105.

X: Max Roach: Drumming the Tales of African and African-American Liberation

1. Marc Crawford, "The Drummer Most Likely to Succeed," *Down Beat,* 30 March 1961, p. 21.

2. This chronology was largely formulated from D.A. Back, *The Freedom Climb* (Dover, Del.: Back Publishing, 1970), pp. 52–53.

3. Bill Coss, "Lennie Tristano Speaks Out," *Down Beat,* 6 December 1962, p. 20.

4. Parallels between Roach's transformations of African music and Moore's transformations of traditional African dance styles warrant further study. Moore's dancing was significantly showcased in "Dance Black America," a documentary film by D.A. Pennebaker and Chris Hegedus, which was aired on the Public Broadcast System, 25 January 1985.

5. *Noi Insistiamo/We Insist,* a 1965 film by Italian director Gianni Amico is described by film historian David Meeker as offering "a visual interpretation of extracts from the 'We insist— freedom now': suite by Max Roach." Roach's suite has appeared on record as both *We Insist: Freedom Now Suite* and *Freedom Now Suite.* I have used the latter to simplify identification. Meeker's description of the film is found under entry number 2317 of the unpaginated David Meeker, *Jazz in the Movies,* New Enlarged Edition (New York: Da Capo Press, 1981).

6. Bret Primack, "Max Roach: There's No Stoppin' the Professor From Boppin'," *Down Beat,* 2 November 1978, p. 22.

7. Ortiz Walton, *Music: Black, White and Blue* (New York: William Morrow, 1972), p. 79.

8. Charles Keil, *Tiv Song* (Chicago: University of Chicago Press, 1979), p. 258.

XI: Pierre Dørge: Travelling Through a New World Jungle Armed With Guitar and Orchestra

1. Mitchell Feldman, "Pierre Dørge and the New Jungle Orchestra: One World, Many Musics," *Down Beat,* November 1970, p. 28.

2. Samuel Charters, *The Roots of the Blues: An African Search* (Boston: Marion Boyars, 1981), pp. 15–16. Also see Charters' liner notes about Jali Nyama Suso, comparing his *kora* and acoustic guitar styles, on *African Journey: A Search for the Roots of the Blues* (Vanguard Nomad SRV-730).

3. J.H. Kwabena Nketia and Jacqueline Cogdell DjeDje, eds., *Selected Reports in Ethnomusicology,* Vol. 5, *Studies in African Music* (Los Angeles: UCLA Dept. of Music, Program in Ethnomusicology, 1984), pp. 8–10.

4. Jurg Solothurnmann, "Johnny Dyani: 'Music Is Like Medicine'," *Jazz Forum,* Issue #87 (1984), p. 47.

5. In letter to the author dated 2/3/88, Pierre Dørge wrote that Dyani's death from liver disease was "very unexpected for everybody." He is survived by his wife and three children in Copenhagen. One is the drummer Thomas Dyani. Dyani has been the subject of numerous musical tributes on record since his death by Billy Bang, Clarinet Summit, and others.

XII: Archie Shepp: Magical Portraits for the Diaspora

1. Jacob Drachler, ed., *Black Homeland, Black Diaspora: Cross-Currents of the African Relationship* (Port Washington, N.Y.: National University Publications/Kennikat Press, 1975), p. 140.

2. A critical analysis of Shepp's departure from traditional African drum rhythms is offered in E. Jost, *Free Jazz* (New York: Da Capo Press, 1975), p. 113.

3. Gunther Schuller, *Early Jazz: Its Roots and Musical Development* (New York: Oxford University Press, 1968), pp. 58–59.

4. One album of Cal Massey's music is currently available, *Blues to Coltrane* (Candid CD 9029). Massey's compositions were covered by Coltrane, most notably, "Bakai" and "The Damned Don't Cry."

5. A pivotal figure in the history of African-American gospel music was the composer and pianist Arizona Dranes who, like Shepp, was comfortable synthesizing gospel with blues styles. Her sole recording in album format, *Arizona Dranes 1926–1928: Barrel House Piano With Sanctified Singing* (Herwin 210) is well worth hearing for a fuller understanding of Shepp and other jazz figures working with gospel themes (Max Roach, Ronald Shannon Jackson).

6. See John Lamphear's "Aspects of Early African History" in Phyllis M. Martin and Patrick O'Meara, *Africa,* 2nd ed. (Bloomington: Indiana University Press, 1986), pp. 68–69. Also see Molefi Kete Asante, *The Afrocentric Idea* (Philadelphia: Temple University Press, 1987), p. 171.

7. Tolia Nikiprowetzky, "Tuareg Music," in Stanley Sadie, ed., *The New Grove Dictionary of Music and Musicians,* Vol. 19 (London: Macmillan, 1980), pp. 236–237.

XIII: Yusef Lateef: Re-Visioning the Geography of the Blues

1. Don Michael Randel, ed., *The New Harvard Dictionary of Music* (Cambridge, Mass.: Belknap Press of Harvard University Press, 1986), p. 98.

2. William Ferris, *Blues From the Delta* (New York: Da Capo Press, 1984), p. 3.

3. David Evans, *Big Road Blues: Tradition and Creativity in the Folk Blues* (New York: Da Capo Press, 1982), p. 114.

4. Lois and Isma'il Faruqi, *The Cultural Atlas of Islam* (New York: Macmillan Publishing Co., 1986), p. 469.

5. Bob Rusch, "Yusef Lateef interview," *Cadence* (January 1989), p. 5.

6. Yusef Lateef, liner notes to *A Flat, G Flat and C* (Impulse A 9117).

7. Henry Louis Gates, Jr., ed., *The Classic Slave Narratives* (New York: Mentor Books/New American Library, 1987), p. 17.

8. Ashenafi Kebede, *Roots of Black Music: The Vocal, Instrumental, and Dance Heritage of Africa and Black America* (Englewood Cliffs, N.J.: Prentice-Hall, Inc., 1982), p. 72.

9. Faruqi, p. 476.
10. Valerie Wilmer, *As Serious As Your Life* (Westport, Conn.: Lawrence Hill, 1980), pp. 9–10.
11. Rusch: 7–8.
12. Lilyan Kesteloot, *Black Writers in French: A Literary History of Negritude,* trans. by Ellen Conroy Kennedy (Philadelphia: Temple University Press, 1974), p. 224.
13. Marcel Griaule, *Conversations With Ogotemmeli: An Introduction to Dogon Religious Ideas* (Oxford: Oxford University Press, 1965), pp. 138–143.
14. Kesteloot, p. 87.

XIV: Sunny Murray and the Creation of Time

1. Anthony Gerard Barthelemy, *Black Face, Maligned Race: The Representation of Blacks in English Drama From Shakespeare to Southern* (Baton Rouge: Louisiana State University Press, 1987), p. 60.
2. Spencer Weston, "Sunny Murray interview," *Cadence* (June 1979), p. 16.
3. For more on reading traditional African cloth metaphorically, see Jean Borgatti, *Cloth As Metaphor: Nigerian Textiles From the Museum of Cultural History* (Los Angeles: UCLA Museum of Cultural History, 1983).
4. Robert Ferris Thompson, *Flash of the Spirit: African and Afro-American Art and Philosophy* (New York: Random House, 1983), pp. 236–237.
5. J.H. Nketia, *Funeral Dirges of the Akan People* (New York: Negro Universities Press, 1969), p. 116.
6. Claudia Zaslavsky, *Africa Counts: Number and Pattern in African Culture* (Boston: Prindle, Weber and Schmidt, Inc., 1973), p. 64.

XV: Ronald Shannon Jackson: Journey to Africa Without End

1. Ronald Shannon Jackson: liner notes to *When Colors Play* (Caravan of Dreams CDP-85009).
2. Gary Giddins, *Rhythm-A-Ning: Jazz Tradition and Innovation*

in the 80's (New York: Oxford University Press, 1985), pp. 96–97.

3. Janheinz Jahn, *Muntu,* trans. by Marjorie Grene (New York: Grove Press, 1961), pp. 132–133.

4. Roger Bastide, *African Civilizations in the New World,* trans. by Peter Green (London: C. Hurst & Co., 1971), p. 222.

5. Bastide, p. 222.

6. Ellington's rainbow of colors in his composition titles are listed in W.E. Timner, *Ellingtonia,* 3rd ed. (Metuchen, N.J.: Scarecrow Press, 1988), a comprehensive discography.

7. Anita Jacobson-Widding, *Red-White-Black as a Mode of Thought: A Study of Triadic Classification by Colours in the Ritual Symbolism and Cognitive Thought of the Peoples of the Lower Congo* (Stockholm: Almqvist and Wiksell International, 1979).

8. Oliver Nelson trenchantly commented on his perception of cultural differences between himself as an African American and Africans he met during his U.S. State Department African Tour in 1969, in Pauline Revelli and Robert Levin, *Black Giants* (New York: World Publishing Co., 1970), pp. 68–77.

XVI: Beyond the Americanization of Ooga Booga: Charting the Pathways of Afrocentric Imagination

1. David V. Erdman, ed., *The Poetry and Prose of William Blake* (Garden City, N.Y.: Doubleday & Co., Inc., 1970), p. 268.

2. Walter Abish, *Alphabetical Africa* (New York: New Directions Publishing Corp., 1974), p. 62.

3. Jean-Paul Sartre, "Black Orpheus," trans. by John MacCombie, *The Massachusetts Review* 6, No. 1 (1964–1965), p. 21.

4. Francis Davis, *In the Moment: Jazz in the 1980s* (New York: Oxford University Press, 1986), p. 153.

5. Louis Armstrong, *Satchmo the Great* (Columbia CL 1077). This album is out of print. This poem by Norman Weinstein was published in *The Village Voice.*

6. The Center for African Art, *Perspectives: Angles on African Art* (New York: The Center for African Art and Harry N. Abrams Inc. 1987), p. 119.

7. Cheryll Weston, liner notes to Randy Weston, *Blues to Africa* (Freedom FCD 41014).

8. John Langston Gwaltney, *Drylongso: A Self-Portrait of Black America* (New York: Random House, 1980), p. 5.

9. Author's interview with John Carter, May 10, 1988.

10. Author's interview with Ronald Shannon Jackson, March 15, 1989. Excerpts from the interview were published in *Rhythm* (May 1989) as "A Spiritual Exercise," pp. 68–70.

11. George F. Butterick, ed., *The Collected Poems of Charles Olson* (Berkeley: University of California Press, 1987), p. 173.

12. Robert Palmer, "Clifford Thornton: Flowers in the Garden of Harlem," *Down Beat,* June 1975, p. 20.

Discography I

The following list of recordings is presented so that readers who wish to pursue the ideas in this book further can do so with ease through intensive listening. As the LPs are phased out in favor of compact discs, a number of these titles will either shift into that format or be available only through import sources. Most of these titles were available at the time of the publication.

Chapter II:

Curtis Hitch and Hoagy Carmichael, *Curtis Hitch and Hoagy Carmichael* (Fountain FJ-109/England). This includes "Ethiopian Nightmare."

Various Artists, *Chicago Jazz 1923–1929* (Biograph BLP-12005). This offers versions of "'Mid the Pyramids" and "Red Hot Hottentot."

Mills Brothers, *From the Beginning,* Volume Three (JSP 1109/England). "Jungle Fever" is included here. It can also be heard within a historical context on the collection *The Human Orchestra: Rhythm Quartets in the Thirties* compiled by Doug Seroff (Clanka Lanka CL-144033/Sweden).

Junie C. Cobb, *South Side Chicago Jazz 1926–1929* (Swaggie 852/Australia). This offers "South African Blues."

Don Redman and Orchestra, *Shakin' the African* (HEP 1001/England). This number is also included on the U.S. compilation *Big Bands Uptown* (MCA 1323).

Various Artists, *Black Bands 1927–1934* (Biograph HLP-35). This includes "The Head-Hunter's Dream."

Wilmoth Houdini, *Calypso Classics From Trinidad* (Folklyric 9040). This offers "African Love Call." Houdini's tribute to the aviation hero Julian (also honored by a Rex Stewart band) is heard on the compilation *Calypso Pioneers 1912–1937* (Rounder 1039).

Chapter III:

Duke Ellington, *Afro-Eurasian Eclipse* (Fantasy 9498).
Black, Brown & Beige (4-Bluebird 6641-1RB29).
Carnegie Hall Concerts: December 1947 (2-Prestige 24075). The first recording of "The Liberian Suite" is offered.
Concert in Virgin Islands (Discovery 841).
The Blanton-Webster Band (4-Bluebird 5659-1-RB29). This includes "Conga Brava" and "Chocolate Shake." The latter can be heard in its original context on *Jump For Joy* (Smithsonian Recordings LP R037DMM1-0722).
The Great Ellington Units (Bluebird 6751-2RB). This includes Rex Stewart's "Menelik (The Lion of Judah)."
Money Jungle (Blue Note BT-85129). This trio album presents "Fleurette Africaine (African Flower)."
New Orleans Suite (Atlantic SD 1580).
Togo Brava Suite (United Artists UXS-92).
Uptown (Columbia Jazz Masterpieces CJ-40836). This offers "The Harlem Suite."
A Drum Is A Woman (Columbia Special Products JCL 951).

Chapter IV:

Sarah Vaughan, *My First 15 Sides* (Official 83003/Denmark).

Dizzy Gillespie, *Dizziest* (2-Bluebird 5785-1-RB11). "A Night in Tunisia" is presented in a big band format.
Compact Jazz (Mercury 832574-2). This compilation offers a small ensemble performing "A Night in Tunisia" at the 1957 Newport Jazz Festival.
Be-Bop's Heartbeat (Savoy Jazz SJL-1177). This captures one of the occasions when Gillespie and Charles Parker played together on "A Night in Tunisia."

Swing Low Sweet Cadillac (Impulse A-9149). Of significance is the inclusion of the composition, "Kush," which has this spoken introduction by Gillespie: "The next tune is an original composition of mine that was inspired by, and dedicated to, Mother Africa. Hope you got with that, baby. I hope that this next one will make some of you feel more or less at home. If it doesn't—shame on you, baby."

Dizzy Gillespie and Arturo Sandoval, *Live at the 1985 Plaza International Jazz Festival* (Egrem LD-4271/Cuba).

Charlie Parker, *Very Best of Bird* (Warner Brothers 2WB-3198). This offers both the famous 47-second aborted take of "A Night in Tunisia" and a complete version.

Anita O'Day, *Sings the Winners* (Verve UMV-2536).

Ella Fitzgerald, *Compact Jazz* (Verve 831367-2).

Eddie Jefferson, *Letter From Home* (Fantasy/OJC OJC-307).
Things Are Getting Better (Muse MR-5043).

Various Artists, *The Smithsonian Collection of Classic Jazz* compiled and annotated by Martin Williams (Smithsonian Recordings R033 P7-19477). This includes Bud Powell's "A Night in Tunisia."

Art Blakey, *Art's Break* (Lotus LOP 14.071/Italy). These are live performances from Tunisia.
The Drum Suite (Columbia 1002).
The African Beat (Blue Note 4097). "Woman of Africa" is offered.
A Night in Tunisia (Blue Note B11E-84049). This presents a 1960 edition of Blakey's Jazz Messengers showcasing Wayne Shorter and Lee Morgan.
Theory of Art (Bluebird 6286-1-R). This was originally released as *A Night in Tunisia* and was the first recording of the standard the author heard.
One Night at Birdland, Volume One (Blue Note BST-81521E). Trumpeter Clifford Brown was fond of "A Night in Tunisia" and this live recording has Brown improvising smartly with Blakey and band.
The Witch Doctor (Blue Note BLP 84258).

Chapter V:

John Coltrane, *Africa/Brass* (MCA/Impulse MCA-42231).
Africa Brass Sessions, Volume II (MCA/Impulse MCA-42232).
Coltrane (Fantasy/OJC OJC-020). This includes "Bakai."
Coltrane's Sound (Atlantic SD-1419). This includes "Liberia."
Dakar (2-Prestige 24104).
His Greatest Years (MCA2-4131). "Afro Blue" is included.
Ole (Atlantic SD-1373). This has "Dahomey Dance."
Om (MCA/Impulse MCAD-39118).
Dial Africa (Savoy Jazz SJL-1110). This includes "Oomba" and "Dial Africa."
Gold Coast (Savoy Jazz SJL-1115). This offers "Taganyika Strut" and "Gold Coast." Both albums have been combined on one compact disc entitled *Africa* (Savoy Jazz ZD-70818).
Ascension (Pioneer 32XD-577/Japan). This Japanese compact disc is available in import stores in the U.S., as are the following four albums.
Jupiter Variation (Pioneer 32XD-600/Japan).
Meditations (Pioneer 32XD-581/Japan).
Expressions (Pioneer 32XD-597/Japan). This includes "Ogunde."
Kulu Se Mama (Pioneer 32XD-5960). Also available in vinyl format (Jasmine JAS-51/England).
Interstellar Space (Impulse 9277Q).
A Love Supreme (MCA/Impulse MCA-5660).

Chapter VI:

George Russell, *The African Game* (Blue Note BT-85103).
Electronic Sonata for Souls Loved by Nature (Strata East 19761).
Outer Thoughts (2-Milestone 47027).
New York Big Band (Soul Note 121039-2).

Chapter VII:

John Carter, *Dauwhe* (Black Saint 120057-1).
Castles of Ghana (Gramavision 188603-1).
Dance of the Love Ghosts (Gramavision 188704-1).
Fields (Gramavision 188809-1).
Shadows on a Wall (Gramavision, R279422).

Clarinet Summit, *In Concert at the Public Theater, Volume I.* (India Navigation IN-1062) and *Volume II* (India Navigation IN1067).

Chapter VIII:

Count Ossie and the Mystic Revelation of Rastafari, *Grounation* (MRR Records/Jamaica).
  Tales of Mozambique (Dynamic DY 3358/Jamaica). These albums are distributed by Ras Records, P.O. Box 42517, Washington, D.C. 20015. In addition to examples of albums with Africanized brass band ensembles offered in this chapter, there are records revealing how the jazz avant-garde has transformed that sound, notably Albert Ayler, *Bells* (ESP 1010) and Lol Coxhill, *Couscous* (Nato 157/-France). A comprehensive anthology of various traditional African horn styles is offered on volume four of "The Music of Africa" series, compiled by High Tracey and available in cassette format through Paul Tracey, 340 Las Casas Ave., Pacific Palisades, CA 90272.

Chapter IX:

Randy Weston, with David Murray, *The Healers* (Black Saint 120118-1).
  Berkshire Blues (Arista/Freedom 1026). "Purple Gazelle" is included.
  Uhuru Africa (Vogue DRY 21006/France).
  Blues to Africa (Freedom FCD 41014). This offers "African Village/Bedford Stuyvestant."
  Carnival (Freedom FCD 41004). This includes African drummer Guy Warren's "Mystery of Love," an African version of "Romeo and Juliet."
  African Cookbook (Atlantic SD-1609). This offers "Congolese Children."

Chapter X:

Max Roach, *Freedom Now Suite* (Candid CCD 9002).
  Drums Unlimited (Atlantic SD-1467-1). "Nommo" is offered.

Chattahoochie Red (Columbia FC37376).

Percussion Bitter Sweet (Impulse 8). This offers "Garvey's Ghost" and "Man From South Africa."

M'Boom (Columbia IC-37066). This percussion ensemble led by Roach includes among its performances "Kulichagalia." The title is the Swahili word for "self determination."

With Archie Shepp and Anthony Braxton, *The Long March* (Hat Art 4026). This includes "South Africa Goddamn."

With Archie Shepp, *Force* (Uniteledia 28976). This includes "South Africa 76."

With Dizzy Gillespie, *Max and Dizzy—Paris 1989* (A&M CD 6404). This includes "Nairobi" and "South Africa Goddamn."

Chapter XI:

Pierre Dørge and New Jungle Orchestra, *Brikama* (SteepleChase SCS-1188).

Pierre Dørge and New Jungle Orchestra (SteepleChase SCS-1162).

Even the Moon Is Dancing (SteepleChase SCS-1208).

Johnny Lives (SteepleChase SCS-1228).

The following recordings of African *kora* players who taught Dørge during his visits to The Gambia are available:

Foday Musa Suso, with Tambu Suso and Jarju Kuyateh, *Mansa Bendung* (Flying Fish FF380). This is an album of traditional compositions.

These two albums represent Suso's attempts to fuse Gambian *kora* music with jazz and funk:

Foday Musa Suso, *Mandingo Griot Society* (Flying Fish FF076) and Mandingo, *Watto Sitta* (Celluloid CELL 6103).

Alhaji Bai Konte, *Alhaji Bai Konte* (Rounder 5001).

Representative showcases for guitar playing by Jimi Hendrix include *Kiss the Sky* (Reprise 25119-1) and *Electric Ladyland* (2-Reprise 2RS-6307).

Albums concentrating exclusively upon Frank Zappa's guitar playing include *Guitar* (2-Barking Pumpkin D12-74212) and *Shut Up N Play Yer Guitar* (2-Rykodisc RCD-10028/ 29).

Chapter XII:

Archie Shepp, *The Cry of My People* (Impulse AS-9231). This includes "African Drum Suite."
  Live at the Panafrican Festival (Affinity 41/England).
  Blase (Affinity 7/England). "Tuareg" is offered.
  Yasima, A Black Woman (Affinity 21/England).
  Goin' Home (SteepleChase 1079).
  Trouble in Mind (SteepleChase 1139).
  Looking at Bird (SteepleChase 1149).
  The Magic of Ju-Ju (Impulse A-9154).
  A Sea of Faces (Black Saint BSR-0002). This includes "Song for Mozambique."
  Jazz A Confronto (Horo HLL 101-27/Italy). Includes "My Heart Cries Out for Africa."
  There's a Trumpet in my Soul (Freedom FCD 41016).

With Family of Percussion, *Here Comes the Family* (Nagara CDMIX 1021/Japan).

With Dollar Brand, *Duets* (DENON C38-7008).

With Cheikh Tidiane Fall, *Things Have Got to Change* (Marge 08SR251/France).

Chapter XIII:

Yusef Lateef, *Eastern Sounds* (Prestige 7319).
  The Gentle Giant (Atlantic SD-1602). "African Woman" is offered.
  In Nigeria (Landmark LLP-502).
  Gong (2-Savoy Jazz SJL-2226).
  A Flat, G Flat and C (Impulse 9117). This incorporates "Nile Valley Blues."

Other musical evocations of water spirits include Ellington's "River Suite" included in Duke Ellington, *The Private Collections,*

Volume V (Saja 90145-2) and Sam Rivers, *Waves* (Tomato TOM-8002).

Chapter XIV:

Sunny Murray, *Homage to Africa* (Byg 529.303/France).
Sonny's Time Now (Jihad 663/DIW-25002/Japan).
An Even Break (Never Give a Sucker) (Affinity AFF 30/-England).
Aigu-Grave (Marge 11/France) with Cheikh Tidiane Fall and Malachi Favors.
African Magic (Circle RK 5679/17/West Germany).

Jimmy Lyons and Sunny Murray Trio, *Jump Up—What to Do About* (Hat Art 2028).

Various Artists, *New American Music, Volume I* (Folkways FTS 33901).

Dave Burrell, *High Won—High Two* (Aristra Freedom 1906).

Albert Ayler, *Spiritual Unity* (ESP 1002).

Chapter XV:

Ronald Shannon Jackson, *Pulse* (Celluloid CELL-5011). "Hottentot Woman" is included. This is a solo drum album where drummming often accompanies poetry readings. The following five albums include Jackson with his band, the Decoding Society:
When Colors Play (Caravan of Dreams CDP-85009).
Texas (Caravan of Dreams CDP-85012).
Mandance (Antilles AN-10080). "Alice in Congoland" is included.
Nasty (Moers Music 0186/West Germany).
Live at the Caravan of Dreams (Caravan of Dreams CDP-85005).

Cecil Taylor, *3 Phasis* (New World NW-303).

Ornette Coleman, *Dancing in Your Head* (Horizon CD-0807). This album is of importance for the African theme in jazz due to one selection, "Midnight Sunrise," where Coleman jams with the legendary North African master musicians of Jajouka. For more on this event, see Drew Franklin, "Ornette in Jajouka: Playing in the Register of Light" *The Village Voice,* Jazz Supplement (23 June 1987), pp. 24–26.

Discography II

This is a selective list of long-playing albums, cassettes, and compact discs containing music related to the theme of Africa in jazz by composers and musicians not discussed in previous chapters. As the compact disc gains in popularity, more titles on vinyl will go out of print. But this list contains a number of vinyl issues which, though officially out of print, might still be available through used record stores or outlets specializing in imported labels. Imported labels are identified by country of origin in parenthesis. Also selections on albums which have particular pertinence to the themes discussed in this book are identified in parenthesis after the album title. While some of these titles may involve a thorough grail hunt, most have been included because they can be located in large metropolitan areas or through large mail order operations.

Ahmed Abdul-Malkik, *Sounds of Africa* (New Jazz LP 8282).

John Abercrombie Quartet, *Abercrombie Quartet* (ECM-1-1164) ("Madagascar").

Muhal Richard Abrams, *Afrisong* (India Navigation IN 1058).

Bob Ackerman, *Pharoah's Gold* (Daagmin JS06) ("Pharoah's Gold").

Cannonball Adderley, *Accent on Africa* (Capitol ST 2987) Includes "Lehadima" (Lightning).
African Waltz (Fantasy/OJC-258) ("African Waltz").

African Roots of Jazz, *African Roots of Jazz* (Plainisphare PL-1267-40-CD/Switzerland.

Ahmed Abdullah and the Solomonic Quintet, *Ahmed Abdullah and the Solomonic Quintet* (Silkheart SHLP-109) ("African Songbird").

Khaliq Al-Rouf & Salaam, *The Elephant Trot Dance* (Nilva NQ3404/France).

Minas Alexiades, *Integra* (Praxis GM 1001/Greece) ("Afrodiet").

Alive, *City Life* (Alive Records 543) ("Afreaka").

David Amram, *At Home/Around the World* (Flying Fish FF 094) ("Kwahare," "Aya Zehu").

Curtis Amy, *Way Down,* (Pacific Jazz PJ 46) ("Liberia").
With Dupree Bolton, *Katanga!* (Affinity AFF 128/England).

Louis Armstrong, *The Hot Fives, Volume I* (Columbia CJ 44049) ("King of the Zulus").
Satchmo the Great (Columbia CL 1077).

Art Ensemble of Chicago, *Tutankhamun* (Freedom FLP 40122).
Urban Bushmen (ECM 829394-2).

Dorothy Ashby, *Afro-harping,* (Cadet LPS 809) ("Afro-harping").

Charles Austin, *At Last* (Man Made Records OP 1) ("Electronic Africa").

Roy Ayers and Fela Anikulapo Kuti, *Music of Many Colors* (Celluloid 6125) ("Africa—Centre of the World").

Albert Ayler, *Music is the Healing Force of the Universe* (Impulse AS-9191).

Donald Ayler, *In Florence 1981, Volume I* (Frame RF 2001/Italy) ("The African Song").

Ginger Baker, *Stratavarious* (Polydor 2480118) ("Ju Ju").

Billy Bang, *Billy Bang Sextet Live at Carlos I* (Soul Note 21136-1) ("Sinawe Mandelas").
Untitled Gift (Anima 3BG9) ("Kora Song").

Gato Barbieri and Dollar Brand, *Confluence* (Arista-Freedom AL 1003).

Thurman Barker, *Voyage* (Up Tee 1001) ("Kalingalinga").

Gary Bartz, *Harlem Bush Music: Uhuru* (Milestone MSP 9032).
Juju Street Songs (Prestige P 10057).

Count Basie, *Afrique* (Doctor Jazz FW 39520).

Sidney Bechet, *Bechet of New Orleans* (RCA LPV-510) ("Egyptian
Fantasy").

Sathima Bea Benjamin, *Lovelight* (Ekapa-008) ("Winnie Mandela—
Beloved Heroine").

Sean Bergin and M.O.B., *Kids Mysteries* (Nimbus NS 502C).

George Benson, *Beyond the Blue Horizon* (CTI/CBS ZK-40810)
("Ode to a Kudu").

Big Black, *Message to the Ancestors* (Uni 73012).

Eubie Blake, *Blues and Ragtime, Volume I 1917–1921* (Biograph
BLP-1011Q) ("Charleston Rag," originally titled "Sounds of
Africa").

John Blake, *Adventures of the Heart* (Gramavision 18-8501-1)
("Mandela—We Are One").
A New Beginning (Gramavision 18-8808-1) ("Serengetti
Dance").

Ran Blake, *The Blue Potato and Other Outrages* (Milestone MSP-
9021) ("Garvey's Ghost").

Paul Bley, *Tango Palace* (Soul Note SN 1090) ("Zebra Walk").

Hamiet Bluiett, *Nali Kola* (Soul Note 121-188-1).

Arthur Blythe, *The Grip* (India Navigation IN 1029) ("Lower
Nile").
Illusions (Columbia JC 36583) ("Bush Baby").

Jean-Francois Bonnel and His English Friends, *What a Dream!*
(Stomp Off SOS 1131) ("Morocco Blues").

Earl Bostic, *Dance to the Best of Bostic* (King 500) ("Jungle Drums").
  Let's Dance With Earl Bostic (King 529) ("Ubangi Stomp").

Allan Botschinsky, *Akili* (M.A. Music International NU 730-1).

Lester Bowie, *African Children* (Horo DP 29-30/Italy).

Dollar Brand, *Africa/Tears and Laughter* (Enja 3039) ("Liberation
  Dance," "When Tarzan Meets the African Freedom Fighter").
  Duke Ellington Presents Dollar Brand (Reprise R-6111).

  The following were issued under the name he has used since the
  Seventies:
  "Abdullah Ibrahim," *Ekaya* (Black Hawk BKH 50205-IDO).
  Water From An Ancient Well, includes "Song of Sathima,"
    "Sameeds," and "Manenburg Revisted" (Black Hawk BKH
    50207).

Anthony Braxton, *Composition 113* (Sound Aspects SAS 003/W.
  Germany).

Roy Brooks, *The Free Slave* (Muse 5003).

Marion Brown, *Duets* (Arista-Freedom 1904) ("Njung - Lumumba
  Malcolm").
  Geechee Recollections (Impulse AS-9252).

Dave Brubeck, *25th Anniversary Reunion* (A&M CD 0806) ("African Times Suite").

Gary Burton, *Live in Tokyo* (Atlantic SD 8280) ("African Flower").

Donald Byrd, *Ethiopian Knights* (Blue Note BST-84380).
  A New Perspective (Blue Note BST-84124X "The Black Disci-
  ple").

Cab Calloway, *Hi De Ho Man* (Columbia CG 32593) ("Jungle
  King").

Joel Chadabe, *Rhythms* (Lovely Music VR 1301).

Tom Chapin, *Nia* (Strata-East SSES-7420) ("Juju").

Charquet & Co., *Jungle Jamboree* (Stomp Off SOS 1076) ("Jungle Jamboree").

Don Cherry, *Mu (Second Part)* (Actuel 529331/France) ("Dollar Brand").
Organic Music Society (Caprice 2001/Sweden) ("Bra Joe From Kilimanjaro").
Relativity Suite (JCOA 1006).

Clarinet Summit, *Southern Bells* (Black Saint 120107-1) ("Mbizo").

Curtis Clark, *Letter to South Africa* (Nimbus NS 501C).

Billy Cobham, *Power Play* (GRP Records GR 1027) ("Summit Afrique").

Al Cohn and Billy Mitchell, *Night Flight to Dakar* (Xanadu 185).
Xanadu in Africa (Xanadu 180).

Ornette Coleman, *In All Languages* (Caravan of Dreams CDP 85508) ("Africa Is the Mirror of All Colors").

Steve Coleman, *Motherland Pulse* (JMT 834401-1) ("Motherland Pulse").

Chick Corea, *Paris Concert/Circle* (ECM 1018/1019) ("Nefertiti").

Jayne Cortez and the Firespitters, *Maintain Control* (Bola Press BP-8601) ("Kai Kai," "Briefing").

Larry Coryell, *Tributaries* (Arista/Novus AN 3017) ("Zimbabwe").

Stanley Cowell, *Musa—Ancestral Streams* (Strata East 19743).

Lol Coxhill, *Couscous* (Nato 157/France).

Marilyn Crispell, *Rhythms Hung in Undrawn Sky* (Leo LR 118/England) ("Song to Abdullah").

Tony Dagradi, *Oasis* (Gramavision GR 8001) ("Ghana Folk Song").

Anthony Davis, *Middle Passage* (Gramavision GR 8401) ("Middle Passage").

Song for the Old World (India Navigation IN 1036) ("African Ballad").

Miles Davis, *Nefertiti* (Columbia PCT 9594) ("Nefertiti").
Panagaea (CBS-Sony SOP 296-97/Japan) ("Zimbabwe").
Tutu (Warner Brothers 25490-1) ("Tutu").
Amandla (Warner Bros. 25873).

Walter Davis Jr., *400 Years Ago, Tomorrow* (Owl 020/France) ("400 Years Ago Tomorrow").

Jack DeJohnette with Lester Bowie, *Zebra* (MCA - 42160).

Claude Delcloo, *Africanasia* (Actuel 529306/France).

Detail, *Okhela: To Make a Fire* (Affinity AFF 125/England).

Al Di Meola, *Scenario* (Columbia FC 38944) ("African Night").

District Six, *To Be Free* (Editions EG EGED-53).

Dixie Rhythm Kings, on Various Artists, *Chicago Jazz,* Volume 2 (Classic Jazz CJM-40) ("Congo Love Song").

Bill Dixon, *Thoughts* (Soul Note SN 1111) ("For Nelson and Winnie").

Eric Dolphy, *Iron Man* (Celluloid 5015) ("Burning Spear").

Kenny Dorham, *Afro-Cuban* (Blue Note BLP - 81535).

Tommy Dorsey, *The Indispensable, Volumes 7/8* (RCA International 90028) ("Night in Sudan").

Johnny Dyani, *African Bass* (Red Record VPA 149/Italy).
Afrika, (SteepleChase SCS 1186) (Includes "Blame It on the Boers").
Angolian Cry (SteepleChase SCS 1209).
Song for Biko (SteepleChase SCS 1109).

Art Farmer, *Farmer's Market* (Prestige P - 24032) ("Mau Mau," "Elephant Walk").

Zusann Kali Fasteau, *Worlds Beyond Words* (Flying Note CD 9001).

Mongezi Feza, Okay Temiz, Johnny Dyani, *Music for Xaba, Volume I* (Sonet SNTF 642/England) and *Music for Xaba, Volume II* (Sonet SNTF-824/England).

Clare Fischer, *Salas Picante* (Discovery DS-817) ("Canto Africano").

Ricky Ford, *Loxodonta Africana* (New World 204).

Sonny Fortune, *Awakening* (Horizon 704) ("Nommo").

Michael Franks, *Sleeping Gypsy* (Warner Bros. BS - 3004) ("B'wana He No Home").

Chico Freeman, *Kings of Mali* (India Navigation 1035).
The Search (India Navigation IN-1059) ("Soweto Suite").

Slim Gaillard and Slam Stewart, *Slim and Slam, Volume III* (Tax 8044/Sweden) ("African Jive").

Ganelin Trio, *Ancora Da Capo, Part II* (Leo LR 109/England).

Jan Garbarek, *Esoteric Circle* (Freedom FCD 41031) ("Nefertiti").

Red Garland, *Red Alert* (Galaxy 5109) ("Theme for a Tarzan Movie").

Giorgio Gaslini, *Africa* (Produttoriassoc LP 61/Italy).

John Gill's Original Sunset Five, *Down Home Blues* (Stomp Off SOS 1126) ("Cleopatra Had a Jazz Band").

Paul Gonsalves, *Cleopatra Feeling Jazzy* (Impulse AS-41).

Dennis Gonzales and New Dallas Sextet, *Namesake* (Silkheart SHLP 106/Sweden) ("Hymn For Mbizo").

Milford Graves and Andrew Cyrille, *Dialogue of the Drums* (IPS001).

Milford Graves and Don Pullen, *Nommo* (SRP LP-290).

Grant Green, *Nigeria* (Blue Note LT-1032).

Robert Greenidge and Michael Utley, *Mad Music* (MCA Master Series MCA-5695) ("African Woman").

Griot Galaxy, *Opus Krampus* (Sound Aspects Records SAS 004/W. Germany).

Cliff Habian Quintet, *Tonal Paintings* (Milestone M-9161) ("The Modernization of Zimbabwe").

Kip Hanrahan, *Conjure: Music for the Texts of Ishmael Reed* (Pangaea PANC-42135).

Edmond Hall, *Rumpus on Rampart St.* (Raecox 1120/England) ("African Fou Fou").

Lionel Hampton, *In Japan/Live* (Glad-Hamp GHL 1006) ("Afrika").

Herbie Hancock and Foday Suso, *Village Life* (Columbia PC-39870).

Roland Hanna, *Sir Elf* (Choice 1003).

Beaver Harris, *Beautiful Africa* (Soul Note SN 1002) ("African Drums").

Craig Harris, *Shelter* (JMT 834408-1) ("Africans Unite").
Tributes (OTC 804) ("African Hi-Life").

Eddie Harris, *For Bud and Bags* (Vee Jay VJS-3058) ("The River Nile").

Gene Harris, *In a Special Way* (Blue Note BNLA 634-6) ("Zulu").

Heath Brothers, *Marchin' On* (Strata-East 19766) ("Smilin Billy Suite, No. 2").

Jimmy Heath, *Jimmy* (Muse MR 5138) ("Aikebu-Lau—Land of the Blacks").

Gerry Hemingway, *Kwambe* (Auricle 78).

Joe Henderson, *Power to the People* (Milestone 9050) ("Afro-Centric").

Woody Herman, *The Woody Herman Collection* (Deja Vu DVMC 2025/Italy) ("Casbah Blues").

Andrew Hill, *Compulsion* (Blue Note 84217).

Jay Hoggard, *Mystic Winds, Tropic Breezes* (India Navigation IN 1049).
  Solo Vibraphone (India Navigation 1040) ("May Those Who Love Apartheid Burn in Hell").

Paul Horn, *Paul Horn + Nexus* (Epic KE 33561) ("Mbiri," "African Funeral Song," "Capetown").

Richard Horowitz and Sussan Deihim, *Desert Equations: Azax Attra* (Crammed Discs MTM-8/Belgium).

Dick Hyman, *Kitten on the Keys: Piano Music of Zez Confrey* (RCA XPLI-4746) ("African Suite").

Robert Irvin III, *Midnight Dream* (Verve Forecast 837034-1) ("Let's Not Wait").

Milt Jackson, *Paris Session* (Phillips (E) BBL 7459) ("Swing 39," "Minor Swing").

Willis Jackson, *West Africa* (Muse 5036).

Ahmed Jamal, *Crystal* (Atlantic 81793-1) ("Swahililand").

Khan Jamal, *Thinking of You* (Storyville 4138/Sweden) ("Theme For Winnie Mandela").

Bob James, *Ivory Coast* (Warner Bros. 25757-1) ("Ashanti").

Joseph Jarman and Don Moye, *Black Paladins* (Black Saint BSR 0042).

Jazz Warriors, *Out of Many, One People* (Antilles New Directions 90681-1) ("In Response to Our Forefathers' Fathers' Dreams").

Elvin Jones, *The Prime Element* (Blue Note LA 506) ("Dido Afrique").

Quincy Jones, *Gula Matari* (A&M SP9 - 3030) ("Gula Matari") *Roots* (A&M SP - 4626).

Richard M. Jones Jazz Wizards, "African Hunch" included on Various Artists, *Jazz Classics in Digital Stereo: Chicago* (BBC CD 589).

Ju Ju, *A Message From Mozambique* (Strata-East SES 19735 A/B).

The Jungle Crawlers, *Stompin' On Down* (Stomp Off SOS 1084) ("The Head-Hunter's Dream," "Jungle Crawl").

Rickey Kelly, *My Kind of Music* (New Note NNR-001) ("The Masai," "Danakil Warriors").

John King Ensemble, *John King Ensemble* (India Street Music 1-1001).

Rahsaan Roland Kirk, *The Best of Rahsaan Roland Kirk* (Atlantic SD 1592) ("Black Roots").

Steve Lacy, *The Door* (Novus 3049-1-N) ("Cliches," "Virgin Jungle"). *The Flame* (Soul Note SN 1035) ("The Flame").

Lambert, Hendricks, and Ross, *The Swingers* (EMI-Manhattan CDP7468492) ("Airegin").

Byard Lancaster, *Mother Africa* (Palm 9/France).

Gretchen Langheld Ensemble, *Desire Brings You Back* (GL Productions).

Hubert Laws, *Wild Flower* (Atlantic SD-1624) ("Ashanti," "Yoruba").

Ted Lewis Orchestra, *Volume I 1926–1933* (Biograph BLP C-7). ("Egyptian Ella") and *Volume II 1928–1932* (Biograph BLP C-8) ("Jungle Blues").

Limehouse Jazzband, *Rhythm Is Our Business* (Stomp Off SOS 1014) ("Zulu Wail").

Abbey Lincoln, *People In Me* (Inner City IC 6040) ("Africa," "People In Me").
Straight Ahead (Candid CCD 79015) ("African Woman").

Theo Loevendie, *Mandela* (Catfish 5C054-24152/Netherlands) ("Timbuktu," "Mandela").

Jimmy Lyons, *Nuba* (Black Saint 0030).

The Machete Ensemble, *Africa* (Machete Records M 102).

Machito and His Orchestra, *Latin Soul Plus Jazz* (original title: *Kenya*) (Tico CLP 1314).

Joe Malinga, *Tears for the Children of Soweto* (Plainisphare C113).

Herbie Mann, *African Suite* (United Artists UA 4042).
The Common Ground (Atlantic 1343).

Shelly Manne, *Daktari* (Atlantic SD 8157).

Hugh Masekela, *The African Connection* (ABC/Impulse 1A-9343/2).
The Americanization of Ooga Booga (MGM 4372).

David Matthews, *Grand Cross* (GNP Crescendo GMP 2157) ("Afro Sax").

Les McCann, *McCanna* (Pacific Jazz 84).

Chris McGregor and Brotherhood of Breath, *Country Cooking* (Virgin STVR 887121).

Maurice McIntyre, *Peace and Blessing* (Black Saint BSR 0037) ("African Procession").
Ram's Run (Cadence Jazz Records CJR 1009) ("African Walk").

Jackie McLean and Michael Carvin, *Antiquity* (SteepleChase SCS 1028), with McCoy Tyner, Woody Shaw, et al., "Appointment in Ghana" included on Various Artists, *One Night With Blue Note, Volume II* (CDP 7 461482).

Mills Blue Rhythm Band, *Volume I* (Everybodys 1013/Sweden) ("African Lullaby").

Blue Rhythm (Help 1008/England) ("Futuristic Jungleism").
Swing—Big Bands (Anthology of Various Artists), "Congo Caravan" (BBC 655).

Charles Mingus, *Cumbia and Jazz Fusion* (Atlantic SD 8801) ("Cumbia and Jazz Fusion").

Miniature, *Miniature* (JMT 834 423-2/W. Germany) ("Ethiopian Boxer").

Blue Mitchell, *African Violet* (ABC AS 9328) ("African Violet").
Bantu Village (Blue Note BNS 4324).

Louis Moholo, *Spirits Rejoice* (Ogun OG520/England).
Tern (SAJ 43/44/W. Germany).

Grachan Moncur III, *Echoes of a Prayer* (JCOA 1009).
New Africa (Byg LP5229321/France) ("New Africa").

James Moody, *Something Special* (Novus 3004-1-N9) ("Nubian Fantasies").

Tim Moran, *Wizard's Dance* (Fretless FR 163) ("Zimbabwe")
City Spirits with Tony Vacca (Philo PH - 9007) ("Homeland").

Mtume and the Umoja Ensemble, *Alkebu-Lau* (Strata-East SES 1972 - 4).

Abdul Malik Muhammad, *Songs for Our children* (Amir-1001).

David Murray, *3-D Family* (Hat Art 2016) ("In Memory of Jomo Kenyatta").

Amina Claudine Myers, *Amina* (Novus 3030-1-N9) ("Nisa-mehe").

Milton Nascimento, *A Barca Dos Amantes* (Verve 831 349-1) ("Southern Tear").

Native Son, *Savanna Hot-Line* (JVC VIJ 6309/Japan).

Oliver Nelson, *Afro/American Sketches* (Prestige 7225).

New Orleans Rascals, *Love Song of the Nile* (Stomp Off SOS 1074) ("Love Song of the Nile").

James Newton, *The African Flower* (Blue Note BT 85109) ("The African Flower," "Virgin Jungle").
Axum (ECM 835019-2).
Luella (Gramavision GR-8304) ("Diamonds Are for Freedom").

Herbie Nichols, *The Complete Blue Note Herbie Nichols* (Mosaic MR5-118) ("The Third World").

Olatunji, *Drums of Passion* (Columbia 8210).
Zungo! (Columbia 1634).

Old and New Dreams, *Old and New Dreams* (ECM 1-1154) ("Togo," "Guinea").

Opposite Corner, *Jazz I Sverige '76* (Caprice 1117/Sweden) ("Melody From Ghana").

Tiny Parham, *Tiny Parham 1926–1930* (Swaggie 833/Australia) ("Back to the Jungle").

Errol Parker, *Errol Parker Tentet* (Sahara 1013) ("African Samba").

Horace Parlan, *Happy Frame of Mind* (Blue Note BST-84134) ("Home Is Africa," "Kucheza Blues").

Passport, *Talk Back* (Atlantic 81937-1) ("Sahara").

John Payne, *Bedtime Stories* (Arista AL 1025) ("African Brothers").

Gary Peacock, *Paradigm* (ECM MSE 1210) ("Moor").

Marvin "Hannibal" Peterson, *Poem Song* (Mole 6/England) ("Africa").

Oscar Peterson, *Nigerian Marketplace* (Pablo D2303-231) ("Nigerian Marketplace").

Werner Pirchner, *Werner Pirchner, Harry Pepl, Jack DeJohnette* (ECM 1237) ("African Godchild").

Jean Luc Ponty and Sahib Shihab, *Jazz Meets Arabia: Noon in Tunisia* (BASF/MPS ST 20640/W. Germany).

Bud Powell, *The Best of Bud Powell* (Blue Note CDP 7932042) ("Cleopatra's Dream").

Perez Prado and His Orchestra, *Voodoo Suite Plus Six All-Time Greats* (RCA Victor LPM-1101) ("Voodoo Suite").

Dudu Pukwana, *In the Townships* (Virgin/Earthworks 7-90884-1).

Ike Quebec, *Easy Living* (Blue Note BST 84103) ("Congo Lament").

Alvin Queen, *Ashanti* (Nilva 3402/France).

Red Roseland Cornpickers, *That's No Bargain* (Stomp Off SOS 1102) ("Egyptian Ella," "Ostrich Walk").

Bob Reid, *Africa Is Calling Me* (Kwela Records 30K010).

Rena Rama Quartet, *Landscapes* (JAPO 60020/W. Germany) ("Royal Song From Dahomey").

Lee Ritenour, *Banded Together* (Elektra Musician EI-60358) ("Mandela").

Sam Rivers, *Black Africa—Perugia,* (Horo HDP-5-6/Italy).
Black Africa—Villalago (Horo HDP-3-4/Italy).

Luckey Roberts, *Harlem Piano* (Good Times 10035) ("Ripples of the Nile").

Shorty Rogers and His Giants, *Short Stops* (2-Bluebird 5917-1-RB11) ("Tale of an African Lobster").

Karel Ruzicka, *Kvarteto Karla Ruzicka* (Sup 01150405/Czechoslovakia) ("Made in Tunisia [Night?]").

George Sams, *Nomadic Winds* (Hat Musics 3506) ("The Path With a Heart for Africa").

Dave Samuels, *Ten Degrees North* (MCA 6328) ("Ivory Coast" "Freetown").

Pancho Sanchez, *La Familia* (Concord Picante CJP-369) ("Senegal").

Pharoah Sanders, *Africa* (Timeless 253).
  Heart Is a Melody (Theresa TR-118) ("Goin' to Africa").
  Izipho Zam (My Gifts) (Strata-East SES - 19733).
  Rejoice (Theresa TR-112/113) ("Highlife," "Nigerian Juju Highlife," "Ntjilo, Ntjilo/Bird Song").
  Thembi (MCA/Impulse MCA 560) ("Ballophone Dance").

Mongo Santamaria, *Afro Roots* (Prestige 24018).

Saheb Sarbib, *UFO—Live on Tour* (Cadence Jazz Records 1008) ("Egypt").

Tony Scott, *African Bird* (Soul Note SN 121083-a).

Gil Scott-Heron and Brian Jackson, *From South Africa to South Carolina* (Arista AL 4044) ("Johannesburg").

Adele Sebastian, *Desert Fairy Princess* (Nimbus N5680) ("Man From Tanganyika").

Artie Shaw, *The Complete Gramercy Five Sessions* (RCA 7637) ("Dr. Livingston, I Presume").
  Artie Shaw and the Rhythmakers Volume II (Swingdom 7003/Sweden) ("Ubangi").
  This Is Artie Shaw (RCA Victor VPM-6039) ("Jungle Drums").

Woody Shaw, *Live Berliner Jazztage* (Muse MR-5139) ("In the Land of the Blacks [Bilad as Sudan]").

Wayne Shorter, *Ju Ju* (Blue Note Bst-84182) ("Ju Ju").
  Odyssey of Iska (Blue Note BST 84363).
  The Soothsayer (Blue Note CDP 7844432) ("Angola").

Horace Silver, *The Cape Verdean Blues* (Blue Note BNS 4220) ("The Cape Verdean Blues").
  Silver With Percussion (Blue Note BN-LP 853-H).

Nina Simone, *Nina Simone at Newport* (Official 6014/Denmark) ("Flo-Me-La").

Leo Smith, *Jah Music* (Kabell K-5).
Human Rights (Kabell/Gramm/24).
Rastafari (Sackville 3030/Canada).

Martial Solal, *Live 1959–1985* (Accord 239963/France).

Sonny Stitt, *Constellation* (Muse MR - 5323) ("Casbah").

Sun Ra, *Discipline 27-11* (El Saturn Records ES 538) ("Pan Afro").
It's After the End of the World (MPS-BASAF 20748/W. Germany) ("Watusi," "Egyptian March").
The Nubians of Plutonia (Impulse 9242).
The Sun Ra Arkestra Meets Salah Ragab in Egypt Plus the Cairo Jazz Band (Praxis CM 106/Greece).

Horace Tapscott, *The Tapscott Sessions, Volume IV* (Nimbus NS 1814) ("Shades of Soweto").
The Tapscott Sessions, Volume VII (Nimbus NS 2147) ("On the Nile").
With Pan-Afrikan Peoples Arkestra, *The Call* (Nimbus 246).

Cecil Taylor, *Nefertiti, The Beautiful One Has Come* (Arista-Freedom AL 1905).

John Tchicai, *Afrodisiaca* (MPS 15249/W. Germany).
Put Up the Fight (Storyville 4141/Sweden) ("For Johnny Dyani").

Kid Thomas, *Love Songs of the Nile* (GHB GHB-183) ("Love Songs of the Nile").

Leon Thomas, *Spirits Unknown and Known* (Flying Dutchman FDS 115).

Clifford Thornton, *The Gardens of Harlem* (JCOA 1008).
Ketchaqua (Byg 529.323/France).

Keith Tippett & Louis Moholo, *No Gossip* (SAJ-28).

Charles Tolliver, *The Ringer* (Arista Freedom 1904) ("On the Nile").

McCoy Tyner, *Asante* (Blue Note BN-LA 223-6).
Sahara (Fantasy/OJC OJC-311) ("Sahara").
Together (Milestone 9037) ("Nubia").
Time for Tyner (Blue Note BST 84307) ("African Village").

Dave Valentin, *Jungle Garden* (GRP Records GR 1015) ("Bones").
Kalahari (GRP Records GR 1009) ("Kalahari").

Various Artists, *Jazz Soul of Cleopatra* (Prestige New Jazz 8292).

Various Artists, *The Young Lions* (Elektra/Musician 60196.1) ("Nigerian Sunset").

Nana Vasconcelos, *Zumbi* (Europa JP 2013).

Joe Venuti, *The Big Bands of Joe Venuti—Fiddlin' Joe, Volume I* (JSP 1111/England) ("Chant of the Jungle").

Voice, *Voice* (Ogun OG 190/England) ("African Breeze").

Fats Waller, *Piano Solos* (Bluebird AXM2-5518) ("African Ripples").

Hasse Walli, Hassan Bah and Afro-Line, *Close to the Line* (Digelius Music HW-2/Finland).

Guy Warren (also recorded under "Kofi Ghanaba"), *Africa Speaks, America Listen* (Decca).

Weather Report, *Mysterious Traveller* (Columbia KC 32494) ("Nubian Sunrise," "Jungle Book").

Chuck Webb and His Orchestra, "Harlem Congo" included on Various Artists, *Big Band Jazz: From the Beginnings to the Fifties* (Smithsonian Collection of Records DMM 6-0610).

West India Company, *Music From New Demons* (Editions EG EGED 61) ("The Lion Sleeps Tonight").

Tony Williams, *Civilization* (Blue Note BT-85138) ("Soweto Nights").

Phil Woods, *Musicque Du Bois* (Muse MR-5037) ("Nefertiti").

Working Week, *Paycheck* (Venture 90997-1) ("South Africa").

World Saxophone Quartet, *Dances and Ballads* (Nonesuch 979164-1) ("West African Snap").

Selected Playlists Spotlighting Facets
of the African Theme

Recognizing how unwieldy lengthy discographies can be, the following lists represent easy entrances to the five major facets of the African theme in jazz: place, nature, portraits, history, and liberation. There are some recordings which fit between the interstices of several categories, and some which seem to fit none, but most of the nearly four hundred recordings mentioned in the text can be situated among these five.

Imagining myself in the position of disc jockey as well as author, I have composed playlists of several hours worth of listening within each category. Readers playing some or all of each list will discover an extra dimension of comprehension in their reading. These lists are not exhaustive. Readers using the discographies can generate alternative selections as well as additional categories (such as collaborative recordings between American and African musicians, or themes of humor, love, and so on.)

While this book has examined the Africa theme solely in recorded jazz, readers might wish to combine their jazz listening with selections from pop music (Paul Simon, Joni Mitchell), blues (Johnny Copeland), and reggae (Bob Marley, Ras Michael). While this author found his hands full dealing with one musical style fertilized by Afrocentric imagination, it is hoped that others might do justice to the African presence in other musical styles. Walt Whitman's phrase comes to mind: "The theme is creative and has vista."

Place:

John Blake, "Serengetti Dance"

John Coltrane, "Liberia"
    "Gold Coast"

"Tanganyika Strut"
"Dakar"
"Africa"

Miles Davis, "Zimbabwe"

Duke Ellington, "The Liberian Suite"
"Togo Brava"
"Virgin Jungle"

Cliff Habian Quartet, "The Modernization of Zimbabwe"

Abbey Lincoln, "Africa"

Mills Brothers, "Jungle Fever"

Old and New Dreams, "Togo," "Gineau"

Pancho Sanchez, "Senegal"

Woody Shaw, "In the Land of the Blacks"

Horace Silver, "The Cape Verdean Blues"

Clifford Thornton, "Ketchaqua"

Charles Tolliver, "On the Nile"

McCoy Tyner, "Sahara" "African Village"

Various Artists, "A Night in Tunisia"

Randy Weston, "African Village/Bedford Stuyvesant"
"Tangier Bay"
"Sahel"

Nature:

Cannonball Adderley, "Lahadima" (Lightning)

Khaliq Al-Rouf, "The Elephant Trot Dance"

Gato Barbieri and Dollar Brand, "The Aloe and the Wildrose"

George Benson, "Ode to a Kudu"

Paul Bley, "Zebra Walk"

Arthur Blythe, "Bush Baby"

Jack deJohnette, *Zebra*

Pierre Dørge, "Suho Ning Samo"
 "Waltz for Two Camels"
 "A Rainbow Over the Bamboo Forest"

Duke Ellington, "The River Suite"
 "Fleurette Africaine"

Ronald Shannon Jackson, *When Colors Play*

Yusef Lateef, "Nile Valley Blues"

Blue Mitchell, "African Violet"

Red Roseland Cornpickers, "Ostrich Walk"

Shorty Rogers, "Tales of an African Lobster"

Pharoah Sanders, "Ntjilo Ntjilo/Bird Song"

Dave Valentin, "Bones"

Randy Weston, "Purple Gazelle"

Portraits:

Billy Bang Sextet, "Sinawe Mandelas"

Sathima Bea Benjamin, "Winnie Mandela—Beloved Heroine"

Art Blakey, "Obirin African (Woman of Africa)"

Anthony Braxton, *Composition 113*

Miles Davis, "Tutu"

Bill Dixon, "For Nelson and Winnie"

Dollar Brand (Abdullah Ibrahim), "Sameeda," "Song for Sathima"

Eric Dolphy, "Burning Spear"

Pierre Dørge, "Mbizo Mbizo"
"Mister Suso"
"To Alhaji Bai Konte"
"Monk in Africa"

Johnny Dyani, "Song for Biko"

Duke Ellington, "La Plus Belle Africaine"

Duke Ellington units, "Menelik (The Lion of Judah)"

Paul Gonsalves, *Cleopatra Goes Jazzy*

Ronald Shannon Jackson, "Hottentot Woman"

Rickey Kelly, "The Masai," "Danakil Warriors"

Steve Lacy, "The Flame"

David Murray, "In Memory of Jomo Kenyatta"

Archie Shepp, "Tuareg"
"Yasima, A Black Woman"

Cecil Taylor, "Nefertiti, The Beautiful One Has Come"

Randy Weston, "Congolese Children"
"Kasbah Kids"

Randy Weston and David Murray, "Blue Moses"

History:

Louis Armstrong, *Satchmo the Great*

Marion Brown, *Geechee Recollections*

John Carter, *Dauwhe*
   Castles of Ghana
   Dance of the Love Ghosts
   Fields
   Shadows on the Wall

Anthony Davis, "Middle Passage"

Duke Ellington, *A Drum Is A Woman*
   "Black, Brown and Beige"

Chico Freeman, *Kings of Mali*

Andrew Hill, *Compulsion*

Jay Hoggard, *Mystic Winds, Tropic Breezes*

Jazz Warriors, "In Reference to Our Forefathers' Fathers' Dreams"

Quincy Jones, *Roots*

Grachan Moncur III, *Echoes of a Prayer*

Count Ossie and Mystic Revelation of Rastafari, *Grounation*
   Tales of Mozambique

Bob Reid, *Africa Is Calling Me*

George Russell, *The African Game*

Clifford Thornton, *The Gardens of Harlem*

Nana Vasconselos, *Zumbi*

Liberation:

Gary Bartz, *Harlem Bush Music, Uhuru*

John Coltrane, *Kulu Se Mama*
  Om

Jayne Cortez, "Kai Kai," "Briefing"

Dollar Brand (Abdullah Ibrahim)
  "Manenburg Revisited"
  "Liberation Dance" ("When Tarzan Meets the African Freedom
    Fighter")

Johnny Dyani, "Blame It On the Boers"
  "Angolian Cry"

Chico Freeman, "Soweto Suite"

Craig Harris, "Africans Unite"

Jay Hoggard, "May Those Who Love Apartheid Burn in Hell"

Wilmoth Houdini, "African Love Call"

Robert Irving III, "Let's Not Wait"

Charles Mingus, "Cumbia and Jazz Fusion"

Sunny Murray, *Sonny's Time Now*

James Newton, "Diamonds Are For Freedom"

Max Roach, *Freedom Now Suite*
  Percussion Bitter Sweet
  "South Africa Goddamn"

Gil Scott-Heron and Brian Jackson, "Johannesburg"

Archie Shepp, "Song for Mozambique"
  There's a Trumpet in My Soul

Goin' Home
The Cry of My People

Leo Smith, *Jah Music*
    Human Rights

Randy Weston, *Uhuru Africa*

Index